THE INTENTIONAL

THREAD

A Guide to Drawing, Gesture, and Color in Stitch

Susan Brandeis

SCHIFFER
PUBLISHING

Printed in China

Designed by Brenda McCallum
Cover design by Brenda McCallum

The following photos are courtesy of Marc Brandeis: photos
in illustrations 01-01, 01-10, 06-05, 06-14, 07-03, 07-07,
08-01, 09-36, 10-13, 10-14, 11-15, and 13-14.

The following photos are courtesy of the author: photos
in illustrations 02-11, 03-04, 03-22, 06-01, 06-20, 08-04,
12-03, 13-04, 13-06, 13-08, 13-10, 13-12, 13-16, 13-18,
and all digital drawings.

All other photos © Sally Van Gorder.

These items are registered or trademarked:
Corel Painter, Adobe Photoshop, Slinky, and Spoonflower.
Type set in Times New Roman/ Colonna MT

ISBN: 978-0-7643-5743-5
Printed in China
6 5 4 3

Published by Schiffer Publishing, Ltd.
4880 Lower Valley Road
Atglen, PA 19310
Phone: (610) 593-1777; Fax: (610) 593-2002
E-mail: Info@schifferbooks.com
Web: www.schifferbooks.com

For our complete selection of fine books on this and related
subjects, please visit our website at www.schifferbooks.com.
You may also write for a free catalog.

Schiffer Publishing's titles are available at special discounts
for bulk purchases for sales promotions or premiums. Special
editions, including personalized covers, corporate imprints,
and excerpts, can be created in large quantities for special
needs. For more information, contact the publisher.

We are always looking for people to write books on new and
related subjects. If you have an idea for a book, please contact
us at proposals@schifferbooks.com.

Other Schiffer Books on Related Subjects:

Threads Around the World: From Arabian Weaving to Batik in Zimbabwe, Deb Brandon, ISBN 978-0-7643-5650-6
Organic Embroidery, Meredith Woolnough, ISBN 978-0-7643-5613-1

Dedicated to
Marc Brandeis,
friend, helpmate, believer, love of my life

CONTENTS

Preface   6

Acknowledgments   9

About This Book   10

Part 1: The Elements of Line   13

Chapter 1: Line Weight   14

Chapter 2: Line Direction   26

Chapter 3: "Natural" Mark-Making: Everybody Does It   36

Chapter 4: Handwriting as Drawing   50

Chapter 5: Large-Scale Gestures   65

Chapter 6: Feathered Strokes and Delicate Lines   77

Chapter 7: Lines on "See-Through" Materials   93

Chapter 8: Contours and Outlines   101

Part 2: Shapes and Spaces: Fills and Shading   107

Chapter 9: Thinking about Color   108

Chapter 10: Fills: Transparent   126

Chapter 11: Fills: Opaque   139

Chapter 12: Fills: Shaded   152

Chapter 13: Fills: Textured   172

Appendix 1: Getting Started: A Guide to Stitching   184

Appendix 2: Getting Started: Help from Samplers   196

Appendix 3: Getting Started: Matching Expression
          and Technique   204

Glossary   214

Bibliography   217

Materials, Tools, and Equipment   220

Index   224

We live in a world where everything, from commerce to transportation to information, moves faster and faster. But the *absence* of speed in the handmade stands in opposition to that hurry, offers an antidote to frenzy and commotion, and is one of the reasons I love handwork. I am drawn to the "meditative" quality of working slowly at human (rather than machine) speed.

Stitchery doesn't require a lot of money or complicated technology. Its gentle repetitions allow my mind to wander, to float, contentedly. I can stitch in silence, or during conversation, or while my favorite music is playing. I can stitch alone or in the companionship of others. I can stitch at home, or—if not in immediate need of a sewing machine for mechanized techniques—in a plane or train or bus, or (as long as someone else does the driving) a car.

I was already stitching by the time I was in elementary school. Raised by women for whom textile crafts were just a natural part of living, I was taught to value hand-made things for their own sake—for the making itself. And while quality of workmanship was valued, and certainly never to be cast aside, "perfection" of technique was not a goal by itself. "Perfect" was something machines did. Imperfect was, inevitably, something that people introduced into the handmade object, and it was honorable. "Perfect" cranked out things that looked the same, repetitive, and anonymous. But imperfections and idiosyncrasies, the evidence of the human hand, and the personality of the maker in pursuit of an idea were what made a thing visibly Mine, or Mom's, or Grandma's.

Since I was never the most coordinated person in the world, this suited me fine. I couldn't have attained "Perfect" even if I'd tried.

I later became an academically trained textile artist, and then an academician myself. I was a professor to young people, and, in summers, a workshop teacher in an assortment of places across America, where many of my students were well past their college years—professional people taking some dedicated time, free of other obligations, to feed their love of fiber work.

Despite my graduate degree in art, my job path had landed me in the design college of a university dominated by science and technology programs. I was surrounded by architects, graphic and industrial designers, animators, and makers of landscapes. Yes, I had students who wanted to do one-of-a-kind artwork. But I also had students who wanted to design upholstery, rugs, "high" and everyday fashion, theater costumes, and liturgical vestments. At the beginning, I thought: *This isn't what I had in mind when I got an art degree.* But I quickly learned to treasure the variety and to accommodate all comers. A good teacher does not, after all, seek to create clones of herself. She tries to nourish her students toward the fulfillment of their own enthusiasms and talents. And hadn't I always said that textiles were inseparable from life itself? Well, now I was getting the chance to put my teaching where my mouth was. I've never been keen on the distinction—the division, the wall—that the art world so often tries to interpose between itself and craft or design. I view art (expressive), craft (handling materials with care, deftness, skill, and mastery), and design (structure and intent, thought and planning) as seamlessly intertwined.

Over the years, my own artwork, previously dominated by highly colored dyed and woven fabric assemblages, began to take on ever more intensive elements of stitchery. I had become deeply fascinated by prehistoric human carvings on rock, by the alphabets of other living and dead civilizations, and by entire languages now lost. Stitchery became ideal as embellishment, mark-making, and color-filling against fabric foundations. As my own repertoire of stitched expressions continually expanded, I knew that my students also needed a firm grounding in thread-based techniques, whether their own interest involved garments or work for the wall. I regularly searched for a book that would provide a truly comprehensive view of what could be done with the threaded needle in textile work. But I couldn't find such a book.

So I had to write my own course materials for my university classes and as handouts for the summer workshops. Over many years, I also accumulated notebooks—oh, so many notebooks!—of stitchery samples and drawings, experiments and brainstormed illustrations, a personal library of the almost infinite possibilities of thread for my own reference and projects and to show to my students. Still, I kept watching for a book—something that went beyond the vast number of publications on how to perform stitches (the means) and onward to the "why" of stitchery (the end, the purpose, the expression). *Why can't I find the right book? There must be a book.*

After 35 years, I retired from university life—but not from the wish to teach and encourage, which, to my way of thinking, are simply forms of "sharing." And since I never did find that all-in-one-place book fully exploring the amazing range of expressive stitchery—the range of the *intentional* thread—I decided to write it.

Welcome.

I can stitch in silence, or during conversation, or while my favorite music is playing. I can stitch alone or in the companionship of others.

ACKNOWLEDGMENTS

It's no secret that the birth of a book requires the work of many kind and talented people, and therefore my debts are also many.

I had been assembling studio notebooks containing hundreds of my own sketches and stitchery samples for decades, but the idea of organizing them, and the techniques and knowledge they represented, into the coherent format of a single-volume book to share with others was first planted in my brain by my husband, Marc Brandeis. His support and enthusiasm for the project never wavered, and his advice and editorial skills greatly improved the manuscript.

Perhaps the single most difficult task in the preparation of this book was the creation of photographs which not only depicted the threads clearly, but also fully conveyed the tactile qualities of cloth. I owe enormous thanks to Sally Van Gorder for accomplishing this with finesse, dedication, and good humor.

During the process of writing, I valued highly the commentary from my two superb readers, Lisa Kriner (Professor of Art in textiles and printmaking at Berea College) and Stephanie Witchger (whose vocations and avocations have included art librarianship, corporate art direction, and—of course—stitchery). These two generous women provided prompt and insightful chapter-by-chapter reviews and superb advice. I am deeply thankful for their time, perception, and belief in the desirability of this book.

For study and sketching access to both contemporary and historic exemplars of world embroidery, and for her willingness to share her own broad knowledge, I am grateful to Mary Hauser, Registrar and Assistant Director of the Gregg Museum of Art & Design at North Carolina State University and former Assistant Registrar at the Textile Museum in Washington, DC. My access to stitchery collections in these museums has enhanced my teaching, artwork, and writing.

I received the gift of professional encouragement from a core group of members of the Southeast Fibers Educators Association (SEFEA): Edwina Bringle, Miyuki Akai Cook, Gabrielle Duggan, Susan Fecho, Robin Haller, Susan Iverson, Jeana Klein, Bethanne Knudson, Kate Kretz, Precious Lovell, Amy Putansu, LM Wood, and Christine Zoller. I extend special thanks to SEFEA members Patricia Mink and Lisa Kriner, who spent portions of our annual conferences reviewing my samples and preliminary writing notes to make suggestions about the content of the book; Katherine Diuguid, who reviewed the chapter on color; and Catharine Ellis, for encouraging me to follow my passion and for recommending Schiffer Publishing.

My creative life has been blessed with many people whose extensive use of embroidery in their artwork spurred my own. My respect and heartfelt thanks to:

Professional colleagues, who demonstrated that a passion for stitching can become a life's work: Renie Breskin Adams, Ilze Aviks, Janice Gatti, Peg Gignoux, Rozanne Hawksley, John Hawthorne, Kate Kretz, Tom Lundberg, Anne McKenzie Nickolson, Carol Shinn, Barbara Lee Smith, and Audrey Walker.

Former graduate students who embraced embroidery with intelligence, joy, and fervor: MacKenzie Bullard, Claudia Dominguez, Julia Feldman, Cheryl Harrison, Jeanine Henderson, Kelly Kye, Adrienne McKenzie, Jacquelyn Nouveau, Pati Reis, Rodica Simon, Shelley Smith, Georgia Springer, and Chrissie Van Hoever.

Although too many to name individually, several decades of *undergraduate students* in my surface embellishment classes at North Carolina State University and *summer workshop participants* of all ages helped me to test and refine the approaches to stitchery now collected here.

I was fortunate to receive the support and guidance of a good publishing team at Schiffer: an enthusiastic editor, Sandra Korinchak, who provided a calm voice, good commonsense advice, and tactfully phrased suggestions; Pete Schiffer, for his faith in the proposal and this first-time book author; production editor Peggy Kellar; book designer Brenda McCallum; and the talented staff in production and marketing who guided the book over many hurdles. Together they made this a pleasurable and rewarding experience.

My readers, colleagues, and publishing team have tried to keep me from making big mistakes and obvious errors, but any remaining flaws are my responsibility.

Finally, I am forever indebted to three people who live on in beloved memory. My mother, Ellen Dowman, and grandmother, Fern Rhodes, treasured textiles and needlework of all kinds, guided my first stitches, and sparked a passion that has enriched and gladdened my life. My father, Harry Dowman, first taught me the use of basic shop tools and the value of good craftsmanship, personally made my first loom warping board (of lovely Indiana cherry wood), and believed there need be no limits on his daughter's possibilities in life.

You hold in your hands a compact reference and guided tour of the possibilities of expressing yourself with the threaded needle, whether deployed by hand or machine.

And those two words—*expressing yourself*—are the keys to the book's purpose and the reasons I've titled it *The Intentional Thread.* Whether your particular interest is pictorial, portraiture, abstract compositions, or actual text, you can "say" almost anything, and depict almost anything, with thread.

Although the book will often use the language of drawing or painting—because good *intentional* stitchery uses many of the same compositional principles—stitch offers possibilities beyond what is attainable with pencil, charcoal, pastel, or paint. Using thread and cloth, you can achieve deep dimensional effects; contrasts of physical textures, colors, and fiber types; drawn or lettered images visible from both sides; "floating" lines on transparent materials; and much more.

This book is intended to offer valuable information to anyone: from the enthusiastic beginner to the accomplished embroiderer, from the person stitching quietly at home to a group of friends in an embroidery circle, from learners in a workshop to a college classroom.

As a long-time teacher, I'll be doing a lot of friendly explaining along the way. I'll be "talking" to you through the text, as if I was standing next to you in a workshop, sharing my thoughts about what you see and about the ways *I* chose to compose a particular image. But my goal as a teacher is always to help individual learners—whatever their age—to find *their* way, regardless of whether it would be *my* way. While the book provides many examples of my own choices and interpretations, they're not meant to be copied but, rather, to spark *your* brainstorming and to encourage you toward finding your own intentional approach to creating with thread.

There are, of course, some principles common to all good design, and I'll be discussing those and providing many illustrations—because good design, combined with good technique, makes for good outcomes. The ideas I present in this volume will answer many fundamental questions you may have about designing and making expressive use of lines, gestures, and color: How do I get started? How do I translate my sketch into stitching? Why and how do marks convey meaning? How can I choose colors or materials for specific expressions? You will find these answers, and more, ahead.

COMPOSITION: TIPS AND CONSIDERATIONS

When I speak of "the intentional thread," I'm mainly talking about *composition,* which may sound like a fancy design term but, reduced to its essentials, is just *the human hand organizing things.* Of course, composition tells us important things about the subject of the composition. But it also reveals much about the vision, aesthetics, attitudes, assumptions, desires, values, and point of view of the "composer."

- Good composition combines all elements—lines, marks, shapes, colors, textures—in ways that are *harmonious* and *coherent* so that the viewer can make sense of our ideas, because we have organized them to be "readable" and understandable.

- Composition applies to both two- and three-dimensional works, to functional and non-functional objects alike. Good composition is just as important in the success of a basket, a garment, or a fashion accessory as it is for a sculpture or a work for the wall.

- The more complex the idea, or the greater the number of parts or variables, the more difficult it is to organize. A common pitfall in composition is getting so excited by so many things simultaneously that you try to throw too much into a single piece—and too many variables may leave you feeling overwhelmed. So: When in doubt or confused, choose simplicity. Good composition is as much about learning what to leave out as what to include. You can always play—later—with adding more. This book explores compositional ideas from simple to complex.

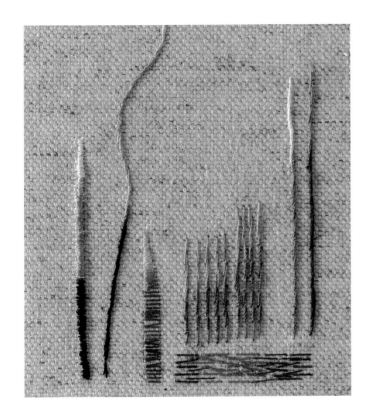

How This Book Is Organized

Each chapter is devoted to a specific design idea and its methods of use and application. The first eight chapters focus on expression with line and shape; the remaining chapters focus on filling shapes and spaces with color, shading, and texture. My goal is to focus chapters on the *separate* effects of various kinds of intentional stitching, but of course, in the actual stitchery work to make a composition, many of these characteristics overlap, and therefore many of the illustrations could have served more than one chapter. I hope this will encourage you to leaf back and forth for multiple ideas and inspiration.

I use straightforward, commonly-used design terms to explain assorted design tools and their multiple effects.

The captions for the images note the materials, stitches, and, where it seems important—such as an image larger than the piece itself—the scale measurements of the actual work.

You'll also find technical "tips" in an array of sidebars and text boxes.

Each chapter concludes with some open-ended projects ("Try this!") inviting you to play with materials, experiment with ideas, test stitch combinations, and invent your own effects. You can, of course, repeat any of these in differing ways as often as you like.

If you are a relative novice at stitching, rest assured that you need to know only a few simple embroidery stitches to tackle the ideas, exercises, or projects. The directions for these stitches are conveniently located in Appendix 1, illustrated for both left- and right-handed stitchers. Appendix 2 gives some basic suggestions on how to design and make exploratory samplers to practice stitches and test new ideas. And finally, Appendix 3 will help you get started on matching expression and technique by showing you some simple examples of expressive gestures.

The glossary defines useful stitchery and design terms. I've also included a bibliography of recommended reading if you'd like to explore further. Finally, I've provided an expanded discussion about the specific properties of the materials, tools, and equipment that I routinely use in my stitching practice, and you'll learn why I choose certain products and which characteristics I find desirable. Because specific vendors come and go with the passage of time, and product offerings change, these lists of desirable characteristics will help you to locate similar products currently on the market, regardless of when you first encounter this book. For a list of current vendors see:

http://www.schifferbooks.com/theintentionalthread

How to Use This Book

Use this book in any way that helps you: as a quick reference for stitch ideas or visual inspiration in the studio; as a self-guided sequence of workshops (for yourself alone or with friends); or as a textbook to teach others. Follow the topics in the order they're presented to build your skills incrementally, or "dip in" anywhere to explore a particular stitchery effect in-depth in your own way.

In the following pages, I invite you to *discover* through creative *play*. You don't have to try everything here at the same time, and you don't have to enjoy all the techniques equally, or even use all of them in your work. Think of the book as a present and future menu—well, actually more like a smorgasbord—of possibilities from which you can choose the things that capture your interest or are appropriate to what you want to make, now or in the future.

Let's start traveling . . .

The Elements of Line

QUITE SIMPLY, *line* refers to any mark that is longer than it is wide—and perhaps that is the only constant characteristic of lines. You may have heard line described as *a point in motion*. You can demonstrate this for yourself. Place the point of a pencil on paper and move it around, continually touching the paper. You will create a line as the *point* of that pencil *moves*. Similarly, if you propel a threaded needle upward from the back of a cloth and down again in another spot, you will create a line. In each case, the motion of your hand holding a tool leaves behind a trail of color.

Lines are the basic tools of drawing, whether made with traditional tools on paper or with a needle and thread on cloth. In practice, they can be fat or thin, sleek or fuzzy, curved or straight, swooping or kinked, but they will always direct your eyes along their length as they *describe* the edges and contours of shapes and add their own color and texture to the surface. When you make lines, some of them will eventually touch or cross, and create *shapes* that are clearly defined against the background.

When you draw with a pencil, the lines record the journey of your hand as your pencil touches the paper—sometimes lightly, sometimes heavily, but rarely with completely equal pressure. Because each person makes lines differently, your lines will immediately express *you*. This is both natural and inevitable.

The chapters in Part 1 explore ways for you to translate the individuality of your marks on paper to the stitched lines you make with needle and thread.

Line weight—a line's length-to-width ratio—is the most basic quality that defines the character of the marks you make on any surface. When describing a line's width or thickness, we use words like *fat* or *thin*, *heavy* or *light*, *chunky* or *delicate*, *solid* or *irregular*, *tapering* or *widening*. Each one describes a different kind of energy and expression. With attention and sensitivity to line width, you control a range of subtle to dynamic drawing effects.

In drawing on paper, line weight is largely controlled by the choice of tool used, the angle at which it contacts the surface, and the amount of pressure applied. For instance, when you press and move a pencil on a surface, you leave a trail of its color behind. If you use the point of the pencil, you will make a thin line; conversely, if you angle the pencil to use the side of the lead, you produce a wider and more transparent line. That trace of your hand movement also records the amount of *pressure* you have exerted. When you increase the pressure, you make darker, fatter marks that are stronger, more visually forceful, and seem to come forward in space. When you decrease the pressure, you make lighter, thinner marks that quietly recede into the background.

Beyond the visible evidence of hand pressure, the trail left by the action of drawing is also a conduit for your internal emotional state, which contributes to the unique qualities of your drawing. For instance, if you are angry you might intentionally, or unconsciously, grip a drawing implement harder, press more firmly, and make more forceful marks. Similarly, if you are nervous, it is likely that your drawn line will express that nervousness by being more erratic in its path, wavering from dark to light in its pressure, and ceaselessly moving around the surface. The trace—that drawn line—captures it all.

ABOVE 01-01 Machine and hand stitching with cotton threads on digitally printed, hand-dyed, discharge-printed, and screen-printed layered cotton twill and silk organza fabric and handwoven cotton accent strip. *Photo credit: Marc Brandeis.*

A sketchbook page (01-02) of rows of drawings of the same series of figures demonstrates how different pencil lead types, from hard to soft, change the weight of the lines. Softer lead tends to force us to make the marks larger and darker, while harder lead leaves slender, tentative, scratchy lines. Each pencil's mark is just slightly different, offering a range of effects and feelings.

Stitching Thin and Fat Lines

Stitching affords a very wide range of options in line weight developed from the interaction of many variables: stitch types and sizes; thread sizes, colors, and textures; value gradations; and combinations and variations of these. While not as direct, immediate, and fluid an action as drawing on paper, the three-dimensional aspects of drawing with thread on cloth compensate by offering a physical dynamism and dimension, close interaction with materials as the thread repeatedly penetrates the plane of the cloth, and textural variety far beyond that of a pencil or pen, while still capturing the spontaneity of your hand.

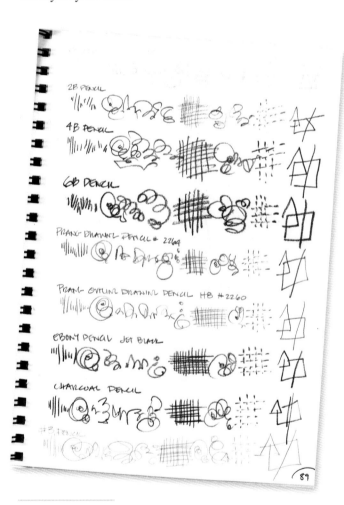

01-02 Pencil drawings on paper using varying line weights and pencil types.

Stitching a sequence of *straight lines* offers a simple starting point to explore line weight. Keep the thread color constant to eliminate the interference of color variables in the study and to focus your emphasis on the gradation of line weights from light to heavy across the surface. In the two studies that follow, each line in the sequence is of equal thickness *from end to end*—that is, the lines do not taper or vary in thickness from top to bottom. But, moving across the surface, each line is a little bit heavier or thicker than its predecessor.

Practicing these gradations, with both hand stitches and machine stitches, will raise your sensitivity to the differences and will help to refine your skills in applying specific line weights when you need them. Each change of thread type requires you to make fresh explorations to understand the limitations and discover the possibilities of the new material.

Sampler of Line Weights:
Hand-Stitched

A single thread has limits of thinness and thickness. Thus, combinations of threads and stitches yield far greater dimensional possibilities. The wider the line, the thicker the thread or group of threads needed. The precise weight of the lines you stitch will depend on your own way of making the stitches and using the threads. Except when using large-scale threads or yarns, wide lines require many more combined small stitches to build, and are therefore slower to produce. Even slight changes in line width can produce dramatically different lines in terms of their visibility, force, and presence.

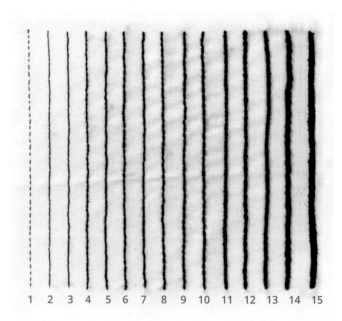

01-03 Hand-stitched sampler of increasing line weights. The wavering in the lines reveals the touch of the hand.
Black cotton threads and rayon tape on cotton.

LINE WEIGHTS: HAND-STITCHED

No.	Stitches	Threads or materials used
1	Running	1 strand cotton sewing
2	Back	1 strand cotton sewing
3	Double running	2 strands cotton sewing
4	Back	2 strands cotton floss
5	Double running	3 strands cotton floss
6	Back	3 strands cotton floss
7	Double running	4 strands cotton floss
8	Back	4 strands cotton floss
9	Back	5 strands cotton floss
10	Back	6 strands cotton floss
11	Chain	2 strands cotton floss
12	Chain	3 strands cotton floss
13	Couching	1 strand low twist cotton moss yarn. Couched or tacked down with 1 strand cotton floss. 2 layers of tacking in overlapping diagonals, stitched from 2 directions.
14	Couching	2 strands low twist cotton moss yarn. Couched or tacked down with 1 strand cotton floss in long, close diagonals.
15	Couching, cross	2 lengths of braided rayon tape couched with 1 strand floss in cross stitches over the tape.

Sampler of Line Weights: Machine-Stitched

A variety of line weights can be created with straight and zigzag machine stitching. Heavier line weights rely on the combination of very short stitch *lengths* with increasingly wider zigzag stitch *widths*—which produces satin stitch (parallel stitches dense enough to cover the cloth). In turn, these wider lines require more stability in the ground material—addressed by strengthening the fabric with a backing or cotton batting, or by stretching it tightly in a hoop during stitching. The maximum width setting on your sewing machine limits the width of the stitched line. To create a solid line that is wider than your machine's limit, overlap multiple parallel lines of satin stitch to maximize stitch density and completely cover the ground cloth.

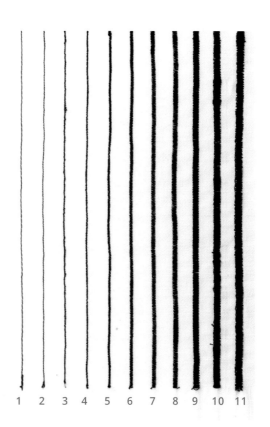

01-04 Machine-stitched sampler of increasing line weights. Even when using the sewing machine, the hand is visible in the making because of slight variations and irregularities in the lines. Cotton sewing thread on cotton.

LINE WEIGHTS: MACHINE-STITCHED

Changing stitch widths using closely spaced zigzag stitching, also called satin stitch
(Stitch width and length settings on the Bernina 930 sewing machine)

No.	Stitch type	Stitch length	Stitch width	Notes:
1	Straight	3 (long)	n/a	
2	Straight	1 (short)	n/a	
3	Straight	1 (short)	n/a	2 strands of thread through the single needle
4	Satin	0.5	0.5	First mark on the dial, narrowest stitch width
5	Satin	0.5	1	
6	Satin	0.5	1.5	
7	Satin	0.5	2	
8	Satin	0.5	2.5	
9	Satin	0.5	3	Needed a second narrow layer to make a clean line
10	Satin	0.5	3.5	Needed 2 complete layers to make solid line
11	Satin	0.5	4	Needed multiple layers to cover breaks in solid line

Heavier Weight Lines

Heavier lines are most easily made by couching down large yarns, cords, or threads—materials too large to be pulled *through* the cloth with a needle—to the *surface* of the cloth. Yarns of almost any weight or fiber content can be couched with hand or machine stitches. This method offers chances to include threads and other materials not usually considered for stitching, such as those typically used in knitting, weaving, or crochet, but also including non-traditional materials like fishing line, wire, plastic cords or tubing, raffia, hemp, twisted paper, spaghetti (dry, not cooked!), reeds, grasses, and many others. Think creatively.

This sampler illustrates a few of the possible choices of materials and densities of machine stitching, couched with a zigzag stitch in varying widths and lengths that change the amount of the laid cord or yarn remaining visible. When the couching completely covers the cord, it resembles hand overcasting. A couched line can travel in any direction—straight, bent, or curved—with each type of cord limiting the angles and flexibility of the curvatures and resulting line qualities.

Machine satin stitch worked over a stiff and stable heavy linen cord creates a very solid line that sits above the surface prominently, firmly, and quite three-dimensionally. Lines can be worked straight or curved, but usually appear even and solid while taking on the texture of the thread chosen for the overcasting. Because they are so stiff from the overcasting, such cords will be naturally rounded in both shape and line, and will resist bending around sharp corners or angles.

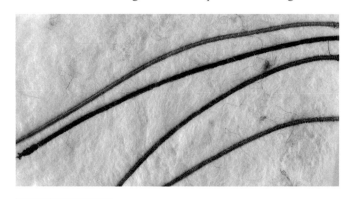

01-06 Bold, dimensional, and solid lines. Overcasting of heavy linen cord on handmade felt. Machine stitching: satin.

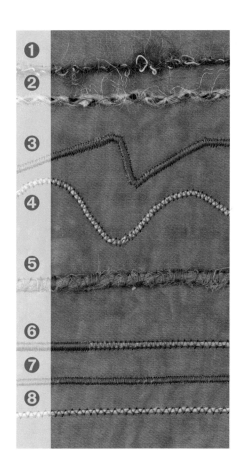

01-05 Variety of heavier weight lines in machine couching.

ROW 1 Highly textured bouclé yarn; openly spaced zigzag. Irregular and flexible.

ROW 2 Multicolored twisted wool yarn; openly spaced zigzag. Stitching aligns with the changes of color in the yarn, adding another line weight to the mix.

ROW 3 Heavy linen cord; tightly spaced satin stitch (overcasting). Highly dimensional, firm, and slightly inflexible solid line.

ROW 4 Heavy linen cord; openly spaced zigzag. Color of machine stitching mixes with the color of the cord. Dimensional and more flexible than overcasting the same cord.

ROW 5 Heavy jute cord; openly spaced zigzag. Color of machine stitching mixes with the color of the cord. Rough, chunky, irregular, flexible.

ROW 6 Medium weight linen cord; half overcast (tight satin stitch), half open zigzag. Presents possibilities for changing the style of couching and the coloration along the length of a line.

ROW 7 Medium weight linen cord; tightly spaced satin stitch (overcasting). Solid and firm.

ROW 8 Medium weight linen cord; openly spaced zigzag. Blended color and firm.

Lines That Change Weight Along Their Length

Quick pencil gestures illustrate differences in pressure along a line's length. The gestures begin at the bottom with force. (Notice the slight skip to the side from the force of the pencil meeting the paper.) They remain dark along nearly the entire length of each line, and then, as the pressure lifts at the top, the line becomes lighter and narrower before trailing off to a slender point. Generally, darkness and wideness of line or gesture conveys more pressure—force, energy, intensity—while lightness and narrowness conveys less pressure—quiet, calm, and delicacy. The specific way your lines change or taper communicates the individuality of your gestures.

01-07 Lines that taper or change in weight. Pencil gestures on paper.

Translating this type of change from drawn hand pressure to stitching requires developing "composite lines"—accumulations of smaller stitches working in combination. The illustrations in this book provide many examples of ways to do this, but you will want to develop a range of your own methods that satisfy your drawing needs. Essentially, the translation from pencil to stitch requires you to manipulate some mixture of stitch types, sizes, variations, colors, and textures.

Tapered Lines: Machine-Stitched

Machine-stitched lines that change in width along their length quickly and easily approximate the character of pencil marks on paper. Where they are darker and wider, they indicate the force of pressure at the beginning of a mark; where they are lighter and thinner, they indicate the release of pressure. Free-motion machine stitching requires some practice to master, but delivers very effective and sophisticated tapered lines. Fortunately, any inaccuracies that occur in the stitching process parallel the idiosyncrasies of drawing with a pencil on paper. They reveal the individual behind the sewing machine and allow direct translation of your natural hand gestures.

MACHINE CONTROLS FOR SATIN STITCH

The key to producing satin stitch lines that widen or narrow smoothly, without jumpy or jagged edges, lies almost entirely in the controls of your sewing machine (bolstered and refined by your technical practice). The smoothest lines can be made on a machine with a stitch width setting that is on a *dial that moves freely*—not one that locks a series of stitch widths into place. Without the freely moving dial, the smooth transition from one width to the next *during stitching* is not possible.

The speed with which you move the hoop determines the stitch length. The width is achieved by adjusting the stitch width dial during sewing *and* while moving the hoop to control the stitch length (the distance from one stitch to the next).

The machine-stitched illustrations in this book were made on a Bernina 930 sewing machine with a movable dial.

Tapering a line in machine stitching can create graceful and fluid gestures. The slender and slightly bent marks in 01-09 widen in the center and taper at *both* ends. When stitched on top of a printed image of long grasses in varying colors, they echo the grass shapes and increase the illusion of depth.

Tapered marks are effective at highlighting or emphasizing details of a composition of plants, adding visual dynamism and sparkle to the surface.

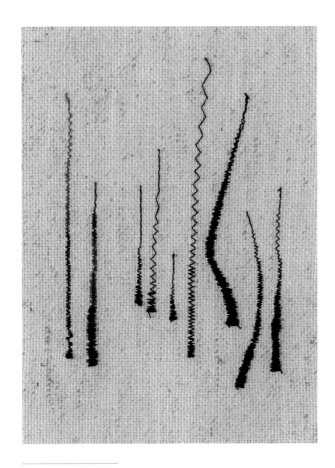

01-08 Tapering marks in free-motion machine stitching. Stitches: straight, zigzag. Cotton sewing thread on linen.

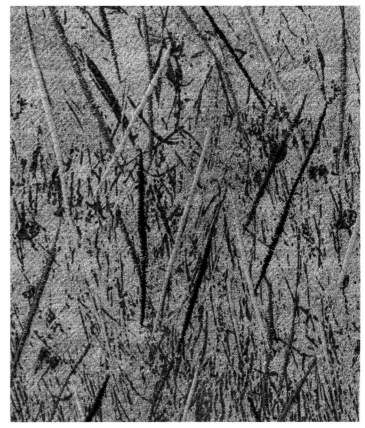

01-09 Lines which taper at both ends. Changes in color add variety and dimensionality. Machine stitching: satin. Cotton thread on hand-dyed and screen-printed parachute silk.

Tapered Lines: Hand-Stitched

Many hand stitches—satin, stem, straight, whip, and back stitches—work well in creating both straight and curved lines that change in weight along their length and that mimic differing pencil pressures. Gradation of color values—changing from light to dark—along a tapered line enhances the tapering effect. As the value of the color approaches the value of the supporting fabric, it will seem to disappear. In other words, stitch with high value contrast at the "fat end" of the line and with low value contrast at the thinner, tapered end.

Using variegated thread potentially introduces both color and value changes faster than re-threading the needle each time, but the process requires careful monitoring of the color changes in the thread for their effective placement along the line. Although slower, choosing a sequence of colors and then re-threading the needle for each change affords more precise value control.

01-10 Machine stitching (satin) on digitally printed and layered cotton sheeting and silk organza. (Collection: Duke University Medical Center, Durham, North Carolina, USA.)
Photo credit: Marc Brandeis.

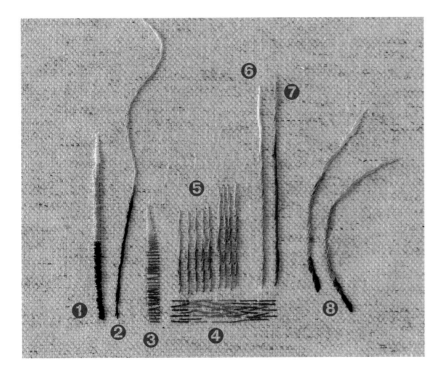

01-11 Tapering marks. Value changes along the length of the lines emphasize the tapering. Hand stitching. Valdani 35 wt. variegated cotton thread and cotton floss on linen.

No.	Stitch	Thread	Notes
1	Satin	Valdani variegated 35 wt., 1 strand	Dark part of thread aligned with bottom of stitch and worked upwards, ending with light value blending with the ground fabric at the tip.
2	Stem	Valdani variegated 35 wt., 1 strand	Stem stitch with the color arranged as in no. 1 Stitch provides a longer line within the changes in the thread's variegation.
3	Straight	Valdani variegated 35 wt., 1 strand	Placed darkest color (medium value) at the base and worked up in separated stitches, narrowing gradually toward the top.
4	Long and short	Valdani variegated 35 wt., 1 strand	Horizontal stitches worked in bands from top to bottom, from left, moving right, like hatching.
5	Stem	Valdani variegated 35 wt., 1 strand	First 5 lines worked simultaneously from bottom to top (1 stitch in each line, then the second, the third, etc.) until third, etc.) until color changed to another dark (purple), then started the second set of 4 lines, worked in the same manner.
6	Stem	Valdani variegated 35 wt., 1 strand	Variegation consisting only of gray and white, and color change therefore more abrupt.
7	Stem	Valdani variegated 35 wt., 1 strand	In this thread, the change from light to dark value is more gradual, but the change from green to yellow is very abrupt and noticeable.
8	Stem	DMC cotton floss—black, 5 warm grays, and natural (2 strands)	Lines marked on fabric and worked from base to tip, changing colors every 3 to 12 stitches, setting the stem stitch very close and making it rather small.

VALDANI THREADS

Many of the illustrations in this book were stitched with the Valdani brand of 35 weight variegated cotton sewing thread, a high-quality thread which is similar in weight to a single strand of cotton floss or to the weight of quilting thread. It is equally effective in the sewing machine (reduce the top tension and try using a top stitch needle) and in hand stitching, and its tighter twist makes it sit up more dimensionally on the surface of the fabric. By comparison, the lower twist of cotton floss makes it settle down more into the fabric surface.

I frequently use Valdani for its sensitive and sophisticated range of colors in its solid threads and the rich and unusual color combinations in its variegated threads. The company also offers cotton and silk embroidery flosses, pearl cottons, and wools. These are available directly from the manufacturer at: https://www.valdani.com. As an alternative to this product, look for a machine thread with similar characteristics, i.e., cotton, high-twist, heavier weight, and a broad spectrum of available color intensities and variations to allow subtle color changes.

Expanding and Contracting Line Weights

Drawing employs many complex variations in line weight. The following studies explore thicknesses that continually expand and contract, back and forth, along the line's length while the lines move in different paths across the cloth. Compare the differences achieved by hand and machine stitches.

01-12 Irregular width and length contribute to a hand-drawn look. Free-motion machine stitching on a base of resist-dyed silk organza laid over hand-dyed silk noil, both then stitched through. Stitch: satin. Cotton thread.

Irregular zigzag (01-12): The dark gold spiral was worked spontaneously and erratically, allowing the spaces between the stitches to vary irregularly. Contrasting thread and ground colors clearly delineate the spiral while irregularity in stitching suggests hand-drawn lines and gesture.

Loosely sketched look (01-13): Irregularly spaced hand stitching allows the fabric color to interact with the stitches for relative transparency or opacity. Stitch width changes alternate between smooth and jerky motions, while variegated thread adds an extra layer of visual change.

Pulsating line (01-14): Continually widening and narrowing line weights make a noticeably pulsating line. With machine satin stitch, the line formed is very solid and firm. The openly spaced hand-stitched line leaves a more delicate and tentative effect, but with similar pulsations.

Smooth and flat (01-15): Regular, short stitch *length* creates a smooth, flat, dense, and controlled satin stitch, while very slight variations in stitch *width* produce a slight visual waver. The dense stitching requires more stabilization to keep the fabric flat. Lower contrast blue threads blend into the ground fabric while the high contrast navy thread at the edge moves forward visually. Combined with the concentric arrangement of the lines, this creates the sense of looking down into a shallow hole.

Machine satin stitching can make a heavy, emphatic line or a slender, piercing edge. In 01-16, complementary contrasts of color, coupled with wavering line weights, define the edges of shapes with great clarity and clearly separate them from the background. The physical presence of the line is enhanced by being stitched on a "quilt sandwich," i.e., the stitching provides depth where it pinches the layers together and the cotton batting provides a contrast of loft on either side of the stitching.

01-13 Irregular spacing produces a more sketch-like and spontaneous line quality. Free-motion machine stitching (satin) on a base of resist-dyed silk organza laid over hand-dyed silk noil, both then stitched through and further enhanced with hand stitching (straight, running). Cotton thread.

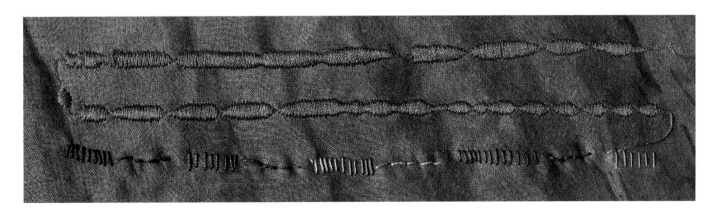

01-14 Upper two rows: closely spaced machine stitching (satin), varying stitch widths. Bottom row: hand stitching (satin and back), openly spaced. Base of resist-dyed silk organza laid over hand-dyed silk noil, both then stitched through using cotton thread.

This stitched translation (01-17) of a small section of a drawing (from a sketchbook of the Dutch master Rembrandt Harmenszoon van Rijn) provides a more complex and dramatic demonstration of the power of changing line weights. The original drawing is masterful and highly communicative, offering a wonderfully inspiring example of contrasting line weights to practice. Its interpretation was a lesson in thoughtful choice of threads in varying sizes and the placement, extension, and continuation of lines with changing stitch types. These combine to approximate the sense of space and living presence in the original drawing.

01-15 Flatter, more regular lines can be achieved with closer control of machine satin stitch. Free-motion machine stitching on a base of resist-dyed silk organza laid over hand-dyed silk noil, both then stitched through. Stitch: satin. Cotton thread.

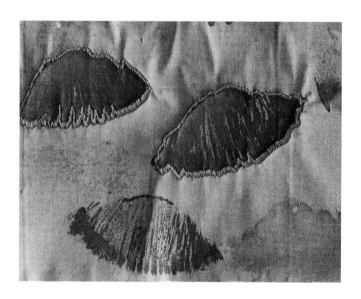

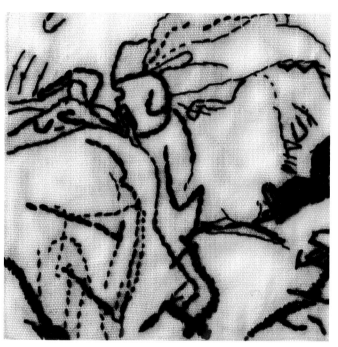

01-16 Changing stitch width, very short stitch length. Complementary color contrast heightens the edge effect. Free-motion machine stitch: satin. Cotton sewing thread on stamp-printed and hand-painted cotton fabric. stem, couching, satin. Scale: 2" × 2".

01-17 Hand-stitched interpretation of Rembrandt drawing detail in cotton threads on cotton cloth. Stitches: running, back, stem, couching, satin. Scale: 2" × 2".

Try this!

1.1 / Sketching Varied Line Weights

Make six to eight simple pencil or charcoal sketches with a variety of line weights. (For examples, see 01-02 and 01-07.) Choose a section from one of the drawings to interpret in stitching, capturing as accurately as possible the various nuances and contrasts of line weight in the sketches.

1.2 / Line Weight in Context

Select a master artist's ink or pencil drawing which contains a variety of line weights. Scan or photocopy a small section or detail to interpret. Paying close attention to contrasts of line weight, select stitches to translate this section using a single color of thread. Use hand stitching, machine stitching, or a combination of the two.

    Follow-up: If you like to draw, do the same with one of your own original drawings containing a variety of line weights.

Because lines are longer than they are wide, they have built-in direction that leads the eye within a composition. Understanding some general rules of thumb about the effects of line direction will help you to achieve a general mood, feeling, or atmosphere in your drawings. This underlying structure sets the tone of the drawing and works in tandem with line weight to convey meaning.

Lines can be placed in three basic positions in a composition: vertical, horizontal, and diagonal. Next we'll take a look at how Western art compositional conventions use these directions to convey distance, hierarchy, and space. People from Eastern cultures, however, may perceive these line uses and their impressions quite differently.

Vertical Lines

Vertical lines—those placed perpendicular to a horizontal base line—exist in a state of equilibrium with natural forces, as we ourselves demonstrate every time we stand or walk despite the force of gravity. Thus, vertical lines tend to look strong, stiff, alert, and rather formal. They convey the structure and solidity of remaining upright despite proximity or individual character. Packed closely together, they reinforce each other and create the appearance of a barrier. In 02-02, vertical lines in differing line weights seem firm and erect, even when they are lightweight or broken.

In 02-03, multiple long, thick vertical lines maintain their overall sense of verticality even when crossed by many small horizontal and diagonal lines and counterbalanced by underlying "organic" circular shapes.

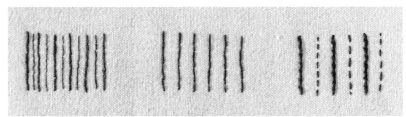

TOP 02-01 Diagonal lines prevail. The more solid the stitched line, the clearer the edges of shapes and the more directly our eyes are led upward. Hand stitching: back, running, stem, chain, couching, coral, overcasting. Cotton thread on digitally printed cotton fabric.

ABOVE 02-02 Vertical lines. Hand stitching: back, chain, running, whip. Valdani 35 wt. cotton thread on linen.

Horizontal Lines

Horizontal lines appear to be stable and at rest. We associate them with the ground plane, the horizon line, and sleeping—directions in nature that provide support and safety. Thus, horizontal lines in compositions tend to convey quiet stability and calm. Even when lines are more visually active by being broken, the overall effect is still restful, an effect enhanced by cool thread colors.

Arrangements of small vertical marks, gestures, or figures, repeated in sufficient number and proximity, combine visually to read as horizontal bands. (See 02-05.) The insertion of the slight diagonals somewhat activates the horizontal bands, but the horizontal emphasis preserves a calm effect.

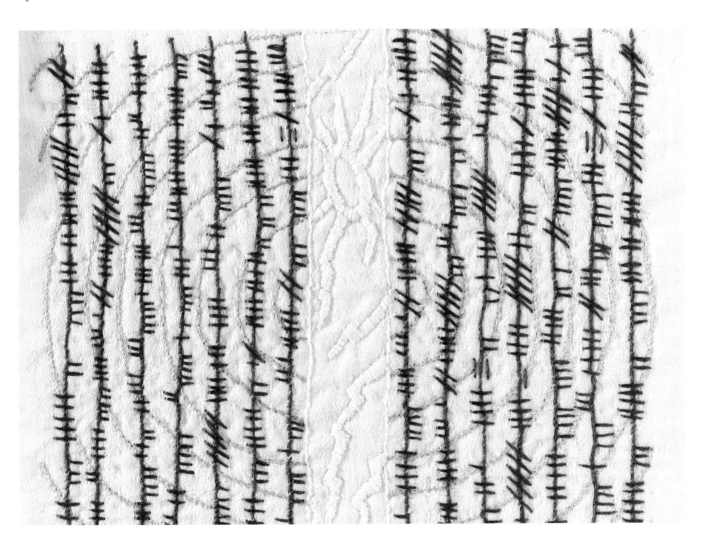

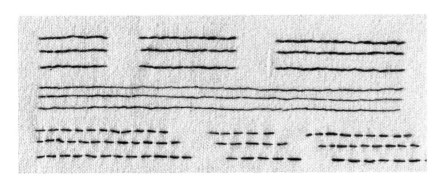

ABOVE 02-03 Hand stitching: back, straight, satin. Cotton floss on heirloom linen.

LEFT 02-04 Horizontal lines in parallel rows. Hand stitching: back, running. Valdani 35 wt. cotton thread on linen.

02-05 Hand stitching: straight, couching, running, cross, back, satin, fly, whip, overcasting, French knots. Cotton floss on heirloom linen.

Oblique or Diagonal Lines

Lines sitting at any angle between the completely vertical and the fully horizontal are referred to as diagonal or oblique. Depending on their placement and character, they can appear to be yielding to the force of gravity by "falling" or resisting the force of gravity by "rising." Because of the tension inherent in their "unbalanced" state, they tend to be perceived as more dynamic, visually active, and energetic. Use of diagonals conveys energy, resistance, conflict, liveliness, or activity.

In 02-06, the lines' angles above the horizontal become progressively smaller as they march across the fabric from left to right. Although in reality they are only a series of diagonal lines, the increasing *tilt* of each individual line causes us to perceive them as "toppling over." (If, on the other hand, the sequence is read from right to left, the lines seem to be

"rising up.") Gradually increasing the lines' weights from left to right would further enhance the effect of tension, dynamism, and falling. But in either way of reading, the lines appear *active*.

Although *straight* lines are often used to illustrate these different orientations, the same effects hold true for lines that bend and curve. Even if curved, lines placed vertically side by side appear stiffer and stronger. If placed horizontally in parallel rows, they appear calmer. If given even a slight oblique leaning, they dance.

Cross stitches are among the quickest and easiest ways to introduce diagonal lines in stitching. The more uneven in length you make their two "legs," the more off-balance and active they will appear.

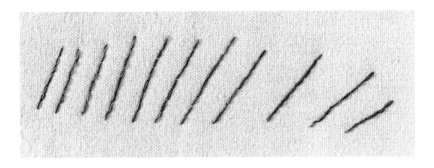

02-06 Diagonal or oblique lines. Hand stitching: back. Three strands of contrasting Valdani 35 wt. variegated threads on linen.

RIGHT 02-07 Hand stitching: running, straight, cross, couching. Valdani variegated 35 wt. cotton thread on heirloom linen.

BELOW 02-08 Hand (satin, cross) and machine (satin) stitching. Cotton thread on hand-dyed cottons and silks.

Combinations of Line Directions

Of course, nearly every composition combines lines that lie in many orientations. The *proportions* of the various line directions will determine the overall effect: the more vertical lines, the stiffer; the more horizontal lines, the calmer; the more diagonal lines, the livelier. Every composition is different—and you yourself control the directions and proportions. This study (02-09) demonstrates a kind of equilibrium, or balanced visual energy. Equal amounts of vertical and horizontal lines combine to cancel out one another's directional energies and to place them in perfect balance.

Symmetry of placement contributes to balance between the straight and curved, verticals and horizontals. (See 02-10.) Equality of visual weight around a central axis establishes equilibrium and stability.

A variety of vertical, horizontal, and diagonal lines arranged in bands and balanced in all directions makes a stable but visually "flickering" effect. In 02-11, alternating light blue-gray vertical and horizontal marks provide a stable and well-balanced foundation for the black oblique marks overlying them.

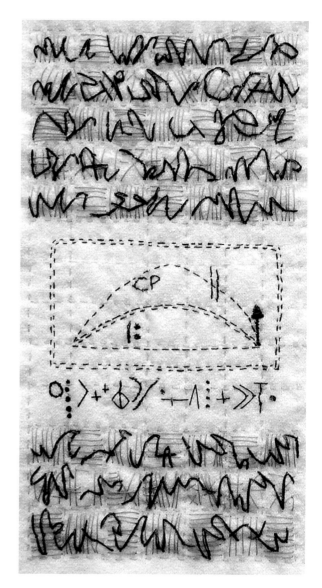

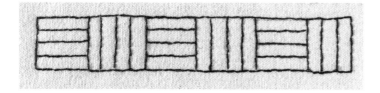

02-09 Horizontal and vertical lines in balance.
Hand stitching: back. Valdani 35 wt. cotton thread on linen.

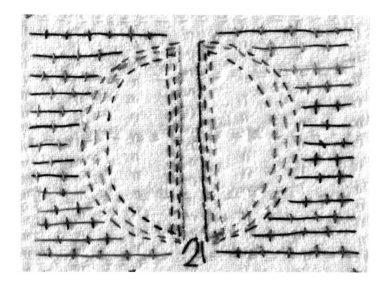

02-10 Horizontal and vertical lines in balance. Hand stitching: running, straight, couching, back, cross, French knots, fly, laced back. Valdani 35 wt. cotton thread on silk noil.

02-11 Stable background built from alternating rows of vertical and horizontal marks overlaid with more active diagonals. Hand stitching: straight, couching, running, cross, back, laced running, French knots. Cotton floss and Valdani 35 wt. cotton thread on silk noil. (Collection: Dolly Perkins, Silver Spring, Maryland, USA.) *Photo credit: Susan Brandeis.*

THREE-DIMENSIONAL ILLUSIONS ON CLOTH

Much image making in Western art employs techniques to suggest the illusion of three-dimensional space—the physical world we live in—on a two-dimensional surface, such as paper or painting canvas. These techniques include:

- **Size:** Smaller objects appear more distant.

- **Overlapping:** Objects that overlap others seem closer than those they partially obscure.

- **Vertical location:** The higher an object is placed toward the top of a composition, the farther away it seems. This is the main way that the illusion of "distance" is created. For example, in an imaginary photograph, your house (if located at the top of the image) appears more distant than your dog (in the middle of the image), which appears more distant than the green lawn (at the bottom of the image)—just as they were actually located, even though the photograph is two-dimensional but the house, dog, and lawn occupied actual three-dimensional space.

- **Aerial/atmospheric perspective:** The use of color and/or value to show depth. As depth increases, value contrast between objects gradually lessens and shape contours are less distinct. Therefore, de-intensified or duller colors, less distinct hue contrasts, and fuzzy shape contours all contribute to the illusion that objects are in the distance.

- **Linear perspective:** Making objects steadily smaller as they are placed on the picture plane closer and closer along the oblique lines (which may be imaginary or an actual part of the composition) radiating from the vanishing point.

Cloth is not a truly two-dimensional surface—or, at least, it is not as two-dimensional as a piece of paper. Although it can be spread flat, it always has both volume and texture. Furthermore, working cloth, unlike drawing on paper with a pencil, always involves adding stitches to *both* sides, even if only the "finished" side is intended to be seen. This physical reality of cloth must be overcome *and used* (think of it as an opportunity, not a barrier) in order to create any desired spatial illusions in imagery on fabric. And that, in turn, usually requires you to *exaggerate* the techniques outlined above. Just think "more." Because cloth and stitching were, of course, made for each other.

Line Direction Applications

While much of this information about line direction may be self-evident, stitching a sampler to explore the ideas will help you to "digest" these general rules for future application. In my own sampler (02-12), laid out like a sketchbook page, I did not try to make the stitches perfectly, or to make each stitch meet the last, or to make lines appear to be solid. I worked quickly and allowed, or sometimes cultivated, spaces between the stitches for aesthetic effect. For example, on the small "ball" in the center, the back stitch was deliberately worked with larger spaces between the stitches to achieve delicacy and suggest shadow. The scale of the linen ground cloth helped in this "sketchiness" and was also easy to needle.

In most cases, the heavier-weight lines were achieved by setting in second lines of stitching *instead of* using two threads in the needle. These wavering double lines of back stitch on the exterior edges of the large cube produce an immediate and *spontaneous* sense of *sketching*. Double threads in the needle would have achieved a line more solid and defined.

The use of line direction can be subtle or obvious, but it allows you to draw the viewer's eye in the direction you intend. It is useful for detailing and defining, creating the illusion of three-dimensional forms, creating textures, and leading the eye through compositional space. In all cases, the changing direction of lines infuses the composition with specific kinds of energy and evokes an emotional or psychological response.

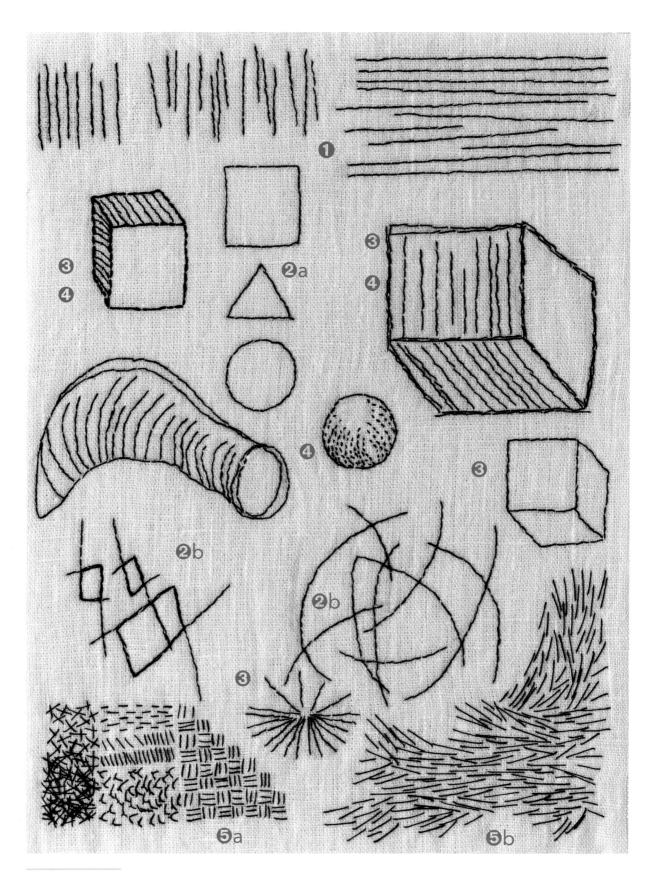

02-12 Sketchbook-style stitched sampler exploring line orientations and directions. Hand stitching: back, running, whip, fly, straight. Valdani 35 wt. cotton thread on softened linen with cotton batting backing.

1	Slight diagonals	Even a very slight tilting to the diagonal injects liveliness by rendering lines more active and energetic, whether they are mostly vertical (top left) or mostly horizontal (top right).
2	Curved and angled lines	Curved and angled lines, placed in proximity, may eventually cross and thereby create shapes which enclose space. This can happen in two ways:
	a) Intentionally:	Lines start and stop precisely to bound a shape, as in the square, triangle, and circle, and a predetermined and often recognizable outline is drawn.
	b) Randomly:	Lines are tossed, and their end points lie well beyond the confines of the shape thus enclosed. They overlap by virtue of their direction and proximity. In accidental enclosures, the shapes can be quite irregular and unique.
3	Illusion of three-dimensional space (perspective)	When straight lines are directed so they converge at a point on an imaginary horizon (known as the *vanishing point*), they create the illusion of three-mensional space on a two-dimensional surface, and thus persuade the eye that it is seeing volume or distance. This type of illusion can be seen in the examples of lines radiating from a central point and lines appearing to form cubes.
4	Flat shapes vs. volumes (slope and surface direction)	The square, triangle, and circle in 2a have no internal lines and are therefore seen as essentially two-dimensional. By contrast, the cubes, the small ball, and the tubular "worm" or "windsock" shape are articulated with parallel internal lines to lead the eye in a particular direction, "pop" the shapes off the surface visually, and make us "read" them as three-dimensional volumes. This is another tactic for creating the illusion of space and volume on the cloth surface.
5	Line direction to create texture	The bottom corners of the sampler demonstrate several ways to use the direction of lines—in particular, lines that repeat—to create the indication of changes in surface qualities or textures.
	a) Bottom left:	Different textures result from using cross and fly stitches when compared to the whip and running stitches adjacent to them. The change of direction (perpendicular juxtaposition) of the straight stitches to the right creates another kind of texture altogether. Each has its own character, and the change from one to the other denotes a change in circumstances or texture on the surface. This can be used to define areas or shapes either abruptly or gradually.
	b) Bottom right:	The clustered straight stitches lead the eye downward and around the corner, flowing and turning. The stitches are never quite parallel, but sit at slight diagonals to each other, infusing the movement with ripples and rhythm. This is simple to work but very effective to suggest a more organic movement.

Every drawing you make will combine lines that run in various directions. It will be your pleasurable task to prioritize those directions, place them in balance with each other, and arrange them on the surface for maximum contribution to the effectiveness of your drawing's composition.

LINE RHYTHM

When lines change direction along their length—i.e., bend back and forth, or zig up and down—they create a *rhythm*. Even minute changes in amplitude, direction, regularity, or irregularity of the marks also change our perception of the rhythm. For instance, *jagged* lines with sharp turns and corners (instead of curves) produce abrupt, sharp rhythms. By contrast, *fluid* lines with long gentle curves, crossings, and intertwinings (instead of sharp angles) produce slow, meandering rhythms. Remember to consider the mutual relationship between line rhythm and line character.

02-13 Vertical, horizontal, and diagonal lines interact and balance in composition. Hand and machine stitching: satin, cross. Cotton thread on hand-dyed, pieced cotton and silk.

Try this!

2.1 / Balance of line directions

Create a composition that combines horizontal, vertical, and diagonal lines in balance. Sketch it on paper first to consolidate your ideas. Then translate the sketch into stitching.

2.2 / Leading the eye

Create a composition in which the lines lead the viewer's eye like a river flowing, winding, or meandering through the space. Pay close attention to the direction of all lines.

2.3 / Rhythm

Create a composition on paper in which there is an intentional rhythm created by the lines and marks. The rhythm can be subtle or dramatic, even or uneven, quiet or forceful. It might echo a heartbeat, a drum beat, a bouncing ball, a rolling marble, a dance step, or a flowing brook. Then translate it into stitching. Be inventive and playful.

2.4 / Interpretation of music

Start with a specific piece of music that you like. Listen to a recording of it, or a section of it, at least twice. On the next play-through, start drawing lines on paper in response to the rhythm and dynamics of the music. Try to equate line weight and direction with the music you hear. What is the character of the music? Is it percussive or smooth? Agitated or peaceful? Loud or soft? Melodious or atonal? Does the nature of the music suggest that your drawn lines should be small and intimate, or large and gestural, or combinations of each as the music itself changes course? (A march with loud drum beats might, for example, require regularly placed vertical lines, but a waltz might suggest lines that gracefully bend back and forth, changing line weights. Jazz might suggest marks that are "syncopated," while rock might suggest bold and "electric.") Then translate your interpretation into stitching.

The urge to pick up a pencil to doodle has struck everyone at one time or another—during a long meeting, a phone call, or while traveling. The marks we make in those moments constitute the most intuitive drawing that we do. Dashes, dots, doodles, scribbles, and ticks seem to come from nowhere and have no explicit purpose. Their watchword is *spontaneity*. These elemental marks are at once highly individual *and* universal in their communication. Therein lies their interest and worth. No matter how common the mark or symbol you make, the *way* you make it is unique to you because it captures the actions of the small muscles of your hand. Marks made *without* thinking can be consciously developed into a personal vocabulary of irregularly spaced, small, sharp, and lively gestures useful for enlivening surfaces or areas of compositions, whether drawn, painted, or stitched.

Capture your own spontaneous marks on paper. As you translate them into stitching, set aside ideas of control and precision, and temporarily ignore what you know about the "correct way" to make stitches. Focus on what you know about the *essence* of making stitches: how to move needle and thread through cloth. In the pursuit of your individual expressive vocabulary, manipulate your stitching—distort, stretch, expand, and modify—to develop your own variations of shape, character, orientation, color, and line weight. Your marks will activate space and simultaneously define and reveal your individual hand. Play around.

ABOVE 03-01 Cotton threads on digitally-printed, hand-dyed, discharge-printed layered linen and silk organza. Machine stitching: satin.

Sharp and Distinct Marks: Dashes, Dots, and Ticks

Tiny marks separated from each other on the surface, numerous in quantity, and distinct from the background, are well-suited to producing with hand stitching. The straighter the mark, the easier it is to approximate with thread. Curling and curving marks require more manipulation and a few tricks to achieve.

Many kinds of small stitches can be used to translate elemental marks: irregular cross, straight, seeding, fly, detached chain, and French knots, to name a few. Many of them combine well for unique effects. Thoughtful or clever fabric choices increase the potential for a complementary relationship between the marks and the surface texture of the fabric.

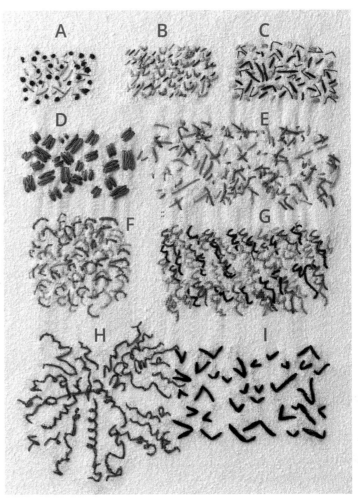

03-03 Hand-stitched interpretation of 03-02.
Stitches: fly, self-couching, straight, French knots.
Cotton floss on silk noil.

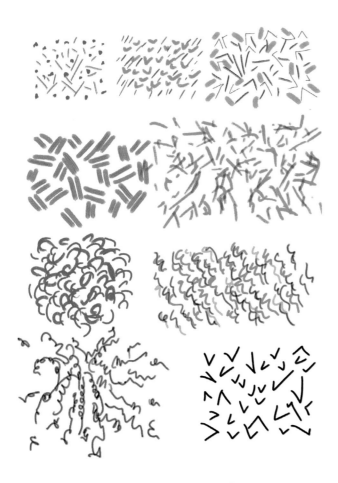

03-02 Quick, sharp, lively gestural marks.
Digital drawing with Corel *Painter*™.

Hand-Stitched Dashes, Dots, and Ticks

Success with hand stitching tiny gestures begins with choosing the right fabric. A "nubby" textured fabric grabs and holds threads in place during stitching—a trick that helps you to manage complex turns, curves, overlaps, and intersections of the threads. Because a nubby fabric is thicker, the more delicate stitches settle "down into" the fabric surface and merge with it both physically and visually. The combination of using nubby, textured fabric and self-couching conquers the technical challenges of producing small and complex elemental marks. Smooth fabric, on the other hand, introduces an extra level of technical challenge to achieve the same marks, because the threads are apt to slip against the fabric.

Because most people feel that the fluidity of gesture is more intuitively and easily achieved in drawing (I certainly do), my exploration began with an initial drawing (03-02) which was then printed on silk noil (a nubby cloth) as a "road map" for the stitching in 03-03. I stitched directly on top of my drawn and digitally printed marks. With my own drawing as a guide, I could concentrate on the specific nuances of my marks, the directions of the threads, and the development of my personal methods of translation. (See previous page.)

A. Dots and Dashes Contrast of tossed diagonal lines in straight stitches and the dots of French knots provides texture and directional contrast. Punchy and active.

B. Dashes and Ticks Contrast of straight and fly stitches yields surface energy. Diagonals and straight lines roughly aligned in a consistent direction.

C. Fat Lines/Thin Lines Contrasts of line weight using 1 to 6 strands of floss in the needle. Color changes add visual variety, depth, and texture.

D. Fat Dashes Chunky and bold marks sit above the fabric surface emphatically. Double seeding arrangement with 6 strands of floss.

E. Irregularly Spaced Marks Irregularly spaced and arbitrarily overlapping marks suggest flattened grass or blown bits of hay. The marks enliven the surface in a quirky, more random way.

F. Curves and Curls Curves and curls grow out from a center point, providing a lively organic texture. Self-couching was used to tack straight stitches into curves.

G. Overlapping Squiggles Layered, squiggling lines combine self-couching with straight stitches. Overlapping and color changes emphasize the layers.

H. Corkscrews Single color, self-couched squiggles in exaggerated irregularity and radiating from a center point suggest growth and liveliness.

I. Chunky Ticks Bold and energetic. Stitches irregular, elongated, and exaggerated. Using 6 strands of high contrast floss color with fly stitches creates simple ticks with counterbalanced diagonals.

Small marks can be stitched onto two separate fabrics, one opaque and one transparent, as in 03-04. When the fabrics are layered with the transparent fabric on top, the misaligned marks create a visual vibration and physical depth.

FABRIC MARKING

To guide the placement and shapes of your initial explorations, I recommend marking the cloth before stitching. There are many products on the market for this purpose, such as markers with disappearing or wash-out inks, tailor's pencils, tracing papers, and iron-on transfers. But you can also just draw what you want directly on the fabric with a pencil, and—although the pencil marks themselves will be permanent—stitch directly on top of them.

If you are digitally adept, digital drawings printed directly on the fabric make clear, though even more permanent, guides.

Choose the method most appropriate for your project. However the drawn or printed marks were made, cover them with your stitching.

RIGHT 03-04 Hand-stitched marks on two layers. Stitch: fly. Cotton floss on silk mesh upper layer and silk noil lower layer which was digitally printed with marks before stitching. (Collection: Dolly Perkins, Silver Spring, Maryland, USA.) *Photo credit: Susan Brandeis.*

Machine-Stitched Dashes, Dots, and Ticks

Generating small distinct marks with free-motion machine stitching requires starting and stopping the machine to relocate the needle for each new mark. Unless they get in your way, the threads can be left joined and then cut when you are done stitching. Each change to a new location can incorporate a new thread color in the mark, but variegated thread will make the changes happen automatically.

On highly textured or dimensional hand-woven fabrics, machine-stitched marks will sink into the surface both physically and visually.

On flatter, thinner, industrially-produced fabrics, dashes sit on top of the surface and are quite distinct. Repeating masses of them across a large surface requires patience and clearly marking the fabric in advance for the location of each discrete mark.

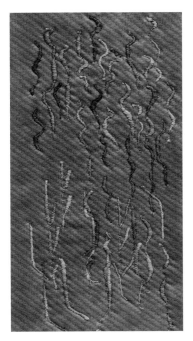

TOP LEFT 03-05 Small, wiggly marks on layered fabrics. Free-motion machine stitching: satin. Valdani 35 wt. variegated cotton on handwoven cotton with silk organza overlay to keep the stitching on the surface.

TOP RIGHT 03-06 Small, wiggly marks. Stitching sinks into the fuzzy wool weft threads. Free-motion machine stitching: satin. Valdani 35 wt. variegated cotton threads on handwoven wool.

ABOVE 03-07 Small marks were printed on organza as guides before machine stitching (satin). Cotton sewing thread through layered silk organza and cotton twill, both of which had been screen-printed, dyed, and discharge-printed.

Fluid Marks: Doodles, Scribbles, and Sketches

Free-motion machine stitching is a perfect tool for making fluid, connected, or larger-scale elemental marks. The machine's uninterrupted motion, combined with the ability to move the stitching line in any direction without turning the fabric, very naturally produces loose, even, and continuous lines. Larger marks, even when disconnected, can be worked more quickly and with spontaneity similar to drawing with a pencil.

RIGHT 03-08 Doodles and scribbles with irregular spacing. Digital drawing with Corel *Painter* ™ pencil tool.

FAR RIGHT 03-09 Increasingly heavier marks produced by overstitching. Top thread color is black, bobbin color is white. Free-motion machine stitching: straight, satin. Cotton thread on silk noil.

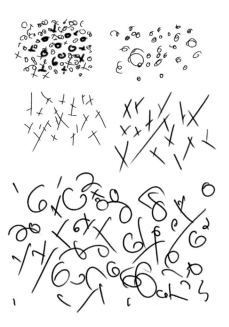

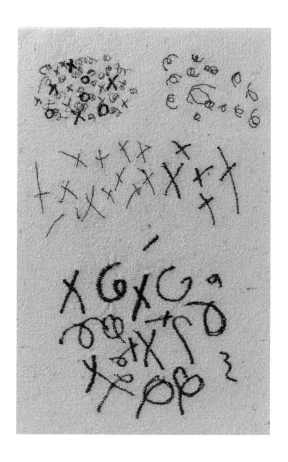

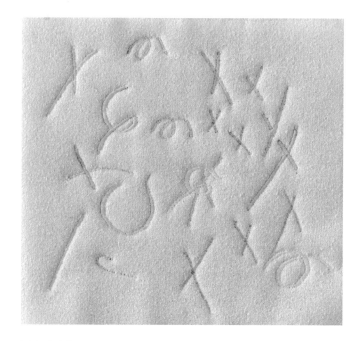

03-10 Free-motion machine stitching: satin. Cotton thread, in matched top and bobbin colors, on silk noil.

Machine-Stitched Doodles, Scribbles, and Sketches

The translation of drawing 03-08 into stitched composition 03-09 on cloth uses black thread on the top spindle of the machine and white thread in the bobbin to increase the sense that the marks are uneven or scratchy, as they might be with pencil on rough paper. This unevenness in color, coupled with the compression of the stitches, makes the marks appear to be etched or scratched into the surface. A bolder line emerges with repeated layers of stitching over the same lines, adding the quirkiness of the slight misalignment to the scratchy quality.

Conversely, in 03-10, matching bobbin thread and top thread colors while keeping stitch length very short builds denser, clearer marks, even when they are stitched in low value contrast with the background. Smooth, dense satin stitch marks are harder to achieve on rough-textured fabric because of its uneven nature, but easily possible on smoother, more tightly woven fabrics.

FREE-MOTION STITCHING TIPS

Stabilizing the Fabric

• Most free-motion stitching works best if the fabric is tightly stretched in a hoop with the small ring of the hoop pressed into the face of the cloth—the opposite of the way you would stretch the fabric in a hoop for hand stitching. This allows the back of the fabric to sit flat and move smoothly over the platform and throat plate of the machine.

• Back the fabric with thin cotton batting or another piece of fabric to increase its stability.

• Always remember to drop the machine's feed dogs so that you aren't fighting against the machine's built-in action.

• Choose a hoop about 8" to 10" in diameter that will sit well on the machine platform and will not knock against the upright of the machine as you move it around to reach different areas.

• When you are stitching, grip the hoop with *both hands* and move it to draw. This is the *opposite* of hand stitching, in which the ground remains stationary but you move the needle. Gripping the hoop lends control and helps to keep your hands away from the rapidly moving needle, which can easily pierce your fingers if they get in its way.

• Highly spontaneous free-motion machine stitching places a lot of tension on the cloth. Backing your fabric with heavy cotton twill, which is especially strong and dimensionally stable while being stitched, will minimize and sometimes even eliminate the need to stretch the fabric in a hoop. But if you decide to work without a hoop, *watch your fingers!*

• Stitching through two fabrics of any weight layered together will add stability, especially if the backing fabric is turned on the bias. This works for dense stitching, whether done by machine or by hand.

• Choose a weight of thread that will best achieve the weight of line you want to create. Adjust your machine's upper tension and use a correspondingly sized needle to accommodate heavier or lighter threads.

The Drawing Process

• Run the machine at full speed. Learn to achieve the desired stitch *length* by moving the hoop at different speeds. Moving it slowly will produce short individual stitches; moving it fast will produce long individual stitches.

• Running the machine at full speed while moving the ground cloth equally quickly and with a bit of a jerk at each change of direction will result in the most agitated or frenzied lines. Moving it slowly will result in the most fluid and elegant lines.

• Thread colors that *contrast* with printed fabrics add a new layer of marks on top of the print. Thread colors that *blend* with the cloth can be manipulated to fill spaces, create textures, and enhance shapes already printed.

Working with black thread on simple white fabric approximates the effect of drawing with black ink on white paper. In this free-motion, machine-stitched study (03-11), the speed of the machine was high, and the motion used to move the fabric (in the hoop) alternated between jerky and smooth, fast and slow, *while stitching*. These variables generated a range of mark types and characters. Quick changes of direction add tension that can pull the bobbin thread from the back to the surface (sometimes called moss stitch). Overlapping zigzag stitches can bunch and wrinkle the fabric, adding dimension. Irregular changes of the zigzag width control *while stitching* form heavier marks. Straight stitching with changes in speed of movement makes different stitch lengths that contribute to the overall wavering quality of the thinner lines.

Printed fabrics offer different opportunities for doodling. You can begin with simple explorations on fabric scraps, using prints or plain colors, singly or pieced in groups, with patterns and colors matched or intentionally mismatched. Start with the kinds of doodles you usually do on scraps of paper and draw a variety of them with the free-motion stitching. Alternatively, make doodles suggested by the fabric's own patterning. (See overleaf.)

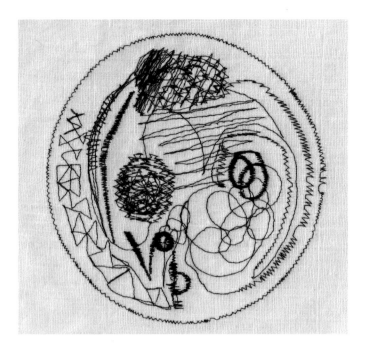

LEFT 03-11 Sketch in free-motion machine stitching: straight, zigzag. Cotton thread on muslin.

BELOW 03-12 Sketch in free-motion machine stitching: straight. Cotton thread on pieced, mismatched cotton fabric prints, embellished with "soutache" braid.

Gesture drawings and contour drawings are yet more advanced types of doodling, and it's a relatively simple matter to change medium and try them in stitching. Experiment to find a workable approach for yourself. Use what you know about making natural marks on scrap paper to guide the way you stitch thread into cloth.

Drawing or sketching spontaneously with the machine is a direct way of translating what we might do with a pencil or pen on paper. Stabilize the fabric in a hoop, grip it on both sides, and practice moving the *ground,* instead of the needle, to stitch lines. When mastered, this approach allows very free drawing with thread. The contours of forms, inner shadings, and details can be simple or complex as your ideas and subject matter vary.

"Scribbling" is a term often used in a derogatory sense to imply vapid, empty movement or activity—something hastily and thoughtlessly "tossed off" and lacking in content or intent. But in the context of natural mark-making, the rapid movement of scribbling can serve as a visual metaphor for emotions such as flight, frenzy, confusion, spontaneity, freedom, or joy. Thus, with a bit of forethought, intent, and creative application, a scribble can carry meanings or emotions. Scribbling is easy to achieve with free-motion machine stitching by using either straight or zigzag stitch settings.

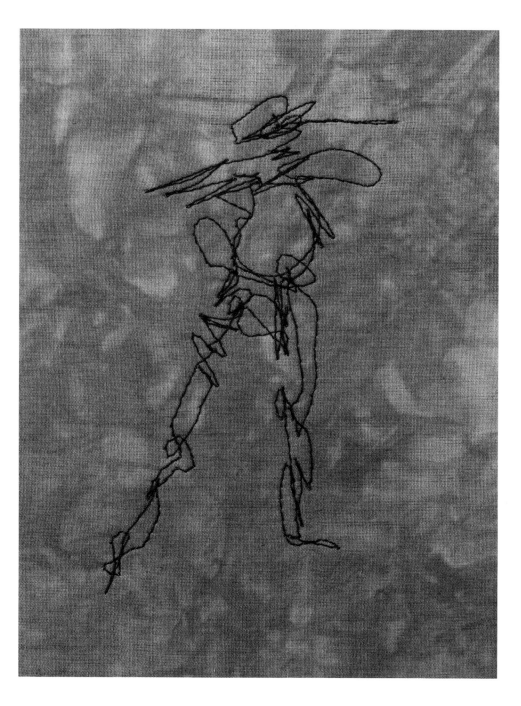

03-13 Quick gesture drawing made from a life pose. Free-motion machine stitching: straight. Cotton thread on hand-dyed cotton fabric.

Scribbling with a medium dark thread in a contrasting hue both emphasizes the darker areas of printing and lays a new set of marks atop the printed fabric. In 03-14 the contrast of hue causes the scribble to appear to move forward visually and the printed marks to sink a bit toward the background, despite the strong color intensities of each.

Scribbling can take many different paths—back and forth, curling, meandering, looping back—for a range of effects, as in 03-15 and 03-16. When the thread color is similar in value to the fabric color, the stitching sinks back into the fabric, creating new textures and details. When it contrasts more highly with the fabric, the scribbling becomes very active and even agitated.

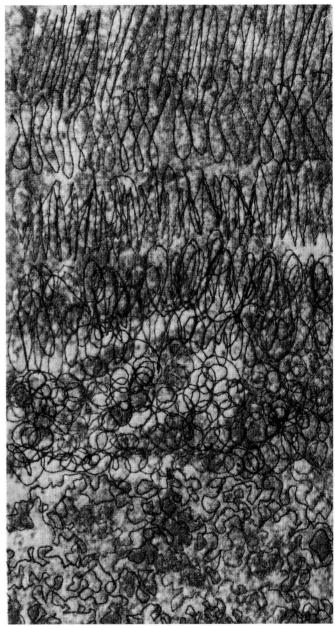

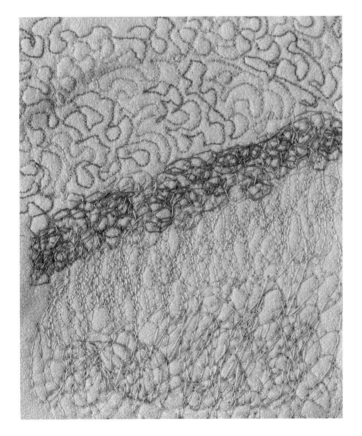

TOP LEFT 03-14 Free-motion machine stitching: straight, zigzag. Cotton thread on screen-printed heavy cotton twill overlaid with hand-dyed and printed silk organza.

BELOW LEFT 03-15 Scribbling. From top: meandering, scratching, looping. Free-motion machine stitch: straight, satin. Valdani 35 wt. cotton thread on digitally printed silk noil backed with cotton batting and heavy cotton twill for dimensional stability.

ABOVE 03-16 Scribbling. From top: back and forth, looping, curling, meandering. Free-motion machine stitch: straight. Valdani 35 wt. cotton thread on digitally printed silk noil backed with cotton batting and heavy cotton twill for dimensional stability.

Hand-Stitched Doodles, Scribbles, and Sketches

Achieving *fluidity* in elemental marks is more challenging in hand stitching, where each stitch represents the shortest distance between two points: a straight line. Most marks that we think of as "fluid" are quite curved or rounded. To assist with making those curved marks, choose a fabric with "tooth" which will grab at the threads and hold them in place as you stitch. Choose threads that are easily bent and shaped, not springy, wiry, or stiff. The low twist of cotton floss is well suited to the task.

Back stitch and couching have long been the "stitches of choice" for drawing on fabric. Both can create clean and clear contours, defined edges, and fluid, continuous lines in hand stitching. Centuries of storytelling in embroidery testify to their effectiveness and usefulness. To study some wonderful examples, look at photographs of the Bayeux Tapestry (which, despite its name, is not an actual woven tapestry but possibly the world's largest and most famous embroidery).

By nature, the back stitch is slightly jumpy or jagged, but lacing it tightly with a second thread smoothes its contours, allowing all manner of curves, spirals, and complex shape contours.

Couching can project many characters (wobbly, smooth, thick, thin), but because it is constructed on one continuous laid thread—tacked or tied to the surface with a second thread—its nature is continuous. Choosing smooth, shiny threads emphasizes the fluidity of the lines, but handling the curves gracefully is more difficult due to the slipperiness of the threads.

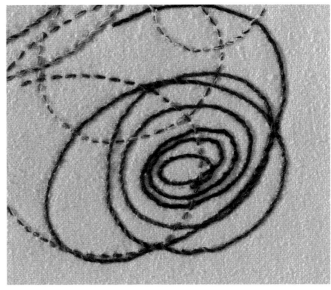

03-18 Laced back stitch. Cotton floss on silk noil.

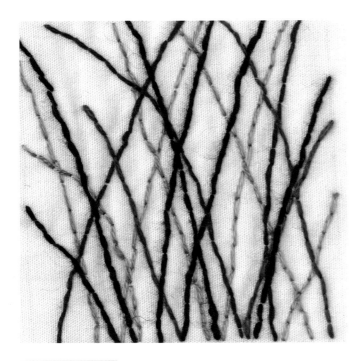

03-17 Back stitch. Cotton floss and fabric.

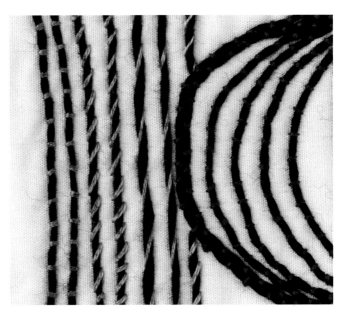

03-19 Couching with contrasting tack stitches.
Cotton floss and fabric.

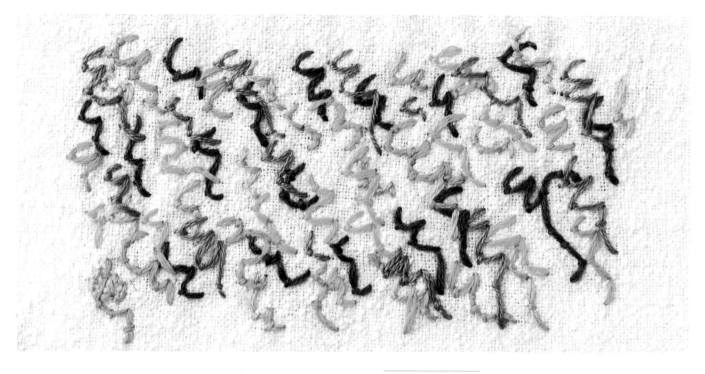

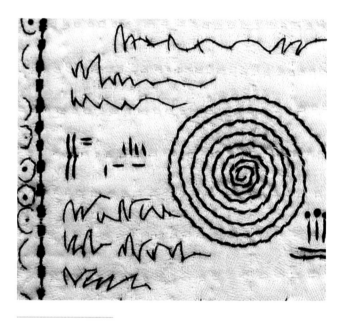

03-20 The nubby quality of the noil "grabs" the thread to assist in making turns and curves. In self-couching, the laid thread is also used as the tacking thread. Hand-stitched cotton floss on silk noil. Detail of 03-03.

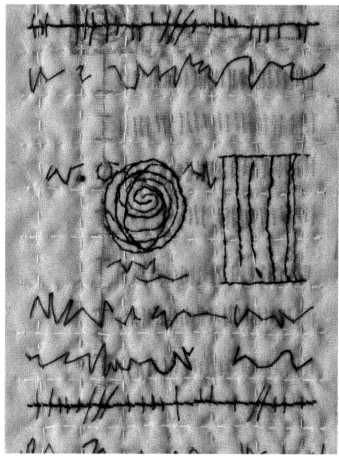

03-22 Hand stitching: straight, cross, couching, fly, running, whip, laced back. Cotton thread on heirloom table linen, nylon netting, and silk organza. (Collection: Dolly Perkins, Silver Spring, Maryland, USA.) *Photo credit: Susan Brandeis.*

03-21 Hand stitching: straight, laced back, running, couching, back, French knots. Cotton thread on silk noil, silk organza, and nylon netting.

A combination of these two versatile stitches, couching and back stitch, works well for many drawings. Both can be clean and crisp, or fuzzy and textured, depending on the materials chosen and the character of your intentional stitching.

Doodles, scribbles, and sketches, printed and stitched, combine in this study (03-23) with complex color relationships. The repetition of small marks, arranged in lines, resembles text. The overlay of larger doodles and gestures rambles around, providing a counterpoint in size and scale.

03-23 Variegated threads add visual changes and irregularity which "soften" or "loosen" regular or even placement of marks. Hand stitching: self-couching, back, fly, laced back, running. Valdani 35 wt. cotton thread on digitally printed silk noil.

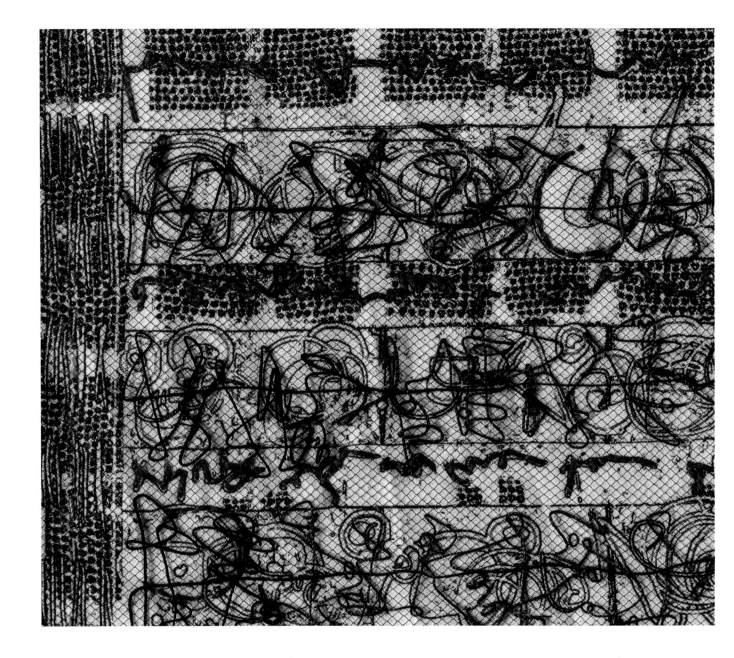

Hand-stitched scribbling can also be achieved by stitching on a "see-through" cloth, such as silk organza or netting made of nylon or silk. The transparency of the fabric reveals both the back and front of the stitch, while the openness of the fabric prevents tight tension. Thus, the thread sits loosely in the fabric and overlies and circles back on itself rather confusedly. In this example (03-24), the hand-stitched netting was laid on top of another printed cloth so that the marks could mingle further. (See Chapter 7 for more tips about stitching on "see-through" fabrics.)

03-24 Hand stitching: straight, couching, whip, cross, back. Cotton floss and Valdani 35 wt. cotton thread on digitally printed cotton damask and nylon netting. (Collection: Sally Van Gorder, Raleigh, North Carolina, USA.)

Try this!

3.1 / Hand-stitched doodling

Sketch six pages of your own hand doodles, dashes, dots, scribbles, ticks—marks that are uniquely yours. Choose a playful arrangement of them to interpret in hand stitching with simple cotton floss on a nubby fabric, such as silk noil. Mark your fabric loosely, but try to stay spontaneous with your stitching. Suggested stitches: self-couching, laced back, laced chain.

3.2 / Machine-stitched doodling

Sketch six pages of doodles, dashes, dots, scribbles, ticks—marks that are uniquely yours to interpret. Select and arrange the best of them into a good composition, paying attention to balance, scale, and proportion in the layout. Choose good quality cotton machine thread and a tightly woven and stable ground fabric, or two stacked layers of a thinner fabric. Mark the fabric directly with pencil, invisible or washable markers, or tailor's chalk to use as a stitching guide, or keep your sketches themselves beside you to serve as visual guides while you stitch directly onto the fabric. Use free-motion machine stitching: straight and/or satin. Emphasize some marks more than others to produce a variety or hierarchy of focal points.

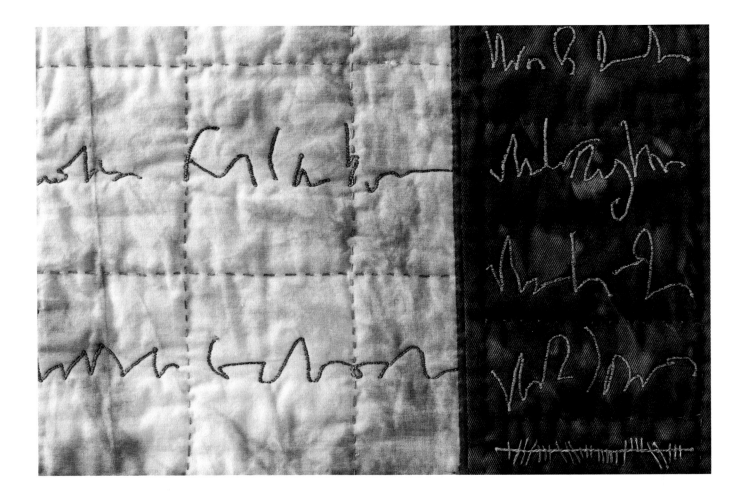

Text and Textiles

In the ancient world, textiles served as important conduits for many forms of human communication—narratives and stories; metaphors and symbols; monograms and identification tags; records of objects, possessions, and animals; commemoration of people and events—embedded within structures, dyed into woven cloths, or stitched onto surfaces. Cultural variations in knots, stitches, inlaid threads, woven figures, and pattern symbols were well established worldwide for thousands of years *before* the invention of written symbols on other kinds of surfaces—rock, papyrus, clay, parchment, vellum, bark, and paper—documented and codified spoken language. The squiggles and doodles we explored in the last chapter could well be imagined as resembling those ancient precursors to accepted standard alphabets.

Thus, it is no accident that we still use the language or imagery of textiles as metaphor: storytellers "weave" tales;

politicians and corporate executives "embellish" the truth; people "weave" their way through a crowd; a salesperson "sews up" a deal; the "fabric" of daily life; the interwoven "fabric" of world cultures; the "patchwork" of agricultural fields; and the "knitting together" of a community or a wound. The words "text" and "textile" come from the same Latin root meaning "woven."

Stitching words onto textiles in modern times—reuniting text and textile—is therefore not only a form of community with other people who share this interest now, but also a kind of poetic connection to our ancestors, recent or distant, who used cloth and thread to tell stories, teach lessons, keep records, and express spirituality. Textiles are ubiquitous in our

ABOVE 04-01 Faux text which mimics personal handwriting forms. Hand (couching, straight, running) and machine (satin) stitching. Cotton threads on hand-dyed cottons.

lives, and we instinctively know how to read their meanings in context and to judge their importance through daily use and cultural familiarity. Thus, your addition of either readable or suggested text to a textile compounds meaning at multiple levels of understanding.

In stark contrast to a world filled with typewritten communications in standardized alphabets, handwriting is by definition very personal and communicates on a more intimate level. Thus, handwritten notes, letters, and journals carry special value and preciousness in their direct person-to-person connection. The way *you* use your hands to create letter forms with a pen or pencil—whether in your own language or another, printed or cursive ("longhand") writing—is unique. Control of the writing tool produces part of the effect: firmness or looseness of grip, amount and evenness of pressure, the slant of the letters, and the angle of tool contact with a surface. The writing style chosen, the character of the lines and marks, the placement and spacing of letters and words, and the nuances of color all enhance the letters, numbers, punctuation, and symbols that indicate inflection and emphasis.

But there is more: Add the three-dimensional qualities of stitching to those technical details of handwriting—through variations in materials, thread weights, line weight and character, and control of the individual hand stitch—and the opportunities to form expressive line, beyond the meanings of the words themselves, are nearly limitless. To develop your own approach to text, start with your own handwriting: printed, cursive, or a combination of both.

Handwriting and Expression

Doubly expressive, handwritten language carries *both* the gesture of the individual writer (the character of the lines) *and* the cultural meaning of the words (the symbols for thoughts or spoken language). Beyond the ideas expressed by the words' definitions are the physical manifestations of the writer's mental state or physical health captured in the lines left behind by the hand movements. When you look at someone's handwriting, especially the writing of a person whose hand you know, you can usually (although often subconsciously) perceive, from nuances in the writing and character of the lines within letters and words, whether the writer was nervous or calm, rushed or contemplative, elated or sad, young or old, well or infirm. Handwriting is really a form of drawing: using line to express and communicate.

Beyond the actual *words* you choose to write—because their definitions convey the meaning you want to express—handwriting adds the individuality of your own unique *way* of making those words appear on paper. Which way do the letters lean? How large are the curves or bowls of the letters?

How tall are the uprights or vertical strokes? How do individual letters relate in size, proximity, and thickness? Do you mix capital and lowercase letters within words? Are there curls or flourishes where letters begin, join, or end? How do the spaces between letters and words vary? These are all unique to you, often without you even thinking about them.

In your textile work, you can emphasize, moderate, or counteract your meaning through the way you construct and control the lines of the letters and words you include. Your choice between block letter printing and cursive ("longhand") writing will also affect the resulting impression.

For example, let's play a bit with the word "anger." If you stitch the word "anger" in cursive with handwriting that is smooth, fluid, and regular in a color that blends with the surface, the emotion is only moderately expressed. (This person is not *seriously* angry.) But starkly contrasted block letters make a bolder, more forceful statement, and bright red jagged lines, agitated and jerky, suggest a person quaking with rage. There has been no change in the word—"anger"—but each change in line character conveys a different shade, intensity, or level of meaning.

So: For maximum expression, combine *what* you say (the meaning of the word) with *how* you say it (the character of the gesture). For extensive and varied information on this type of manipulation of text, consult graphic design and calligraphy books, where these ideas are discussed in depth.

04-02 Experiments with altering tone of expression through choices of color and letter style. Free-motion machine stitching: satin. Cotton threads on hand-dyed cotton fabric.

04-03 Words digitally printed on fabrics, layered, stitched, misaligned in the overlay, and then stitched again through all layers. Hand stitching: running, couching. Cotton floss on digitally printed silk noil and silk organza.

Printed Text

When you were a child, the alphabet was undoubtedly the first thing you learned about written language. You may have played with brightly colored plastic letters or lettered toy blocks. Later, a parent or teacher may have helped you to name and then shape *each letter* or to remember the letters in proper sequence by means of a rhyming song. You mastered letters and numbers, step by step, with a crayon, marker, or pencil gripped very firmly in hand. The first *word* you wrote was probably your own name. Mastering the symbols of writing became a way of claiming your conscious presence in the world: knowing who you were, finding your place, and learning that lettered shapes *mean* something. Much of standard early schooling emphasizes increased mastery of spoken and written language and develops the ability to communicate through written thought.

And, of course, your first "writing," which is still available to you now, was *printed* text in *individual* letters.

While there are many designed typefaces and styles of text you could stitch into cloth for individual block letters,

the most immediately expressive choice—and the most comfortably familiar—is your own hand printing, which combines your particular way of making letters and your specific way of making stitches.

Printed Text: Hand-Stitched

This study (04-03) uses layers to contrast hand-printed antonyms (pairs of words with opposite meanings). The translucency of the top fabric and the visual interference of the overlaid words (which describe "positive" human attributes) combine to mask the words on the bottom layer ("negative" attributes), rendering them nearly unreadable. The positive attributes triumph in visual importance because they are bolder and more clearly readable, and the overlapping organization (positive placed *over* negative) also signals a clear belief in their superiority. Broken stitches make the words quiver or pulsate, infusing them with a rumble of emotional intensity.

Printed Text: Machine-Stitched

Free-motion machine stitching (as in 04-04) more closely approximates the speed and fluidity with which you might actually print by hand with a pencil. Much faster and more spontaneous than hand stitching, it captures the curves and the slight curls at the end of each stroke which start to connect the letters and reveal the speed and path of your hand motions over the surface. If you use a pencil to write the letters directly on the fabric, then stitch over them exactly, you will capture your printing quirks and idiosyncrasies. Emphasize changing line weights by controlling the stitch widths sensitively and following the markings carefully.

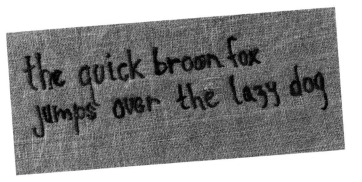

04-04 Stitched pangram (a sentence containing all the letters of the American/English alphabet). Free-motion machine stitching: satin. Cotton thread on linen.

MARKING FABRICS FOR MACHINE STITCHING

Common graphite pencil markings are usually permanent on fabric, although if the marks are lightly made, a white Staedtler Mars plastic eraser may remove them. Washing is usually unsuccessful. If your stitching will not conform to or completely cover your markings, use another type of removable marking tool. Fabric stores and sewing supply sources sell an array of fabric-marking tools, such as disappearing ink markers, tailor's chalks or pencils, water soluble ink pens, or washable graphite pencils. Each has its own advantages and disadvantages. Before marking a large piece of the fabric, always test a marking tool on a sample swatch of that same fabric.

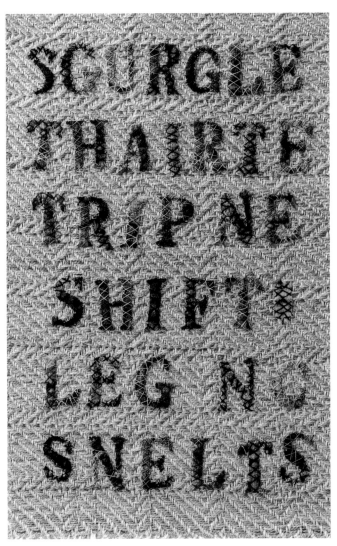

04-05 Appliquéd words and letters. Hand stitching: cross. Cotton thread on handwoven cotton fabric (point twill structure).

Individualizing Generic Printed Text

Manipulating and changing generic letter forms provides another good starting point for using text, with many opportunities for spontaneity and invention. Most sources that sell office supplies also sell plastic or cardboard stencils of alphabets, allowing you to trace letter forms onto signs and posters. Most arc based on popular typcfaccs such as Times or Helvetica. While these machine-cut stencils do not, of course, capture *your own* hand, clever manipulation allows them to assume aspects of your personality and to convey your ideas.

In 04-05, I traced letters from a stencil onto fabric, cut around them with sharp scissors, then used cross stitches to appliqué the cut letters, one by one, onto another piece of handwoven fabric. These generic letterforms are transformed into a quirky, more personal text by the irregularities of construction: the handwoven background fabric, the irregular cross stitches, the slight tilt to the placement of the letters, the color shifts in the thread variegations, the unevenness of the color on the letterforms, and the varying degrees of value contrast which make some parts of the letters more readable than others. The bulk, thread size, and loft of the handwoven fabric beneath the letters make them mound up slightly and appear "stuffed" and dimensional. Raw fabric edges and a certain amount of fraying lend an aged or worn look. The letters now have the appearance of being cut from different pages of a newspaper, in a way reminiscent of the mysterious anonymous warnings sent by mail in some murder mysteries: free of personal hand printing, but nevertheless leaving clues to identity.

The meaning of the text offers many opportunities for individuality. Here the letters are arranged to form words, but those words are surrounded by extraneous letters, making them hard to pick out. The words chosen were not meant to link together to form meaning. They were random. (Imagine the game of Scrabble, in which the players don't fashion phrases or sentences but instead try to form words from the letters available.) Alternatively, this kind of "hiding words in plain sight" could contain an actual message, but camouflaged by extra letters added.

APPLIQUÉD LETTER FORMS

Appliqué of cut fabric letterforms is tricky work, which at certain moments almost seems to require more than two hands. To make the process less awkward: 1) Pin the letters down to the fabric in the desired arrangement; 2) stabilize the fabric by stretching it tightly in a hoop; and 3) insert the hoop in a floor, tabletop, or clamp-on embroidery frame to provide that "third hand" to hold the work in place as you stitch. The frame frees up both of your hands for the stitching.

Cursive Text
(Also Known as "Longhand")

Somewhat later in your childhood school years, after you had mastered reading and printed text, you probably learned *cursive* handwriting, a system of connecting the letters to each other to form words, clearly indicating where a word starts and stops. Cursive provides a hand action more fluid and quickly performed than hand printing's requirement of frequent starts and stops to achieve complete separation of the letters. Cursive focuses much attention on the slope of the letters, the ways they connect, and how the connections modify the shapes of the letters. This approach results in a more rounded, curved, and fluid appearance which evolves into a wholly personal way of writing as a person matures. The look of a one's handwriting, and especially one's signature, changes throughout life, but its core aspects remain constant or stable—as handwriting analysis experts would surely tell us!

Cursive Text:
Hand-Stitched

If you already mastered the techniques of stitching fluid, natural marks in Chapter 3, hand stitching of cursive writing will present few additional hurdles. Like those doodles, dots, dashes, and ticks, letter forms are composed of straight and curved parts assembled in predictable ways, but subject to your own alterations. Keep in mind that stitching words for clear readability and comprehension requires extra care, attention to detail, and time.

Your handwriting might be elegant or chunky, sloped or straight upright, bold or delicate, combining your own variations of line weight, line direction, and natural mark-making. (See Chapters 1, 2, and 3.) While retaining aspects of the writing that are identifiably yours, you can alter, modulate, or distort your writing with the stitches you choose and your methods of working them. Self-couching, back stitch, laced back stitch, running stitch, stem stitch, chain stitch, and laced chain stitch have distinct individual characters. (See 04-06.) Notice how the text, written only once and with a single implement, changes appearance on each line with the substitution of a different stitch.

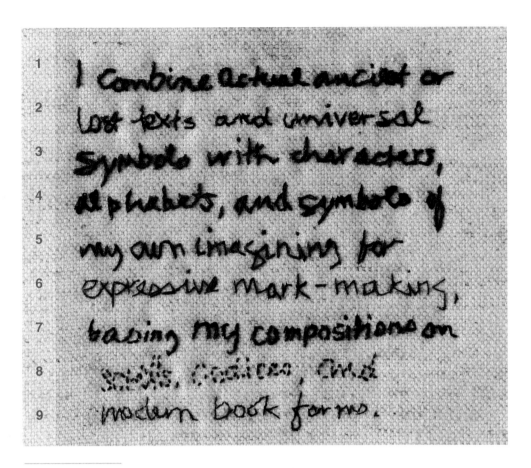

1
2
3
4
5
6
7
8
9

04-06 Hand-stitched cursive. Each line uses a different line weight and/or stitch for comparison. Stitches: laced back, back, laced chain, self-couching, stem, outline, running. Valdani 35 wt. variegated cotton thread on linen.

ROW 1	Laced back stitch, 2 strands. Bolder, chunkier, smooth, and more dimensional.
ROW 2	Back stitch, 2 strands. Solid, slightly jagged, and readable.
ROW 3	Laced chain stitch, 1 strand. Boldest and most dimensional.
ROW 4	Chain stitch, 1 strand. Slightly transparent, more angular, and distorted.
ROW 5	Self-couching, 2 strands. Quickest to stitch, slightly angular, altered.
ROW 6	Self-couching, 1 strand. Readable, more delicate, fast to stitch.
ROW 7	Stem stitch and outline stitch combined, 2 strands. Solid and very readable, quick.
ROW 8	Running stitch, 2 strands. Slow to stitch, harder to read, tentative.
ROW 9	Back stitch, 1 strand. Delicate, readable, and quick.

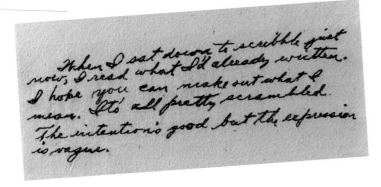

04-07 Cursive paragraph. Words digitally printed onto the fabric as a guide before stitching. Free-motion machine stitch: straight. Valdani 35 wt. variegated cotton thread on silk noil.

Cursive Text: Machine-Stitched

Free-motion machine stitching is the fastest—and potentially most controlled—way to transfer your cursive text to cloth. Writing directly on the fabric with pen or pencil, then stitching over it precisely, captures the nuances of your hand movements. Use it to sign your works, or more interestingly, to insert your own words in your own hand, thus doubling the power of your meaning. Satin or straight stitches are both useful, depending on the desired weight of the line.

In 04-07, the writer's cursive idiosyncrasies are easily seen: broken connections between letters in words, letters cramped or made larger than others, dots misaligned over "i" or "j," and letter shapes which vary depending on where they fall within a word. All of these collectively identify the writer's manner—whether intentional or based on long-time habit—of moving the hand to form words. And *all* of us have such handwriting idiosyncrasies.

PROGRAMMED MACHINE TEXT

There are many (usually expensive) sewing machines allowing the quick stitching of a variety of pre-programmed texts onto cloth. Text that is machine-programmed *looks* programmed. It is even, regular, and the characters are often attached at the base, making it appear to be underlined. Precisely *because* they are pre-programmed, these texts are also usually unalterable. They are most useful for applications in which the character of the human hand is not needed or desirable, i.e., where the precise words themselves are sufficient for the desired content and an individual rendering style is irrelevant.

Writing as Background Texture or "Subliminal" Message

Text can be highly visible or blend into the background, depending largely on the degree of *value contrast* between the text and the ground. We are most accustomed to the high contrast of black text on white ground used to make books, computer pages, and many other forms of writing maximally visible to most people. But in artwork you can alter that value relationship to serve your ideas.

When text and ground are nearly the same value, the *low value contrast* transforms text into texture, rendering the words readable only at certain close distances or angles of view. Low contrast introduces ideas subtly by drawing the viewer closer in—trying to read and decipher the meaning—and the words can then deliver a powerful or unexpected close-up "punch."

Rows of low-contrast print or cursive become so soft and blended into background when viewed from a distance (04-08) that they "read" almost as horizontal lines or stripes, and can even be overlaid with other images and marks. Different line weights yield different levels of readability: back or straight stitches in single strands are more subtle, delicate, or almost non-existent, while dense satin stitch is more prominent, textural, three-dimensional, and readable, even in low contrast.

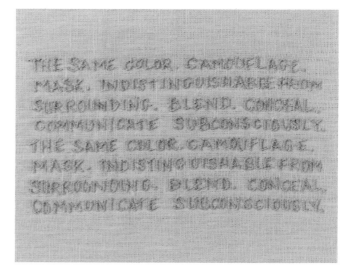

04-08 Hand printing. When low contrast colors are being used, satin stitch is more readable because of its density and dimension. Free-motion machine stitching. Valdani 35 wt. solid color cotton thread on linen.

Invented
and Borrowed Texts

All alphabets, whether of your own language or another, have one thing in common: Some group of people, somewhere, over some course of time, invented them. And they are *symbolic*. They have meaning only because a society using them *agrees* that they have a certain meaning. For example, the following, considered in its most basic essence, is just a collection of printed shapes: *girl.* But English-speaking people agree that these symbols represent a specific pronounceable word sound and mental concept, both of which designate a female young person.

Because humans have invented alphabets, or symbols serving the purpose of alphabets, for as long as humans themselves have been literate, *there is nothing to stop you from inventing your own* and putting them into stitch. You can create an actual alphabet in which each invented letter substitutes for its traditional counterpart in your own everyday language, or you can create shapes which resemble letters in some imaginary language but have no particular meaning at all.

"Faux text"—line work that looks like real text, but when examined carefully is not a recognizable language at all—can be suggestive, idiosyncratic, mysterious, and intriguing. Whether rendered with hand or machine stitching, you can make it up as you go along, base it on ancient scripts or lost languages, abstract it from handwritten English, or combine all these approaches for an evocative composite. You may relish the idea of inventing your own alphabet and writing in "code"—or simply make swooping lines arranged in horizontal rows or vertical columns to suggest "writing."

Here (04-09) is an example of free-motion stitched faux text on a larger scale. There are no real words, just the suggestion of cursive writing or an ancient script in a layout whose format suggests a scroll or large codex. Contrasting colors make the lines quite visible, although unreadable.

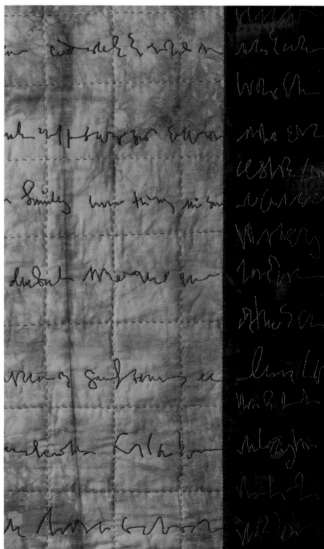

TOP RIGHT 04-09 Lines formed like cursive are used to *suggest* text. Hand and machine stitching. Cotton thread on hand-dyed cotton fabrics. Scale: 26.5" × 35" (left half of whole work). (See 04-01 and 04-10 for other details.)

RIGHT 04-10 Right edge detail of 04-09. Lines formed like handwriting are used to *suggest* text on a page. Hand (running) and machine (satin) stitching. Cotton thread on hand-dyed cotton fabrics.

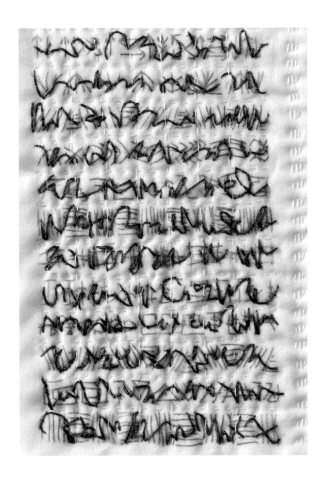

Layers of faux text can suggest an ancient "palimpsest," (imperfectly erased layers of different texts that are visually mingled, confused, or contain multiple layers of meaning). In 04-11, the lower layer of marks remains slightly visible, pushed into the background by the boldness of the clearer text on top. Layering of faux text in this way suggests the passage of time and evolution of thought, or the "recycling" of a previously used scroll or parchment.

We live, of course, in a world of many alphabets. Encountering one of them from outside our own cultural tradition, unless we read the language shared by that group of people, may leave us bewildered about what we are seeing and what it means, but the texts themselves may still be *aesthetically* beautiful even considered solely as marks and shapes. Hebrew and Arabic come to mind as examples of alphabets which are lovely to look at, even if we don't know the pronunciation or meaning of the words we see. Still other alphabets or word symbols are no longer used by any living group of people. They might be found in rock carvings or paintings in caves, and their meaning, if known at all, is limited to the explorations of scholars.

For our purposes here, the point is that alphabets and symbol systems of many kinds, living or "dead," incorporate visually interesting characters which can be adapted for drawing and stitching based on an aesthetic attraction to their shapes and visual variety alone.

ABOVE 04-11 Hand stitching: couching, straight, running, French knots. Cotton floss on heirloom linen with silk organza overlay.

RIGHT 04-12 Hand stitching: straight, fly, cross, French knot, running, back. Valdani 35 weight variegated cotton thread on custom woven cotton fabric.

In 04-12, some of the marks are simply invented (by me), while others were borrowed from, or inspired by, ancient Phoenician script and later Germanic runes. The common scale, stitches, spacing, and visual interlocking give them the appearance of a readable sequence of letters or symbols. They have no actual "meaning" known to me—I just selected shapes I liked and then put them together—but the outcome resembles a detailed readable text in a mysterious language. The long floats (longer, looser surface threads) and the ridges of the woven structure slightly "swallow" the delicate characters into the cloth, further suggesting a rough ancient writing surface such as bark, vellum, or parchment.

Changes in color in a row of script can highlight or emphasize certain marks, letters, or points in the sequence. Like the previous example, 04-13 borrows extensively from Phoenician symbols and German runes. The red on certain characters draws attention and adds emphasis. Changes in the scale of the marks on the different layers—smaller on the bottom, larger on the top—help to distinguish or separate the two layers visually.

Combining Text, Symbols, and Shapes

Starting with the illustrated books of your childhood, you began to tacitly understand the powerful link between text and image for rich storytelling. As an adult with a lifetime of reading experience, you quite naturally assume that if you have the words *and* the images together in a book, you will have the *entire* story. There is a completeness about this combination, and the physicality of books themselves, that we accept almost without question.

04-13 Hand stitching on digitally printed cloth. Stitches: straight, running, back, cross, French knots, fly, couching, detached chain. Valdani 35 wt. thread on silk noil overlaid with Chinese cheesecloth and silk organza.

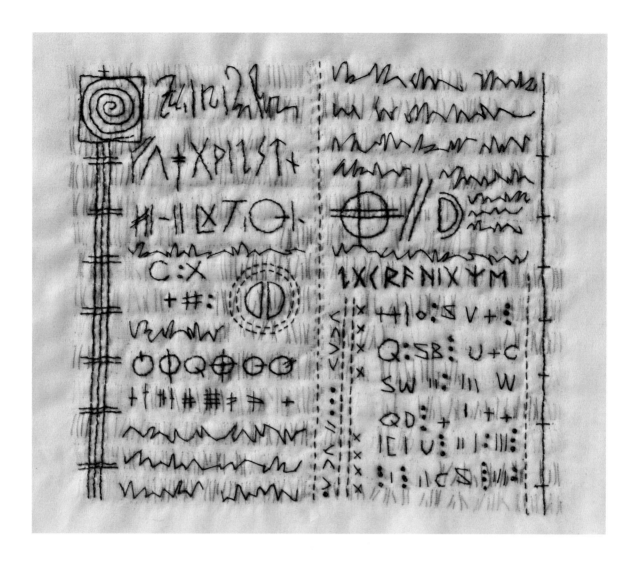

Likewise, there is a strong possibility that text will not exist alone in your fabric work, but that you will combine it with other diverse marks, gestures, shapes, or images to complete your ideas. To integrate well, the text should fit with other elements in harmony and balance, like the pieces of a jigsaw puzzle. Knowing which elements are most important is key to making decisions about the placement, size, color, and balance of each in the composition. Because stitching is slow, labor-intensive, and hard to rip out (!), it is important to plan your strategy *before* the work begins.

In scientific books, you typically find text mixed with diagrams, symbols, graphs, and numbers, each element helping to describe and illuminate the other. The stitched exploration 04-14 suggests a page from a scientific book, but sports a variety of *faux texts* in layers combined with *invented* symbols, diagrams, and figures. The scientific reference is clear, although the symbols and text are playfully unreadable. The translucent cloth behind the darkly stitched faux text and

symbols blurs, but does not obscure, the lighter and simpler "accounting" marks separately stitched on the background fabric.

In the next composition, 04-15, symbols inspired by petroglyphs, rendered in white satin stitch on white cloth, lie behind faux text resembling cursive. The combination suggests that the text on top is translating, commenting on, or overruling the meaning of the symbols underneath. The faux text scratches across the surface, rushed and irregular, suggesting urgency of intent, while the symbols beneath appear painstakingly embedded and permanent.

ABOVE 04-14 Hand stitching: running, back, couching, straight, French knots, fly, cross, straight. Valdani 35 wt. thread on heirloom linen with silk organza overlay.

Text as Labeling

On this digital print (04-16), the images are more important than the text, which adds supporting information and a bit of humor, rather like labeling things for someone learning a new language. The text explores various names for rocks while simultaneously demonstrating the different effects of various hand stitches for rendering printed text. The character of each stitch contributes an impression to the word it spells: satin stitch, the traditional choice for monograms, makes the boldest statement. Back stitch and various laced stitches make clear and readable, though quieter, communications. Running stitch tends to look tentative, hesitant, faded, or temporary.

04-16 Hand stitching: straight, running, back, laced back, self-couching, satin. Cotton floss on digitally printed cotton.

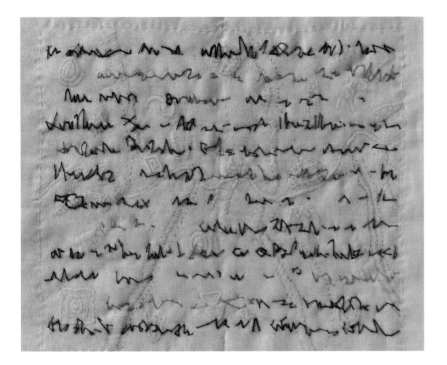

04-15 Hand stitching: self-couching, satin stitch, straight stitch, French knots. Cotton floss on heirloom linen with silk organza netting overlay.

Text in the Classic Sampler

In an era when most linens and clothing were embroidered, early English and American embroidery samplers were a practical necessity. From the early sixteenth through nineteenth centuries, there were few books of patterns and stitches, and therefore samplers functioned as learning tools, as pattern books, and as proof of the embroiderer's skill. Nearly all samplers included text, which was liberally used in labeling household linens and belongings, and was therefore a valued stitching skill.

The classic compositional layout of the sampler was usually symmetrical, especially regarding text, with the letters of the alphabet, both lowercase and uppercase, dutifully and precisely rendered. Additionally, letters composed verses from hymns or folk songs, passages from the Bible, quotations of common wisdom, or warnings against bad behavior. Leaves, flowers, people, animals, and sinuous vines often surrounded and illustrated the text, and the sampler was signed and dated by the maker upon completion. For the schoolchild, samplers represented skills achieved; for the professional, skills for hire.

As you experiment with expressive stitching, you may find small samplers a good way to organize your practice, test your ideas, or focus your explorations. To practice stitching text, transcribe your favorite aphorism, poem, quote, or lyrics. Or more simply, stitch labels on your experiments for future reference. All your practice at stitching *readable* text will sharpen your eye-to-hand coordination in the precise placement of stitches. (See the Bibliography for sources on historic samplers.)

04-17 Contemporary interpretation of traditional American sampler layout including the alphabet, a favorite quotation, and small pictorial images (in this case petroglyph symbols, which would never be found in a traditional sampler, let alone associated with Oliver Wendell Holmes). Hand stitching: French knots, laced back, satin. Silk floss on silk noil.

INVESTIGATING ALTERNATIVE KINDS OF TEXT

If expressive text interests you beyond explorations of your own hand printing and writing, I recommend that you research ancient (extinct) written and symbolic languages—those not in modern usage—from which you can learn or imaginatively borrow.

Tapping other languages—those still being spoken or written today—presents special challenges. If you use *real* foreign words and letters, be sure that you know *exactly* how they translate and what they will mean to a person for whom they are "the mother tongue." To avoid giving unintentional offense with your text, exercise knowledge and careful intent when using actual foreign words.

To expand your research, examine scripts and text that other artists have used in a variety of media and environments: carved or scratched into wood, metal, or ceramic; printed on papers in lithographs, intaglios, or etchings; hand inked in calligraphy; burned into wood; constructed into sculpture; and woven into, or stitched onto, textiles. Investigate symbols in cave paintings, pictographs, and petroglyphs. Investigate the vast world of designed typefaces to discover an enormous range of line qualities and delicate nuances of letterforms and fonts. These sources all provide rich inspiration, clearly defined models, and excellent springboards for your invention and manipulation. (See the Bibliography for sources that will help you to get started.)

Try this!

4.1 / Contemporary sampler

Research traditional American samplers. Roughly sketch some of their layouts or usual compositions. Make note of the elements included—usually an assortment of alphabets, numbers, quotes, and images—and where they are located and how they are balanced. Look carefully for interesting deviations or inventions.

Use one of the sample layouts you discover to design your own contemporary sampler. Replace traditional elements with your own choices and combinations of letters, numbers, quotes, and images. To increase the meaning, use words and images from a passionately felt experience or concept from your own life. Select stitches, threads, fabric, and colors that support your ideas.

Since this project takes time, and may require working in different areas of the layout simultaneously, place the fabric in a large enough hoop or frame to allow a view of the entire composition.

4.2 / Write a letter in stitch

Compose on paper, in print or cursive, a *brief* letter or note to someone about a simple subject of interest to you. Transfer the text to cloth with a pencil, transfer pencil, or digital printing. Hand- or machine-stitch that writing onto fabric. Consider altering the thread color to emphasize certain more important words.

4.3 / Abstract your own writing

In artistic terms, you may usually think of "abstraction" in terms of paintings of the real world—landscapes or portraits—in which the artist has stripped away much realistic detail in order to capture the essence of a place or person. This "visual distillation" process requires looking closely, and carefully choosing a rendering style well-suited for expressive purposes. With a similar kind of process, you can create abstract versions of your own handwriting to render it unreadable or unidentifiable to create a sense of mystery, to camouflage it among other marks, to provide a level of personal privacy, or to heighten emotional expression.

Working first on paper, try some classic "idea generation" mechanisms to alter the line of your handwriting. For example: distort, exaggerate, stretch, compress, layer, fragment, or simply change the slope of the letters and words. Each of these actions will change the way your handwriting appears and simultaneously make it more difficult to read or to identify as "yours." The lines that result will still *refer* to writing (capture the essence of the line configuration from your hand), but without providing clear, readable words for the viewer (the details of letter formation).

Compose a few sentences that have actual meaning for you—anything from a shopping list to a love letter. Write the message on paper in your normal handwriting. Next, select parts of the communication to change into your abstracted handwriting, parts you would like to "hide" or obscure. Re-write the message on paper with the combination of normal and abstracted writing, then transfer the entire message to a nubby fabric to prepare for stitching. Use a single dark color of thread and your choice of one or more stitches. Recommendations: free-motion machine stitches (straight, satin) or hand stitches (self-couching, back, laced back, running, stem).

4.4 / Research and experiment
with ancient scripts

Do some research about specific ancient (extinct) scripts and (universal) symbols that interest you. Some have been translated, and some have not. Choose a few characters that seem relevant to the meaning you want to express or that convey a feeling you like, even if you don't know what they mean. Make some sketches of compositions including these characters or symbols. Decide how prominent or subtle you want them to be. Choose colors and threads that will help you control the level of expression. Stitch the composition by hand or machine.

4.5 / Invent an alphabet and write in "code"

Write down the alphabet of your native language. Beside each letter or character, invent a new mark to represent it. Referring to this "key" to your new alternative "alphabet," stitch a few simple sentences in your invented "language."

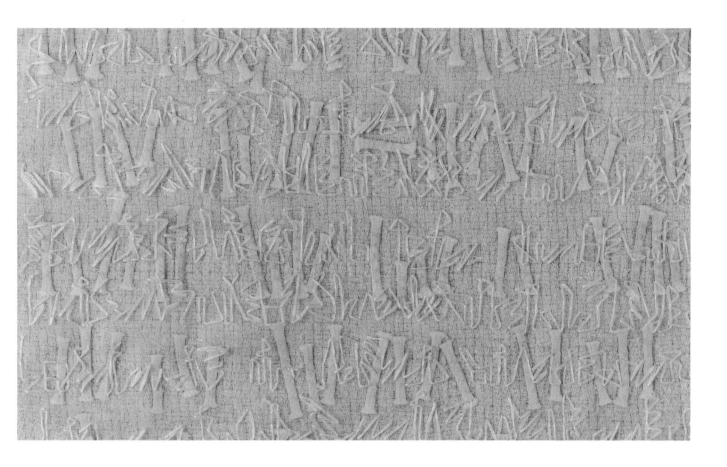

When you write or draw with a pen, you probably prop the outside heel of your hand on the table for support, swivel from that point, and use the muscles of your hand and fingers. This physical position encourages you to make marks that are short (about 0.5" to 1"). Simply picking up your hand from the table allows you to swing your lower arm from the elbow and to very naturally make longer gestures (about 6" to 18"). When you stand up or move back further from the surface and pivot your whole arm from the shoulder, your gestures can become very large (24" to 30") or quite enormous (60" to 72", or limited only by your arm span). You experienced this freedom of movement and scale if you played with finger paints as a child. "Stitching large" revisits that joyful and spontaneous experience.

Very large marks offer a bold, even sassy, scale of expression that is routinely available to painters (often men) but seldom embraced by stitchers (often women). If you are so inclined, embroidery's heritage of "ladylike," sedate, and restrained expressions can be discarded for a bolder and brassier practice. Like the action painters of the mid-twentieth century, you can involve, position, and use your whole body as you draw or

stitch. The sheer scale of large mark-making necessitates your moving freely from the larger joints of your upper body—the shoulders and elbows.

Drawing large-scale, especially with needle and thread, may seem both startling and a bit daunting, but doing it is like singing out loud: energetic, vigorous, oxygenating, and liberating. Larger marks (longer and/or thicker), chunkier threads, and larger pieces of cloth demand new stitching strategies, with the reward of giving voice to more powerful expressions. Try experimenting with larger gestures—to loosen up, to challenge your preconceptions about stitching, to discover new perspectives, to enlarge your stitching repertoire, and to build your confidence in working spontaneously.

ABOVE 05-01 Hand stitching: couching, straight, back, cross, whip. Cotton floss and braided shoe string on layered cotton damask, cheesecloth, silk noil, and silk organza mesh. Scale: Detail of a composition 35" × 43"; the larger marks are 1" to 2" long.

Long Marks

Ease into larger scale by using both your hand muscles *and* your arm to draw or stitch. Functionally speaking, when you pivot from the elbow, you engage the muscles of your lower arm, which overpower the tiny muscles of the hand, making fine detail more difficult, but larger marks *easier*. Test this out on paper using pencils, markers, charcoal, or paint/pigment with large brushes to make as many different types of lines as you can invent.

The marks track and record your arm movements, uniquely reflecting them through character, placement on the paper, and variations of pressure and emphasis.

Working from your own gestures, select stitches to interpret the character of the marks.

Experiment with long directional strokes in varying lengths and thicknesses using a digital drawing program. A stylus and graphics tablet will allow you to hold an implement

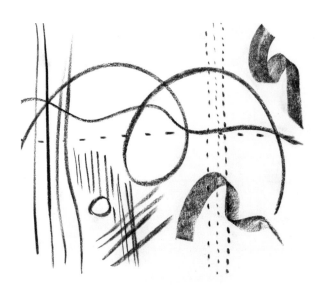 

ABOVE LEFT 05-02 Charcoal stick on drawing paper, using both the ends and sides of the charcoal to vary weights and characters. Scale: 16" × 20".

ABOVE RIGHT 05-03 Pencil on drawing paper, using both the sides and the points of the lead to vary marks. Scale: 16" × 20".

RIGHT 05-04 Hand-stitched interpretation of pencil drawing in 05-03. Stitches: Back, stem, laced stem, laced back, cross, running, seeding, couching, laced chain. Cotton floss on linen. Scale: 8" × 9.5".

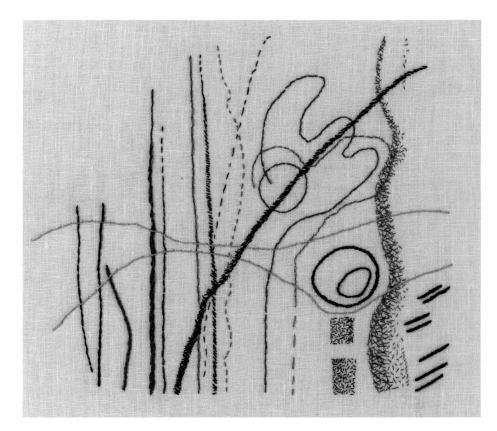

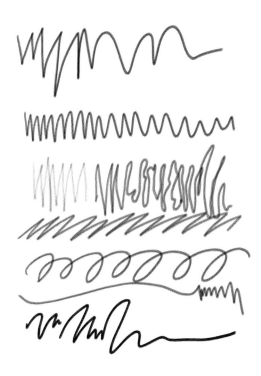

as you normally would a pen, but to create marks that mimic pencil, charcoal, ink, watercolor, oils, pastels, or airbrush, with variations in size, color, opacity, and grain. This captures your own large gestures in the appearance of different media, with the added advantage of allowing you to print them directly onto fabric to guide your stitching.

Machine satin stitch produces long, smooth lines and gestures resembling the marks of a fat ink pen or marker, which flatly sink into the fabric surface.

Hand stitching with a thicker bundle of threads makes a larger, more dimensional mark that stands above the fabric surface. The slight deviations and imperfections of hand stitching render the gestures more lively and individual.

ABOVE 05-05 Long marks with thicker line weight. Digital drawing with Corel *Painter*™. Scale: 8.5" × 11"; gestures 6" wide × 0.75" to 2" high.

BELOW LEFT 05-06 Interpretation of 05-05 in grays and blacks. Free-motion machine stitching: satin. Cotton machine embroidery thread on silk noil. Scale: 8.5" × 11"; gestures 6" wide × 2" high.

BELOW RIGHT 05-07 Interpretation of 05-05 in color. Hand stitching. From top: laced chain, chain, laced back, stem, back, long stem, back, short stem. Valdani variegated silk floss on silk noil. Scale: 8.5" × 11"; gestures 6" wide × 2" high.

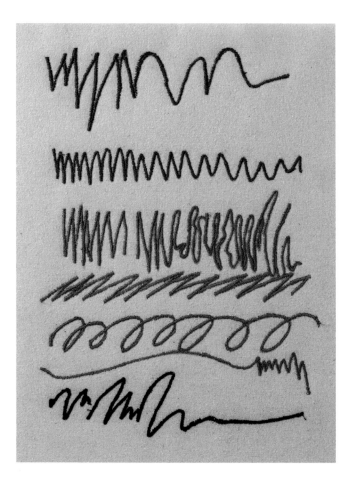

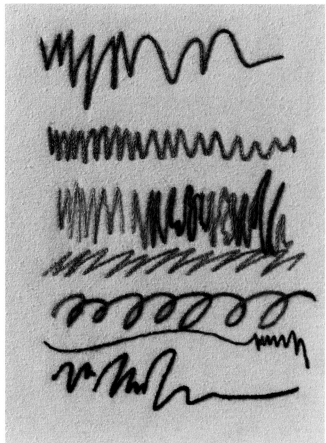

Clusters of overlapping long lines or curved gestures more boldly fill space and convey energy, whether hand- or machine-stitched.

ABOVE 05-08 Larger gestures with the arm and hand. Digital drawing with Corel *Painter*™. Scale: 8.5" × 11"; gestures 3" to 4" long.

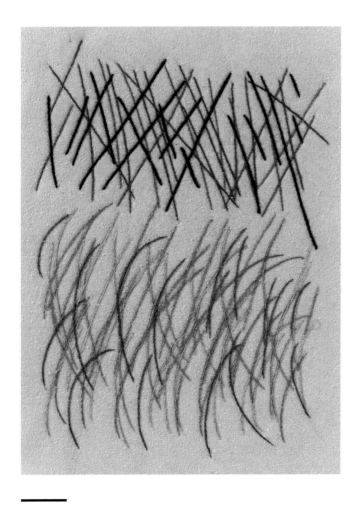

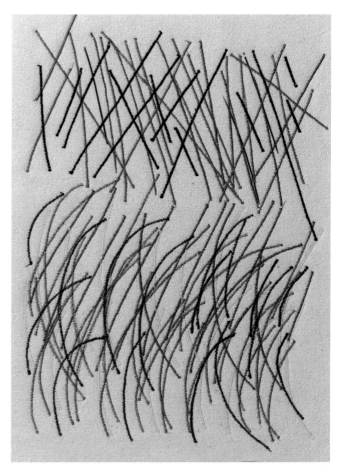

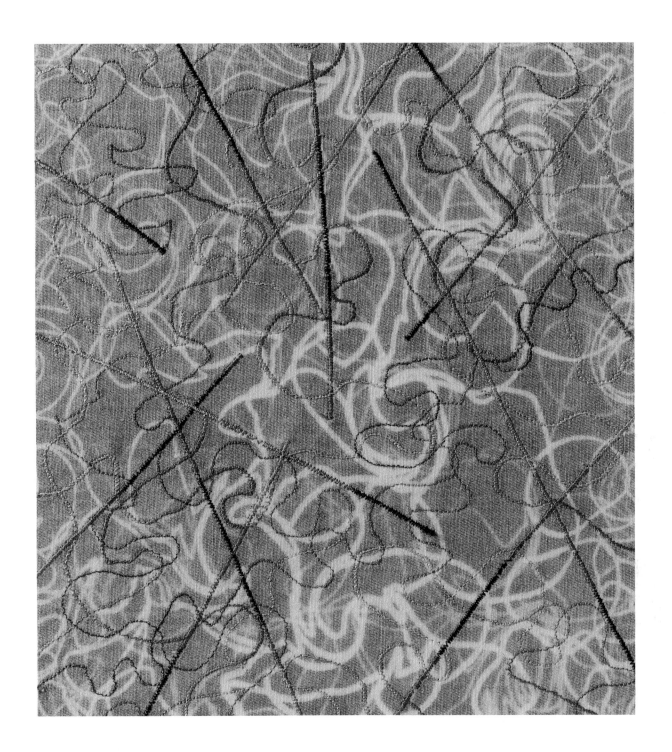

OPPOSITE LEFT 05-09 Long gestures, more dimensional line character. Hand stitched: back, stem, laced back, laced stem. Cotton floss on digitally printed silk noil. Scale: 8" × 10"; gestures 3" to 4" long.

OPPOSITE RIGHT 05-10 Flatter and less dense line character. Machine stitched: satin. Cotton machine embroidery thread on digitally printed silk noil.Scale: 8" × 10"; gestures 3" to 4" long.

Use what you know about scale relationships to your advantage to make marks *look larger* than they are. For instance, 6" marks look larger and bolder on an 8.5" × 11" surface than on a 48" × 72" surface. Our perception of their size is largely dependent on the context and scale relationship.

ABOVE 05-11 Machine stitching: satin. Cotton threads on digitally printed heavy cotton twill. Scale: 8.5" × 11"; straight marks 4.5" to 7" long.

Very Large Marks:
Using the Muscles of the Shoulder, Arm, *and* Hand

Making very large marks on paper—those longer than 18" to 24"—requires the use of the shoulder, arm, and hand *working together*. The gestures made naturally by rotating the entire arm communicate the force and action of your whole body. (This could be a good opportunity to get out of your sewing chair and put something *big* on the *wall*!) In scale, the marks might be as short as your lower arm, or as long as your entire arm span, and as thick as your arm or leg. Playing with paint or pigment and a variety of implements on paper builds a vocabulary of your own marks ripe for translation into stitching,

and provides a useful guide. (For excellent tutorials on large-scale drawing on paper, see Steven Aimone: *Expressive Drawing* in the Bibliography.)

Your goal is to translate your large-scale marks by shifting to thicker lines; by selecting or assembling chunkier thread bundles; and by combining different types and sizes of stitches, laid side by side, overlapped, or clustered for effect. Zoom in, magnify, or blow up the details. Make stitches that are like splashes of ink or daubs of paint from huge brushes. Work boldly and spontaneously.

05-12 Pigment drawings on paper, using brushes, forks, and cotton swabs. Scale: 10" × 16".

05-13 Pigment drawings on paper, using brushes and forks. Scale: 7" × 9".

05-14 Pigment drawings on paper, using brushes and forks. Scale: 14" × 9".

STABILIZING LARGE PIECES OF FABRIC

Facilitate working large and freely by stretching the piece of fabric so that you can work across the entire surface at one time. Try these alternative ways of stretching:

- Wooden frame: Wooden painting stretchers offer inexpensive and modular frames. Use closely set tacks or staples to stretch fabric onto the frame. (An electric staple gun will make the tacking easier.) Place the frame on an easel or wall to work vertically or on blocks on a table to work horizontally. Either gives easy access to the fabric back during stitching.

- Wall: If you have a tack wall, you can stretch and T-pin the fabric directly to the wall at a height comfortable for working at a standing or sitting position. Use open-weave fabric and blunt needles. No access to fabric back during stitching.

- Pinned to tabletop: On a *padded* tabletop or portable screen printing surface, stretch out loosely woven linen (or other openly woven fabric) with small T-pins (for example, size 20). Work with smaller *blunt* tapestry needles (size 16 or smaller) which will go through the linen, but use care to avoid snagging the table covering. No access to fabric back during stitching.

- When you don't have access to the back of the fabric during stitching, leave *long* loose ends on the front, moved out of your way, as you continue to work. When you are done stitching, re-thread the ends and pull them through to the back of the fabric to tie off. The longer the pieces of thread you use in the needle, the fewer loose ends will be left to pull through.

RIGHT 05-15 Hand-stitched interpretation of detail of 05-12. Stitches: straight, cross, back, fly, self-couching. Cotton floss, knitting cotton, rayon, and linen threads on natural linen. Scale: 28" × 36"; gestures (total length) 12" to 24".

OPPOSITE 05-16 Detail of 05-15.

BELOW 05-17 Detail of 05-15.

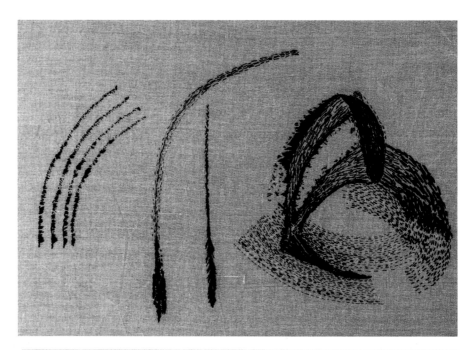

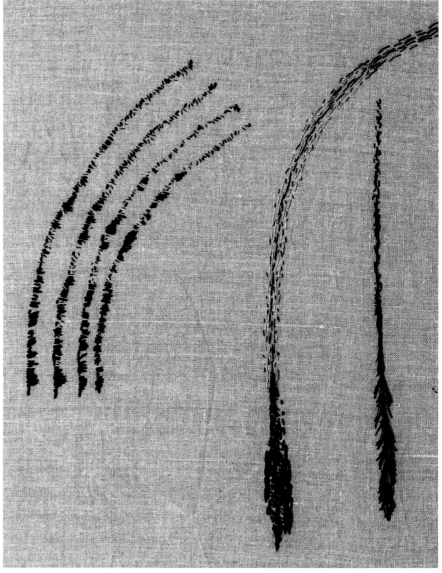

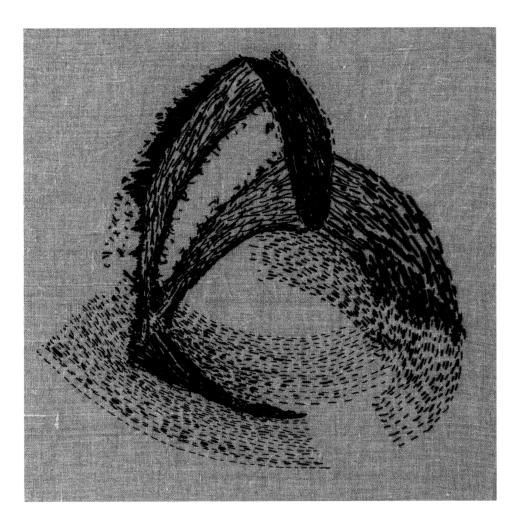

Large gestures may sometimes be more effectively expressed (05-18) with unusual or non-traditional materials: raffia, braided shoestring, waxed linen, rug wools, fishing line. Experiment with materials you already have on hand around your home.

RIGHT 05-18 Large marks with various materials. Hand stitching on linen with raffia, braided shoestring, rug wool, waxed linen. Stitches: running, straight, back, cross, whip.

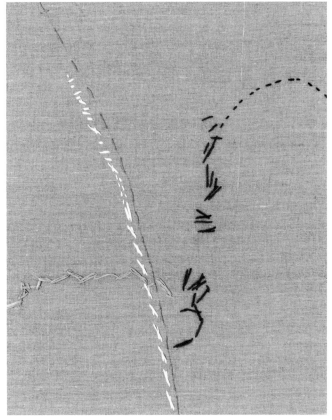

STITCHING AT VERY LARGE SCALE

- On large pieces of paper, use black paint or textile pigment with a variety of mark-making tools or found objects to make the large marks you will interpret in stitch. Stand up to do this so that you use the muscles of your shoulder, arm, and hand freely. Invent a lot of different kinds of marks.

- Use larger threads to compose and interpret larger marks.

- When threads you have on hand are not large enough, use multiple threads in the needle to compose fatter thread bundles.

- Try knitting yarns, weaving threads, or other non-traditional linear materials.

- Use larger needles with bigger eyes—tapestry, crewel—to accommodate the thicker threads.

- Use strong, but more loosely woven, fabrics—linen, burlap, netting, meshes—to accommodate larger needles.

- Cluster smaller stitches or lines into composite gestures to achieve appropriately large-scale or thicker lines. (See Chapter 1 for more about heavy line weight.)

- Stitch from the center of the fabric outward toward the edges to minimize wrinkling or bunching the fabric.

- At very large scale, standing to stitch can become a dynamic physical activity that involves your whole body quite naturally in the mark-making. But standing to work can be tiring. Once you have the marks on paper as a guide, you can sit to stitch and still capture the spontaneity and energy of the marks on the fabric.

- Tightly stretching the entire piece of fabric in front of you will ease your ability to reach all areas, working spontaneously back and forth. But you can also mark the composition basics on the fabric, use a large quilting hoop, and stitch the cloth in sections. This allows use of a floor stand for support and frees both hands for stitching.

- Try it! Don't be afraid. *Play* a little. Even if you later revert to working smaller, you will never again think quite the same way about stitching, and you may discover a new spontaneity in your work.

Try this!

5.1 / Translating a pencil drawing into stitching

Part 1: Pencil drawing (see 05-03 for an example)

Working with a pencil on paper, experiment with a variety of marks to discover the individuality of your own hand. Fill several large sheets of paper with large-scale lines and marks by responding to the following series of word prompts. Don't worry about the composition, where the marks are placed on the page, or how they relate to each other. They can overlap spontaneously and run into each other.

Suggested prompts: Several downward strokes, pressing harder each time, then several upward strokes. Try angry marks, floating horizontal marks, bumpy marks, large swirls that overlap, a grid of overlapping horizontal and vertical marks. Use the *side* of the pencil to make fat lines, long looping marks, and a batch of circles. Try to depict these words: jagged, cracked, chunky, dotted, fragmented, spiky, curling, splintered, blunt, blurred, meandering, bold, broken, thick, thin, elegant, hesitant, compressed, scratchy, twisted, flowing, irregular, uneven.

Variations: Change the drawing tools with each new drawing, or mix tools to get more variety and experience. Try drawing pencils, black markers (large, medium, and small tips), charcoal, Conté crayons, crayons, or pen and ink.

Part 2: Stitching (see 05-04 for an example)

Choose a section of your drawing to interpret, looking for an area with variety, interest, and diversely contrasting marks. Work on white fabric with black or dark gray cotton floss. Examine the different marks in your selection and think about which stitches will best represent each one. For example, if the mark is broken or dotted, a running stitch might work best. If the mark is fuzzy, you might use a sequence of straight stitches laid side by side. Try to capture the undulations, changes in direction, and variations in line weight in your drawing. Mimic them with one color of thread, expressing the changes in the marks through the weight of the thread (using one, two, or more strands) rather than changes of thread color. Capture all the marks in the section, varying stitches as needed.

5.2 / Painting very large marks on paper

Make large marks in paint or textile pigment on large sheets of paper as a "warm-up" and guide for stitching. To make very large gestures, secure large sheets of paper to the wall or the surface of your work table so they don't move around. If possible, stand while making the gestures.

Use a combination of traditional and non-traditional implements: found objects or natural debris; discarded kitchen, shop, or garden tools; sticks, rocks, or grasses; brushes, styluses, or sponge brushes; spatulas, cut cardboard, or cotton swabs. Use only black textile pigment for mark-making. You can saturate a folded cloth with pigment (protect the table underneath with some sheet plastic first!) and then press your implements into the wet pigmented cloth before making marks on the paper; or use a sponge brush to dab pigment on the implement and then make the marks; or combine techniques to see what works for your imagery.

Working freely with the muscles of shoulder, arm, and hand (loosen up!), make as many different types of marks as possible, but allow the *tools* to produce their character and the *marks* to reflect the gestures of your body. Remember: nothing "dainty." Investigate as many different kinds of *large* marks as each implement will produce, testing all sides and positions of the tools. Don't stop after filling just one piece of paper. Do three to five, or more. Play, invent, and experiment. Hang completed drawings on a line or on the wall to dry and compare.

5.3 / Large-scale gestural stitching

Note: This project is more understandable and likely to succeed if you first complete the Rhythmic Stitching "Try this!" project 10.3 at the end of Chapter 10.

Choose a section of one of your large-scale drawings in project 5.2 above to translate into stitched marks. Stretch a one-yard piece of linen, burlap, or other openly-woven fabric on a print table, wall, or around a wooden frame. Keep the grain of the fabric straight and stretch out wrinkles. Choose larger-scale black or dark blue threads (weaving threads are often good choices). Examine your drawing section and choose stitches that will closely translate or replicate the marks. Working with the large muscles of the arm, stitch with large tapestry needles on the stretched fabric and try to capture the scale, spontaneity, and nuances of the marks from your paper drawing. Feel free to make the stitched marks even larger than the painted ones. (Note: If you are working with fabric stretched on a print table, take care not to snag the table covering while stitching. Since you cannot reach the back of the work while stitching is in process, just leave long tails where you run out of thread so that you can pull them to the back later to finish off.)

Drawing at a smaller scale with a light touch produces a calmer emotional tone, like a visual whisper. Slender, delicate lines imply a quiet mind, light pressure on a drawing tool, and the small movements of a steady hand. Marks that "fade off" or "feather" at the ends or edges suggest the soft grazing of the surface as a tool is lifted. Feathered strokes and delicate lines possess qualities perfectly suited to quieter expressions, smaller-sized works, sensitive or intricate drawings, and softer, painterly effects.

06-01 Hand stitching: straight, stem. Cotton floss on digitally printed silk noil. Scale: 2" × 2". (Collection: Fleur Bresler, Rockville, Maryland, USA.) *Photo credit: Susan Brandeis.*

Feathered Strokes

Marks made on paper with charcoal or pastel sticks naturally "fade off" at the ends or edges. Chalk-like media "disintegrate" as you move them from the contact point across the paper, leaving behind soft, grainy strokes with fuzzy borders. Experiment with some of the following techniques to produce feathered effects in stitching.

06-02 Soft and grainy, with lines tapering to mimic pastels.
Digital drawing with Corel *Painter*™ pastel chalk tool.

Feathering with Tapering

As you lessen the pressure on a drawing tool toward the end of a stroke, the line weight narrows and the mark tapers. An upward stroke direction enhances the light and feathery feeling.

In 06-03, single strands of thread nearly matching the ground fabric offer a simple interpretation of upward strokes.

In 06-04, machine satin stitch allows a simultaneous *narrowing* of stitch *width* and an *increase* of stitch *length* to taper the marks and create a sensation of fading off.

Feathered marks can be used to suggest plant life details such as leaf veins.

06-03 Hand-stitched interpretation of 06-02. Stitch: straight.
Single-strand Valdani variegated cotton thread on silk dupioni. Scale: 1" × 6".

06-04 Machine-stitched interpretation of 06-02. Stitch: satin.
Left: cotton sewing thread. Right: rayon 40 wt. thread. Scale: 1.5" × 6".

06-05 Hand stitching. Stitches: straight, loose overcasting. Cotton thread and floss on hand-dyed, handwoven cotton twill. Scale: 7" × 12". (Collection: College of Design Library, North Carolina State University, Raleigh, USA.) *Photo credit: Marc Brandeis.*

Feathering with Transparency

Lines need not be thin to seem feathery or delicate. Transparency compensates for width, rendering even flat wide marks filmy or wispy.

To approximate this transparency, combine single strands of thread with open spacing, allowing the fabric to peek through between stitches. Make the marks quickly and spontaneously.

With machine stitching, manipulate *both* the stitch width *and* the length, allowing imperfect spacing to contribute to the spontaneity and transparency.

06-06 Flat, wide marks. Digital drawing with
Corel *Painter*™, smeary palette knife tool. Scale: 1.5" × 6".

06-07 Hand-stitched interpretation of 06-06. Stitches: stem, straight, self-couching.
Valdani cotton thread on linen. Scale:1" × 5.5".

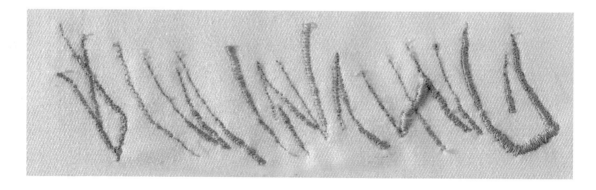

06-08 Machine-stitched interpretation of 06-06. Stitch: satin.
Cotton sewing thread on cotton. Scale: 1.5" × 6".

Feathering with Changing Value

Gradations of thread colors make gestures seem to "fade away." The rules to remember are: When the thread matches the fabric in value (*same* lightness or darkness), it will seem to disappear. When the thread contrasts strongly with the fabric (*very different* lightness or darkness), it will become much more visible. This knowledge will help you to arrange gradations of thread colors that seem to make parts of any line "disappear."

For example: Choose several graded values (light to dark) of the same color and a lighter value fabric color. If you stitch the centers of your marks with the darkest value and grade the color values steadily lighter toward the tips, then the center will be quite clear, but the ends will seem to dissolve into the cloth. The result resembles the fading of marks made with ikat dyeing or (in 06-09, using brown thread) scorch marks.

Construct the value gradations with either separate colors of thread in sequence (as on the left in 06-10) or by using variegated thread with its own "built in" gradation (as on the right in 06-10). The latter, varying in both *value* and *hue*, creates added expressive possibility.

Feathering with a Gradation of Spacing

Spacing stitches increasingly farther apart—a gradation of spacing—results in an airy, dispersed effect. (See 06-11 on overleaf.) Your eye composes the line by connecting the stitches (perceptual *closure*), while the bits of intervening cloth cause a visual interference that makes the line seem to dissolve.

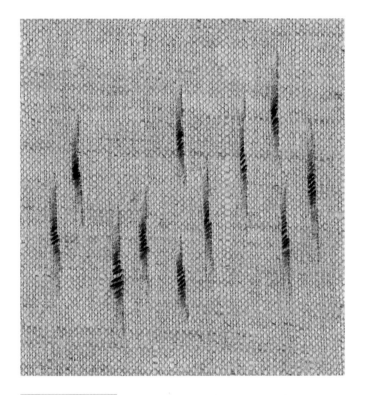

06-09 Hand-stitched fading marks. Stitch: straight.
Cotton floss on linen. Scale: 3" × 3".

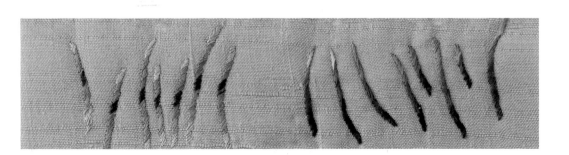

06-10 Hand-stitched value gradation. Stitches: stem, straight. Rayon threads (left) and variegated cotton threads (right) on silk dupioni. Scale: 1.5" × 5.5".

06-11 Feathering achieved through gradations of spacing. Hand stitching: straight, stem, cross. Valdani 35 wt. cotton thread on softened linen. Scale: 3" × 3".

06-12 Airbrushing. Digital drawing with Corel *Painter*™ airbrush tool. Scale: 2" × 6".

06-13 Machine-stitched interpretation of 06-12. Stitch: zigzag. Rayon sewing thread, Valdani 35 wt. variegated cotton thread. Scale: 2" × 6".

Feathering with Airbrush Effects

An airbrush creates feathering on all edges of a mark. It disperses paint in an airborne mist that concentrates most of the color in the center of the mark but allows a dusting of small dots to fall around the sides in a soft shower of color (06-12).

Free-motion machine zigzag stitching is very effective for interpreting the spattered color patterns of airbrushing. Moving the hoop quickly and erratically from side-to-side *and* back-and-forth will leave a scattering of open "tips" around all sides of the mark, allowing bits of fabric color to show through. Shiny rayon thread overstitching (as on the left in 06-13) adds sheen and lighter colors that break up and blend the darker colors underneath. Without the rayon overstitching, the marks appear more forceful, solid, and visible (as on the right in 06-13).

06-14 Feathering softens and blends edges. Free-motion machine stitching: zigzag. Cotton thread on edges and "veins" of cotton velveteen leaf shapes, which were appliquéd over silk organza and silk noil. Scale: 12" × 18". (Collection: Duke University Medical Center, Durham, North Carolina, USA.)
Photo credit: Marc Brandeis.

Applied to the edges of the leaf shapes in 06-14, this airbrush effect softens and blends their contours smoothly into the background.

A straightforward way to interpret this in hand stitching is to combine strong, densely placed stitches in the center of a mark surrounded by scatterings of "seeding." (See Chapter 10.)

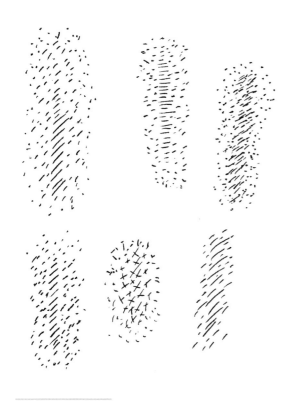

06-15 Excerpt from sketchbook ideas for translating airbrush effects into hand stitching. Hand drawing, fine-tipped ink marker on paper. Scale: 3.5" × 4.5".

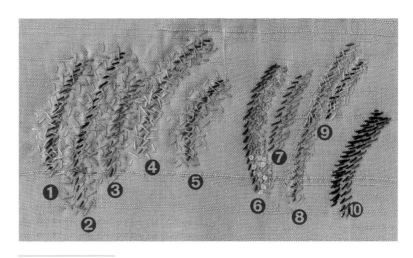

06-16 Hand-stitched interpretation of 06-15. Stitches: straight, whip, seeding, French knots. Valdani 35 wt. variegated cotton threads on silk dupioni. Scale: 2.25" × 5.5".

TRANSLATIONS OF AIRBRUSH EFFECTS

Marks 1–5	Lower layer: whip stitch. Over-stitched with seeding in a color nearly matching the cloth.	This dimples the fabric, obscures some of the lower layer, and visually disperses the color very effectively.
Mark 6	Lower layer: whip stitch. Over-stitched with French knots and straight stitch seeding.	This mark is more distinct, with less dispersion of color. Good choice for larger scale marks.
Mark 7	3 rows of whip stitch, set in saw tooth or dovetail.	With careful color balance, this works well and is fast to stitch. Try fuzzy threads.
Marks 8–9	Lower layer: 2 rows of whip stitch. Over-stitched with seeding in rayon 40 wt. thread.	The sheen and lighter color of the rayon obscures the cotton beneath to break up and soften the mark.
Mark 10	Pair of parallel double rows of whip stitch.	The "shadow row" makes a heavier mark useful for a "painterly" or dimensional look.

These composite marks can be shaped to mimic the look of painted brushstrokes. Layering the thread colors blends, tints, tones, and shades the overall perceived color. (See Chapter 9 on color mixing.)

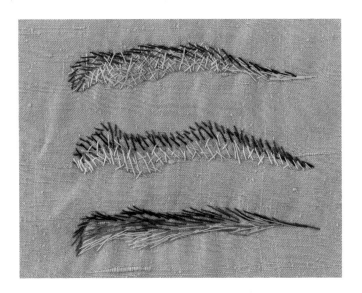

06-17 Painterly strokes. Hand stitching: straight, cross, whip. Cotton on silk dupioni. Scale: 4" × 4.5"; strokes 0.5" × 4".

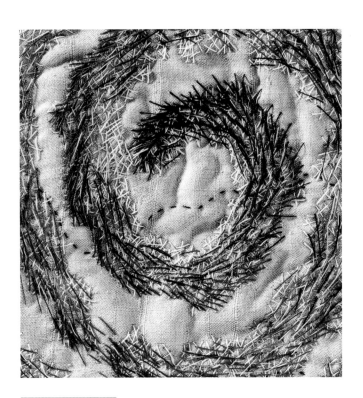

06-18 Painterly strokes. Hand stitching: straight, cross, running, back. Cotton thread on silk. Scale: 7" × 8".

Feathering Effects with Wool

To more closely mimic the soft look of airbrush, charcoal, pastels, or blended paint colors, use naturally fuzzy protein fibers (animal hair or fur) such as wool, mohair, or angora. These threads have tiny fibers projecting from the central spun core, which leave a soft halo around the marks.

USING WOOL KNITTING YARNS

Wool knitting yarns are generally more loosely spun and fuzzier—but also weaker—than those threads spun more tightly for weaving, canvas work, or crewel work. Even so, they make fine stitching threads when handled gently. They have the advantage of availability in a wide variety of colors, sizes, and spins. If you want to stitch the yarn *through* the cloth, avoid "novelty" yarns or threads with dramatic nubs, loops, or other projecting textural elements.

Use a large, sharp needle with an eye large enough to easily accommodate your yarns, and choose openly woven fabric, such as softened linen, to ease the task of pulling plump threads through the cloth. Stretch the cloth tightly and leave easy access to the back of the fabric. Lightly brushing the threads *after stitching* fluffs them and increases the soft halo.

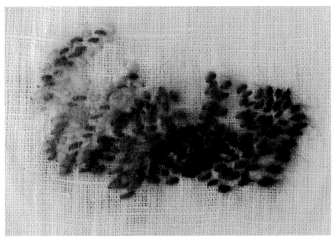

06-19 Hand-stitched and hand-brushed wool knitting yarns on softened linen use the fuzziness of wool to achieve the look of pastels or painterly strokes. Stitches: straight, back.

Delicate Lines

Very thin lines create delicate, spidery, or filmy drawing effects. Very thin threads—those as small as, or smaller than, the threads in the background fabric—convey a similar kind of intricacy and delicacy. The smaller the thread, the more diaphanous the stitching.

06-20 Delicate thin threads in high contrast suggest the outward extension of cactus thorns. Hand stitching: straight, laced back. Cotton and metallic threads on digitally printed silk noil. Scale: 2" × 3". (Collection: Janice Gatti, Seattle, Washington, USA.) *Photo credit: Susan Brandeis.*

FINE LINE STITCHING TIPS

- Try *hand* stitching with thin threads of any type (cottons, nylons, silks, rayons) made for *machine* use or single strands of cotton or silk floss—or even human hair.

- Machine embroidery thread—a strong but very thin thread that comes in a wide array of colors—offers an easy way to stitch thin lines by *either* hand or machine.

- Thin materials challenge your hand stitching coordination, control, and workmanship. The thinner the thread, the harder to see, the more difficult to thread through the needle, and the more awkward to handle.

- Small-scale work demands keen eyesight (or magnifying tools), good work lighting, lots of patience, and personal strategies for handling the threads.

- At this scale, each small action, misplaced stitch, or slight change of line weight is clearly noticeable. Small misalignments in stitch direction can cause a line to acquire a jerky, jagged edge.

- Use a more tightly woven fabric and fine needles. Stitching fine, smooth lines depends on carefully orienting the needle insertions from both front and back. The needle's "path of least resistance" is at thread intersections in the fabric. More tightly woven cloth provides more intersections per square inch, so that you can more precisely place the ends of tiny stitches.

Delicate Scratchy Lines

Single strands of light colors translate the scratchy, slightly curving lines from the sketchbook drawing with alternating running and back stitches.

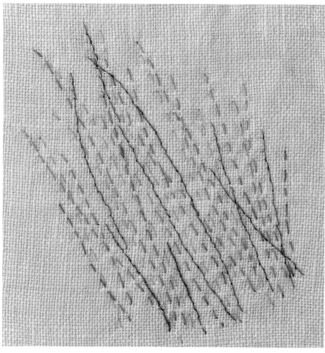

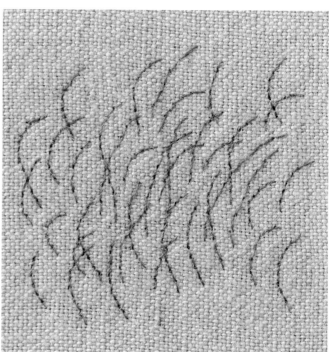

TOP 06-21 Scratchy, delicate lines with some line weight changes. Sketchbook excerpt, hand-drawn with fine-tipped ink marker. Scale: 2" × 2.5".

ABOVE 06-22 Hand-stitched interpretation of 06-21. Stitches: back, running. Cotton machine embroidery thread. Scale: 3" × 3".

TOP 06-23 Small, thin arcs. Sketchbook drawing, hand-drawn with fine-tipped ink marker. Scale: 1" × 1.5".

ABOVE 06-24 Hand-stitched interpretation of 06-23. Stitches: back, running, double running. Cotton machine embroidery thread on linen. Scale: 2.5" × 2.5".

ABOVE 06-25 Hesitant vertical marks. Sketchbook excerpt, hand-drawn with fine-tipped ink marker. Scale: 0.75" × 2".

RIGHT 06-26 Hand-stitched interpretation of 06-25. Stitches: back, running, double running. Cotton machine embroidery thread on linen. Scale: 2.5" × 2.5".

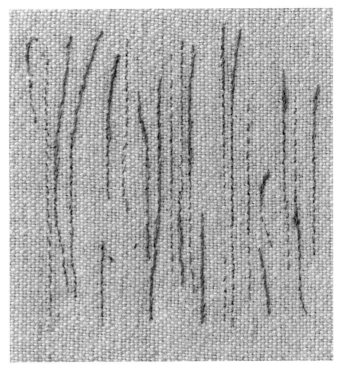

Mimicking Fine Marks

Sharp pencils with hard lead (for example, 6H), light pressure with a softer pencil (for example, 2B), or fine-tipped ink pens produce a fine, light line that does not dent the paper. Pencils naturally produce a drawing style and emotional tone that is intimate, delicate, and quiet. You can suggest or mimic pencil on fabric with thin, dark gray threads (the color of graphite) that share these qualities of thinness, delicacy, and tiny scale.

BELOW LEFT 06-27 Long, slightly wavy verticals. Sketchbook excerpt, hand-drawn with fine-tipped ink marker. Scale: 1" × 2".

BELOW RIGHT 06-28 Hand-stitched interpretation of 06-27. Stitches: back, running, double running. Single strands of variegated machine thread on linen. Scale: 2.5" × 2.5".

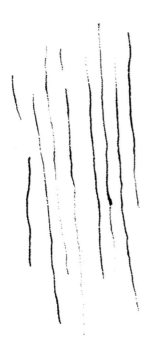

06-29 Vertical and horizontal dashes. Sketchbook excerpt, hand-drawn with fine-tipped ink marker. Scale: 1.25" × 1.75".

06-30 Hand-stitched interpretation of 06-29. Stitches: back, running, double running. Cotton machine embroidery thread on linen. Scale: 2.5" × 2.5".

Delicate Marks in Color

Colored pencils used with a light touch produce soft, fuzzy, slender lines that are easily translated with thin colored threads. Color adds sparkle and depth to thin lines and adds subtle shadings to stitched drawings. If similar in hue and value to the fabric itself, fine lines barely seem to exist, while those high in contrast resemble the gossamer of spiderwebs.

Overlapping, repeating, and clustering tiny colored marks will create texture, enrich color, and energize surfaces.

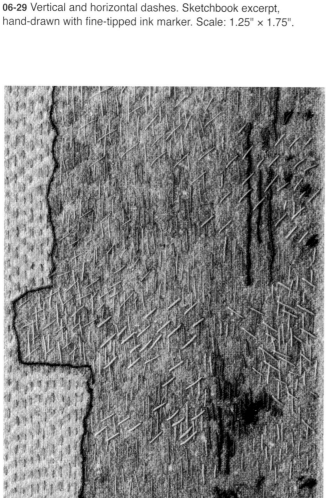

LEFT 06-31 Hand-stitched interpretation of colored pencil marks and shading. Stitches: back, running, straight. Cotton machine embroidery thread on digitally printed silk noil. Scale: 3.5" × 5.5".

Drawing with Fine, Even Lines

Ink drawings on paper often employ cartridge ink pens with calibrated interchangeable tips that control the flow of ink to maintain consistent line weights. A uniform line produces a delicate and intricate drawing which conveys both clarity and detail.

Combining a single color of thin thread with a single stitch type mimics that rendering style on fabric. Even line weights can still range widely in character, generating considerable surface energy from their curvature, spacing, direction, and path.

Fine lines are essential tools in standard contour and gesture drawing exercises to build hand and eye skills. Very small changes in line weight convey a great deal of depth and sense of volume.

The interpretation of a small section of a drawing by early twentieth-century French master Henri Matisse demonstrates the artist's skill with economy of line, delineating space, and suggesting volume with very few gestures and minimal internal shading on the figure. You can experiment with delicate lines to stitch contour and gesture drawings directly on the fabric or learn from the masters by making your own translations of small sections of their drawings.

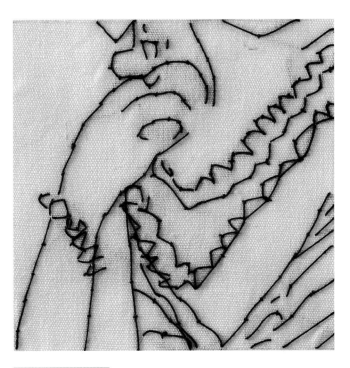

ABOVE 06-33 Hand-stitched interpretation of Henri Matisse drawing detail. Thin lines contour the figure, giving minimal form which is filled in by the eye and the brain of the observer. Stitches: straight, self-couching. Cotton thread on cotton fabric. Scale: 2" × 2".

Human Hair: A *Very* Fine Line Indeed

There are many available lightweight manufactured threads, but the finest weight (and perhaps most evocative) "thread" for stitching is human hair. If your hair (or a gift of hair from a helpful friend or styling salon) is long enough (at least 12"), try it for yourself! In addition to being very delicate, hair carries powerful associations—and sometimes aversions— from its very personal origin on the human body.

While there is no other stitching "thread" quite like hair, it can be challenging to use. Different types of hair vary in character, effect, and suitability according to the age, health, gender, and race of the source. But generally speaking, hair is springy, stretchy, slightly brittle (breaks easily), and (even if cut long ago) still feels very much *alive*. I stitched 06-34 with my own *childhood* hair (a ponytail lovingly preserved by my father). I found it to be very fine, smooth, and very springy: it wanted to jump back out of the needle. My childhood hair was blonde, which, set against black fabric, resulted in a shiny, glittering, delicate web. Stitching with it was oddly personal, and the effect magically ethereal. But because my childhood hair was also curly, it was difficult to control while stitching, and it broke frequently. The creation of this composition was accompanied by generous amounts of both delight and grumbling.

06-34 Human hair on black silk noil. Hand stitching: straight, back, cross, stem. Scale: 4" × 5".

TIPS FOR HAND STITCHING WITH HAIR

- Each hair requires patience and time to handle. Move slowly, stay calm, and limit stitching to short periods of time.

- Do *not* work anywhere near an electric fan or other strong air current!

- Choose a very small grouping of hairs to lay out as straight as possible on a contrasting fabric where they can be easily seen and distinguished from each other. A "grabby" fabric like silk noil or velveteen helps to hold them in place. Cover them when not in use.

- Work in daylight, augmented by overhead lights. A focused, *adjustable* angle-arm lamp positioned directly over the work will be helpful.

- To free up both hands to work, tightly stretch the fabric in a wooden hoop and clamp the hoop into a tabletop frame or floor stand.

- Hair work is so delicate that a thimble is not only unnecessary, but may actually interfere by making the hair difficult to grasp.

- Use a very small, short, sharp needle and thread it in good light.

- Use a quilter's knot to secure the end (wrap 6 to 9 times around the needle).

- Because hair can be brittle, fold it over in the needle and keep adjusting its position in the eye as you stitch to prevent it breaking.

- Pull the hair through the fabric from the back very carefully, feeling for the knot with your other hand, and (to minimize chance of breakage) slow down your pulling as the knot nears the back of the fabric.

- Start and end each line of stitching with two small back stitches to further anchor the hair.

- Handle the hair slowly and delicately as you work, pulling very gently to set the stitches.

- To minimize the hair springing up out of place, consistently use your non-dominant hand to hold each stitch in place as you make the next.

- Grip the needle near the eye, also pinching the folded hair at the same time. This helps keep the needle threaded and the hair in place, especially when tying knots to finish.

- Caveat: You *must* be able to *see* the hair in order to stitch with it. This might seem a completely obvious point, but I emphasize it because hair has very little "substance" or weight. Therefore, you may barely feel the hair in your hands while stitching with it, and you must be guided by sight rather than touch.

Try this!

6.1 / Airbrush effects

Start with some digital (or real) airbrush markings and gestures arranged in a composition or drawing. Print them on paper as a guide for your stitching. Choose a white fabric and colors appropriate to your ideas. Work in a 6" square for the first experiments. Try to capture the sense of the scattered dots of color and feathered strokes as you translate the marks into stitching.

Follow-up: If you have good success with the small square, enlarge the bounding box and work larger.

6.2 / Fine, even lines

Choose a subject matter that lends itself to fine, even lines—topographical maps, mazes, labyrinths, clusters of hieroglyphs or other symbols, striations in rocks, floating lengths of seaweed—and make a sketch of them as a guide for stitching. Choose a closely woven cloth and thin thread. Use back stitch or laced back stitch in a single line weight throughout. Use consistent thread tension to keep the background cloth flat and to prevent puckering.

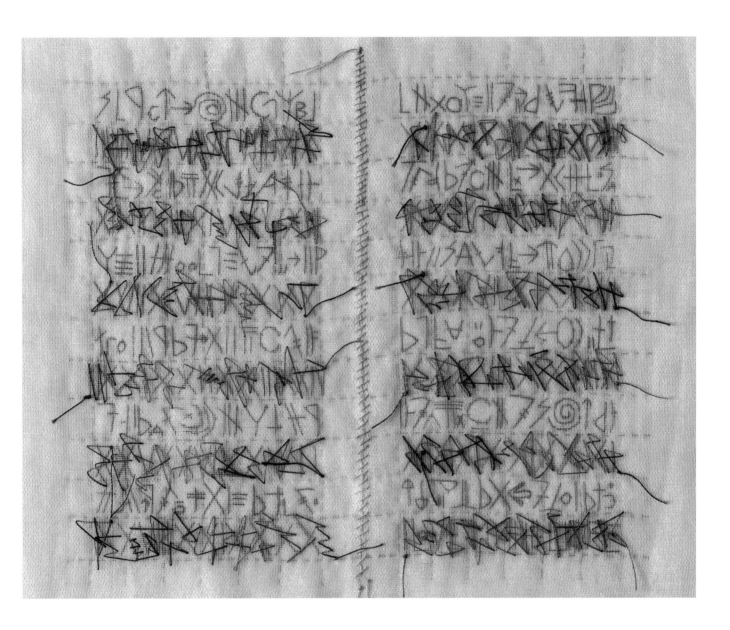

We're accustomed to thinking of most cloth as a solid surface, but some fabrics allow light, or the colors of other fabrics and threads, to pass through them. All of these "see-through" fabrics are made with fine threads but differ in the "openness" of their weave structures. The looser the weave, the more it can be seen through.

See-through fabrics offer many possibilities for evoking mystery, suggesting concealment, or achieving ethereal effects. The *ability* to see through a material immediately invites viewers to *try* to see through it by examining the surface more closely.

You control the surprises awaiting beneath. Layering these fabrics can blend or obscure while producing both the reality and illusion of depth. The degree of transparency of each material determines how much of the underlying layer is revealed.

ABOVE 07-01 Hand stitching: straight, cross, whip, back, self-couching, running. Cotton floss on layered heirloom linen, nylon netting, and silk mesh.

If you draw with a marker on a piece of clear acetate, the drawing acquires a front and back. That is, from the front you can see the image as drawn; from the back you will see that image *in reverse*—a view you *don't* have when you draw on opaque paper.

A stitched drawing, however, is unlike either of those. The act of stitching creates a "public face" on the front of the fabric, but simultaneously creates a "private face" on the back—a labyrinth or network of connecting threads formed by your movements from one stitch to the next as you trail the thread behind and leave knots at starting and stopping points. The back can be quite visually exciting, usually reflecting a sense of the front, but more chaotic, irregular, and visually erratic.

Stitching on see-through fabrics simultaneously reveals (and combines) both the "public face" (quite clearly) *and* the "private face" (perhaps slightly concealed). Both are visible from *either side*—doubling the number of visible lines, revealing the process of stitching, and extending the language of mark-making. Continuous reconnecting and intersecting lines are formed, as in blind contour drawings on paper, in which the pencil never leaves the page.

To add contrast, use stitches that are naturally opaque (for example, back or satin stitches) to make dense areas on a transparent ground; or apply stitches to *both* sides for even more complex two-sided effects; or combine or contrast see-through and opaque stitched fabrics. The more nearly transparent the fabric, the more the stitching will appear to mysteriously "float" in space.

I think of these fabrics, in order from least transparent to most, as *translucent, semi-transparent, transparent, layered transparent,* and . . . well, *none* (disappearing, because the former ground dissolved away).

Translucent Fabrics

The main translucent fabrics are organza, organdy, and cheesecloth. Whether made from natural or synthetic fibers, translucent fabrics create visual complexity and depth by revealing the "ghost" of what lies beneath them.

In 07-02, hand stitching on a single layer of translucent fabric produces solid lines on the surface of the fabric and lighter "ghost" images where the threads traveled behind it.

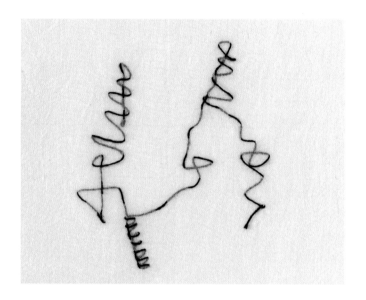

ABOVE 07-02 Hand-stitched cotton floss on silk organza. Stitches: fly, straight, running, whip.

LEFT 07-03 Free-motion machine stitching: satin. Cotton on a band of silk organza, appliquéd onto handwoven, dyed, and stitched grounds. (Collection: Duke University Medical Center, Durham, North Carolina, USA.) *Photo credit: Marc Brandeis.*

Mid-value fabric colors are more transparent. White, very light, and very dark dye colors, on the other hand, are nearly opaque. In 07-03, the horizontal gold translucent organza band overlies the woven central structure but reveals both the underlying weave structure *and* the additional hand stitching added to the weave itself *before* the organza was placed above it.

In 07-04, stitching is done on a stand-alone piece of translucent organza without an underlying fabric base. Because organza is thin and delicate, free-motion machine stitching stands above and slightly separate from the surface. The *stitched* shapes echo the *printed* shapes, visually connecting the two.

TIPS FOR MACHINE STITCHING ON SILK ORGANZA

Free-motion machine stitching on silk organza looks simple but takes practice. It requires coordination of the machine's foot-operated stitching speed, hand-operated stitch width dial, and your own manual movement of the stitching hoop. (Sometimes it can feel as if you don't have enough limbs in the right places at the right times!) Stabilizing the organza with a dissolvable web and tightly stretching it in a muslin-wrapped hoop helps greatly. To prevent the needle tearing the fabric, avoid jerky motions.

Semi-Transparent Fabrics

For a bit more transparency, try silk organza *mesh*, a material more transparent than silk organza but woven with the same threads. Stiffer, stronger, and more substantial than nylon netting—but also more opaque—it can be dyed any color. It stabilizes easily and stretches tightly in a hoop or frame. It is strong enough to hold both heavy and delicate effects. The mesh is transparent enough to see through, revealing the threads on the back at color value and intensity nearly equal to those on the front, and producing the effect of the lines floating in space.

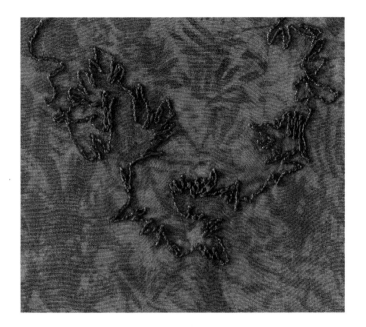

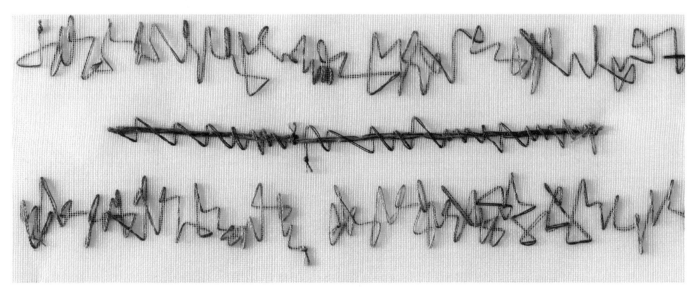

TOP 07-04 Free-motion machine stitching: moss stitch, a type of straight stitch in which loose bobbin tension has allowed the thread to bunch. Cotton thread on hand-dyed and printed silk organza.

ABOVE 07-05 Hand stitching: straight, running, whip, cross, couching. Valdani variegated cotton thread on silk organza mesh.

Both one-sided stitches (running, French knots) and two-sided stitches (back, double running, satin) look about the same on front and back: connected, continuous, and suspended.

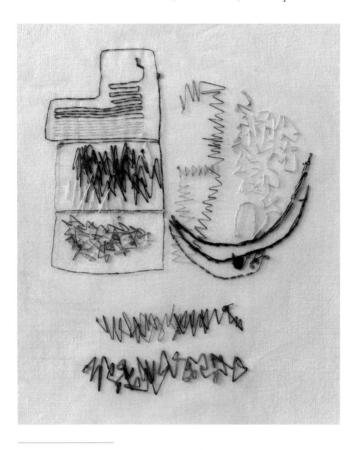

07-06 Hand stitching: cross, straight, running, chain, French knots, stem, fly, satin, back. Variegated cotton threads on silk organza mesh.

Transparent Fabrics

The extreme transparency of fabrics such as nylon netting only slightly alters the color of surfaces beneath it. However, you can combine several layers of netting to compose richer colors and denser surfaces that are still quite transparent. Netting can be stretched in a hoop or onto a tack wall for stability and then effortlessly stitched with a blunt needle. Conversely, machine stitching on netting requires *very stable* support (perhaps dissolvable web) and slow movements.

When the color of the netting matches the color of the background behind it, the stitching creates the illusion of a pile of random or dropped threads suspended in space.

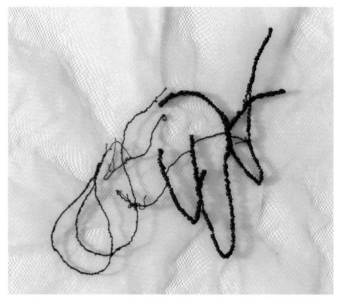

ABOVE 07-08 Hand stitching: running. Synthetic chenille thread on white nylon netting, photographed against white background.

LEFT 07-07 Hand stitching. Cotton floss (6 strands) on nylon netting overlaid on pieced fabrics. (Collection: Credit Suisse, Research Triangle Park, North Carolina, USA.) *Photo credit: Marc Brandeis.*

Layered Transparent Fabrics

You can control the *degree* of transparency by layering different types of translucent, semi-transparent, and transparent fabrics.

You can control the *perceived* color of the finished work through your choice of colors in the layered fabrics being combined.

The slight misalignment of two gridded fabric structures, whether intended or accidental, will also produce a moiré effect—and, if sufficiently misaligned, may even produce a classic moiré pattern, which can be either interesting or distracting.

In any case, the greater the number of fabric layers, the more dimly you will see the backs of the stitches themselves from the front of the layered stack.

Appliquéing transparent fabric *shapes* onto a transparent ground mixes the colors and provides a light, delicate composite ground for stitching. When viewed from the front, the thread colors on the back are tinted or shaded by the intervening fabric colors.

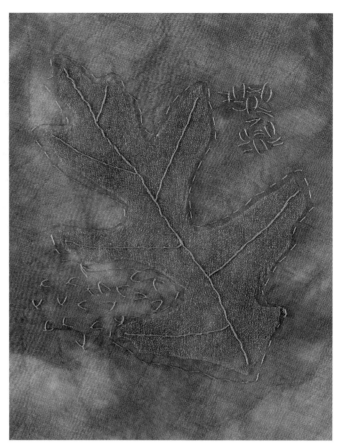

ABOVE 07-09 Novelty threads on layered nylon netting and silk organza mesh, which combine to become less transparent than either material alone. Hand stitching: running, back.

TOP RIGHT 07-10 Organza color shades the connecting stitches of the yellow thread running behind the fabric. Silk and metallic blend fabric appliquéd with cotton and metallic threads onto hand-dyed silk organza. Hand stitching: couching, seeding.

Disappearing Ground: Only the Lines Remain

The most transparent stitching ground is *none at all*. You may ask, "How can I stitch on *nothing*?" Well, you can machine-stitch a network of lines directly onto a web or gel material that will later dissolve in hot water.

Dissolvable webs come in various weights and allow you to stitch an independent "thread web" and then, in essence, to draw "in space."

The stitching must be fairly dense, with clear and frequent connection points, so that the stitches alone produce a lacy cloth sufficient to sustain itself—i.e., not fall apart—when immersed in hot water to remove the ground. Like lace itself, lacy stitch structures can then exist in space without need of a permanent ground fabric. But they can also be clustered or layered onto other fabrics or assembled into three-dimensional forms.

The stitched lines can be spontaneous, meandering, busy, and erratic; or organized, structured, and linear.

As with other transparent constructions, bobbin threads (both top and bottom) will be visible, especially if differently colored.

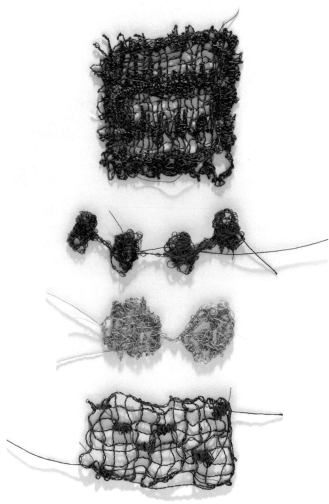

ABOVE 07-11 Cotton thread stitched on dissolvable web, which was removed after stitching so that only the thread structure remains. Machine stitching: straight, zigzag.

RIGHT 07-12 Simple and complex shapes. Cotton thread on dissolvable web removed after stitching. Machine stitching: straight, zigzag.

Something Different: Metal Mesh

The world abounds in various sizes of transparent metal, nylon, and synthetic meshes ripe for experimentation. Try some if you'd find it interesting to step beyond "traditional" stitching fabrics.

RIGHT 07-13 Hand-stitched cotton and linen threads on metal mesh. The stitching could also have used thin wire (also a linear "thread" material, but less likely to break if abraded by the mesh).

Try this!

7.1 / Textured drawing on transparent materials

Choose a transparent or translucent material (netting, organza, meshes, or plastics) and threads of appropriate size. Look at pictures of the shapes of jellyfish, seashells, or crumpled clear plastic wrappers for inspiration. Create a textured stitched "drawing," allowing the fabric(s) to pucker and distort in response to the stitches. Choose stitches and color according to the source of inspiration.

7.2 / Back and front

Choose very transparent materials like nylon netting or clear plastic. Look for inspiration in photographs of ice, frozen streams, swirling water, tide pools, or textured glass. Design and create a stitched drawing in which you can clearly see *both the back and front* of the stitching from either side. Follow-up: design and create a stitched drawing on the same transparent fabric in which the front and back look *the same, but reversed in orientation*.

7.3 / Layering transparent fabrics

Layer transparent materials, slightly misaligning the grids to create a moiré effect. Add stitching that accentuates the moiré effect. Follow-up: apply stitches to each layer of transparent fabric *before* you layer and misalign them.

7.4 / Groundless stitching

Look for visual inspiration in spider webs, tree branches against the sky, natural sponges, or clothes dryer lint. Design and create a 4" round or square composition using free-motion machine stitching on dissolvable web. Think of the stitching as irregular lace, a thread web, or ground-free embroidery. Stitch densely so that all stitches cross many times to hold their shape when you wash away the web to finish.

7.5 / Non-traditional materials

Working with non-traditional (i.e., non-cloth and non-thread) materials is one good way to practice innovation in stitching. Often this also means working at larger scale, but it nearly always involves a base—such as plastic or metal meshes or screens, or drilled wood, metal, or fired clay—that is perforated with holes and therefore at least partly transparent. Gather any materials that seem likely or appealing. The guiding principle is that *linear elements must pass through another material.* (This *may* mean that *you* have to do the drilling or hole-punching!) Gather any special tools necessary to work with your materials (scissors, pliers, awls, metal punches, drills, or other shop tools) and make sure to wear protective work gloves. Linear elements for stitching might include: plastic tubing, knitted or leather shoelaces, metal wires, coated or uncoated electrical wire, leather strips, paper, or . . . imagine! Additionally, you may be able to make your own linear elements by stripping other materials: window screens, plastic bags, interfacing, felt, old clothing, or . . . imagine! The materials themselves will both constrain and inspire your choices of stitches, which probably need to be simple. The pattern or organization of holes in the ground material will both constrain and inspire your composition. (Note for the astonished: This may sound bizarre, because it involves linking materials you may never previously have associated with stitchery. *"Electrical wire through perforated sheet metal? Really? Is this some kind of joke?"* But have some fun. If non-traditional materials interest you, think of this as an experiment in "pushing my embroidery to new limits." You may even have to invent new ways to "stitch" with your chosen materials. Try several different combinations to compare the possibilities.)

Lines that bend or curve with sufficient angle or curvature, or overlap in their pathways, eventually cross and enclose space, forming shapes distinguishable from the surrounding space. Each shape has expressive potential, largely determined by the combination of its external boundary (*outline* or *contour*) and its interior markings, shadings, or coloring (*fill*).

Weight and Character

Applied to shape contours, *line weight* contributes to the relative delicacy, strength, or character of the edge or outline. This quality will affect the visibility and perception of that edge from a distance. Contour line weights imply the pressure of your hand pressing a pencil against paper, or turning a drawing tool to make thick and thin wavering lines, thus expressing different emphases or intensities. (See Chapter 1 about line weight options.)

A simple comparison of similar stalks of leaf shapes (08-02) first stitched with a *single* upper thread and then with *double* upper threads (in a double needle) shows the difference in effects. The heavier contour causes the leaves to look clear, heavy, and closer to us. The lighter contour, on the other hand, causes the leaves to look delicate, indistinct, and farther away. Combinations and refinements of these effects contribute to the illusion of space, indicate layers of shapes, or emphasize selected shapes. If you want a shape to seem closer, to appear to lie on top of another, or to seem more important, make its contour line weight heavier.

ABOVE 08-01 Free-motion machine-stitched shapes on layered silk organza and linen. Stitches: straight, zigzag. *Photo credit: Marc Brandeis.*

Shapes can be transformed by the *character* of their contours: solid or broken, jagged or smooth, fluid or jerky. Outlines can vary from sharply defined to softly indefinite, depending on the character of their boundaries (as in 08-03). Varying the value, intensity, and composition of a contour determines whether the perimeter appears to be heavy or light, strong or weak, defined or vague. Your style of rendering the contour controls the extent to which a shape blends into, or stands out from, the background.

LEFT 08-02 Machine-stitched comparison of differing line weights. Cotton sewing thread on silk. Stitch setting: straight.

BELOW 08-03 Hand stitching: cross, blanket, back, straight, stem, running, laced running, laced back, satin. Cotton floss on linen.

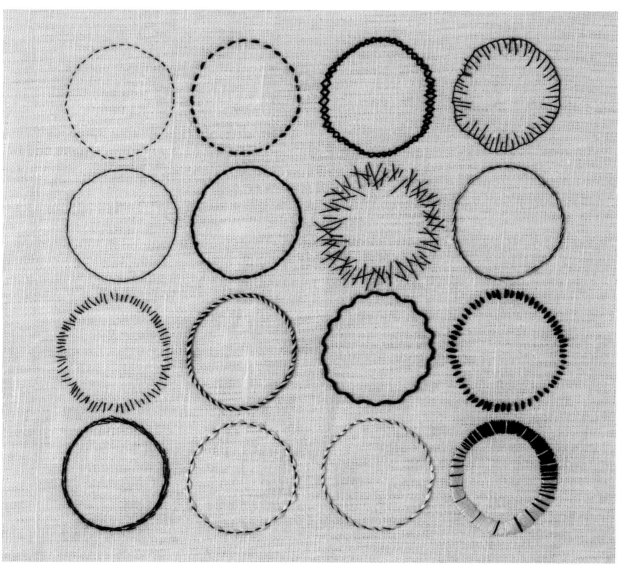

High contrasts of color and dimension accentuate and clearly define the edges of shapes or divisions in a composition. In 08-04, a seeded line of red beads dramatically defines and highlights the edges of geographic contours in the printed image.

Conversely, in 08-05 subtly colored beads blend into the background colors, adding texture and light reflection *without* high contrast. The edge is defined, but the effect is subdued and calm.

Multiple outlines can suggest a wavering or expanding contour, simultaneously enlarging the shape and making it seem to radiate or glow (08-06).

While the solidity of a machine-stitched line makes a firm boundary (08-07), a lighter hand-produced running stitch causes the same shape to appear soft and delicate (08-08).

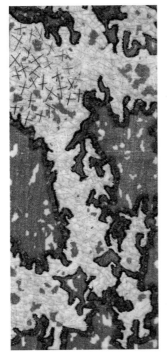
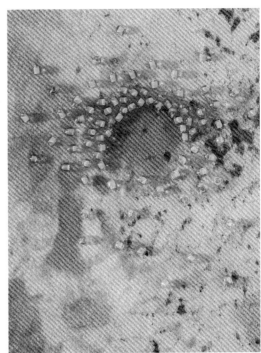

TOP LEFT 08-04 Stippling in red glass and plastic beads (to define edges) and in cross stitch (to enhance texture in the cream-colored areas). Cotton thread on digitally printed linen. (Collection: Duke University Medical Center, Durham, North Carolina, USA.) *Photo credit: Susan Brandeis.*

TOP RIGHT 08-05 Stippling with glass beads and cotton thread on digitally printed heavy cotton twill.

LEFT 08-06 Multiple wavering contours on layered silk organza and printed parachute silk. Machine stitching: varying width satin.

Contour Drawings

Like the relationship of hand printing to handwriting, contour drawing techniques capture the unique lines of your hand while you draw what is in front of you. This is an exercise that is well-suited for you to try with free-motion machine straight stitching, simultaneously building your eye-hand coordination and your machine drawing skills.

In traditional contour drawings, where only the perimeters of the objects in your field of view are traced, the character of the line becomes quite important. In a "blind contour" drawing, you look only at the source objects themselves, but not at what you are drawing, never lifting your pencil from the paper, and thereby capture shapes and details in a single continuous line. This lack of interruption causes the lines to double back on themselves, misalign, and assume a lively energy.

This approach appeals to those who love to draw and are searching for direct ways to translate their skills to cloth.

 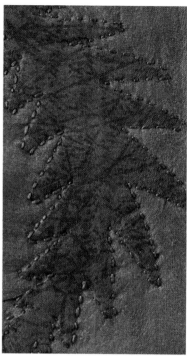

TOP LEFT 08-07 Free-motion machine-stitched cotton sewing threads through silk organza layered over printed cotton. Stitch: straight.

TOP RIGHT 08-08 Hand-stitched cotton floss through silk organza layered over dyed silk noil. Stitch: running.

LEFT 08-09 Contour drawings can be stitched directly at the machine, or hand drawings (in this case, a sketch of the author's home studio) can first be transferred to the cloth as a guide. Free-motion machine stitching: straight. Cotton machine embroidery thread on silk noil.

Try this!

8.1 / Varying contours

Start with a simple geometric shape like a circle, square, or triangle. Using a pencil, draw that shape at least 12 times on a piece of white fabric. Using a variety of stitches, threads, and line characters, render at least 12 different kinds of contours for the shape. Compare the effects.

8.2 / Machine contour drawing

As a subject for drawing, choose a familiar space in your home, an assembled still life, or a section of your garden. First, do a contour or blind contour drawing with paper and pencil. This will get your eyes accustomed to looking at the subject and your hands accustomed to following where your eyes focus, moving in tandem. You may want to try this several times. Choose the best of your drawings on paper as a guide. Transfer your drawing to fabric with a light pencil mark (a light table or sunny window will help you see through the fabric to the drawing on the paper). Stitch directly on top of your drawn line. Alternatively: Set up your sewing machine for free-motion stitching using black or dark gray thread. Then do a contour drawing with your machine, directly on fabric, without first doing an intermediary drawing on paper. Be careful to keep your fingers away from the needle!

Shapes and Spaces:
Fills and Shading

SHAPES CAN HAVE NEARLY INFINITE VARIETY, but they fall into broad categories which may be familiar to you: geometric, organic, irregular, descriptive, figurative, abstract, or random.

Within these broad categories lie thousands of variations you can use and combine at different sizes and scales. You can capture shapes from the real world, invent them from your imagination, or develop them by drawing in your sketchbook.

Once a *shape* has an outline, its inner dimensions invite "fill." Filling shapes requires using many smaller marks, lines, or stitches, which in turn contribute to form, color, and surface texture. Choose fill stitches for their individual character: some are naturally quiet and gentle, others are naturally energetic or dynamic.

Fills can make shapes appear flat or dimensional, opaque or transparent, close or far away, realistic or abstract.

In Part 2 we'll explore fills that define shapes and spaces by rendering them transparent (revealing large or small bits of the fabric); opaque (covering the fabric); shaded (grading from transparent to opaque); or highly textured—starting with color considerations that affect them all.

Keep in mind that, although I've devoted a separate chapter to each kind of fill, in "real life" stitching they're not mutually exclusive, and any composition could incorporate some of each. As always when using *intentional* thread, it's important to match the chosen technique (or *mix* of techniques) to your subject and the impressions you want to create.

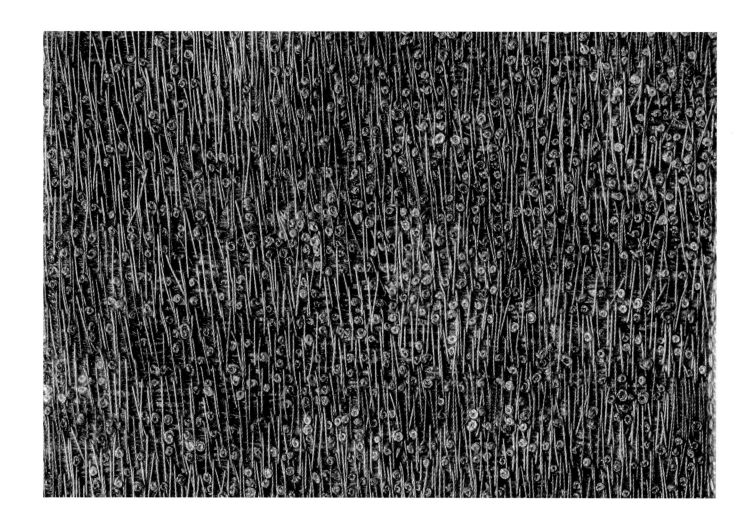

Humans are uniquely capable of perceiving millions of individual colors, stimulated by the combination of light reflections and the surface qualities of objects, which are then translated by the cone cells in the eye and, in turn, the brain. The characteristics of the light source (time of day, weather conditions, nature of artificial light) and the surface characteristics of materials (rough, smooth, bumpy, slick) change our perceptions of color. To further complicate matters, each individual person carries varied capacities for perceiving colors and their subtle variations.

In everyday practical terms, differences in color allow us to distinguish shapes and objects from each other and from their surroundings. In subjective terms, color can trigger emotions, associations, and memories by providing visual "cues" we associate with safety or warning; pleasure or discomfort; agitation or peace of mind. And, more universally, of course, our capacity to perceive color transforms our world into a richly "decorated" and lively place.

Responses to color are often emotional and largely culturally rooted. You respond to certain colors in predictable ways because you learned the "correct meaning" of colors from those around you. Cultural norms—uses, associations, practices, and choices—tempered by your own individual perceptions allow you to "read" psychological and emotional messages in the colors of objects in your environment. For example, some cultures associate white with cleanliness, but for others white is the color of death. In some Western cultures, red is associated with raciness or immodesty; in some Eastern cultures, red is the color used in marriage ceremonies; and in some religions, shades of red are the colors worn by high clergy.

ABOVE 09-01 Hand stitching: straight, back, French knots. Cotton floss and threads on cotton ground. Scale: 3" × 4".

Color is a complex, powerful, and essential tool for the expression of emotion or mood. Adding color infuses the marks and gestures you make with dynamism, nuance, and meaning.

Context

Colors are perceived *only* in relationship to the colors around them—that is, *in context.* This means that the same series of colors will look entirely different when viewed against a green background, a white background, or a bright pink background. (See 09-02 below.) You can create interesting effects by manipulating the relationships between the cloth and stitch colors.

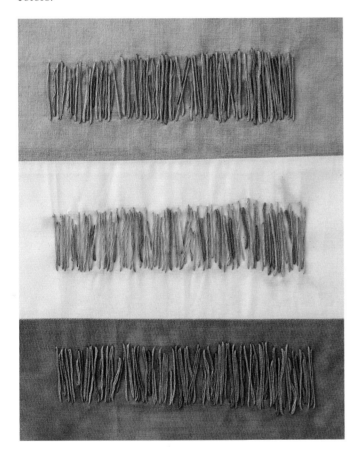

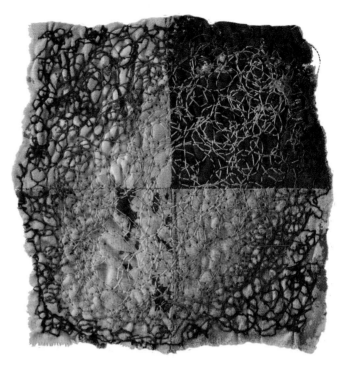

Test this maxim on a pieced fabric square with four different base colors. (See 09-03 above.) Stitch scribbles, working in concentric rings from the center out toward the edges, with a sequence of analogous colors—such as yellow, orange, scarlet, and dark red. As each color of thread crosses a different color of ground fabric, it either recedes or advances because of its low or high contrast—its *context.* (See Josef Albers: *Interaction of Color* in the Bibliography.)

Low contrasts of hue, value, and intensity (concepts I'll discuss in the pages ahead) blend with the background. The repetition of similar hues within a narrow dynamic range maintains harmony, while inserting some variety (09-04).

Higher contrasts of hue, value, and intensity stand out from the background clearly, for emphasis (09-05).

ABOVE 09-02 Hand stitching in identical thread colors and amounts. Stitch: straight. Cotton floss on 3 colors of cotton fabric.

TOP RIGHT 09-03 Machine-stitched scribbling. Stitch: straight. Cotton sewing thread on pieced fabric square. Scale: 3" × 3".

RIGHT 09-04 Machine stitching on pigment-stamped cotton fabric. Stitch: satin.

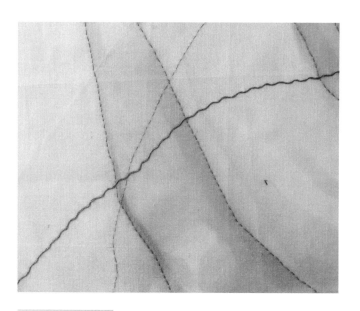

09-05 Cotton floss on digitally printed cotton fabric.
Stitches: running, laced running.

Characteristics of Color

The *color wheel*, which arranges hues in a sequence referring to their mixing potentials, presents colors at their highest intensities. The primary colors are laid out at equidistant points (the points of an equilateral triangle inscribed inside the circle), the secondary colors about midway between them, and the intermediary colors between them in sequence. Manufactured color wheels are readily available from art suppliers; I recommend that you keep one handy for reference.

Description and control of color hinge on understanding three terms—*hue, value,* and *intensity/saturation*—which indicate the linked and interacting characteristics present in any color. Manipulating these aspects allows you to fine-tune colors to more precisely match your visual experiences or your ideas. Repetition of color across a composition provides coherence, harmony, and rhythm, while deft placement of color can emphasize the illusion of three-dimensional space.

09-06 Color wheel. Hand stitching: French knots (primary colors), chain (secondary colors), satin (intermediary colors). Cotton floss on silk noil.

Hue

Thinking about color usually begins with *hue*—the name of a color or its place on the color wheel—for example, green. What we call the *primary colors* are the basic hues from which all others are mixed (09-07). Particularly when using paint, inks, dyes, or pigments, the primaries (also known as the *subtractive primaries*) are cyan, magenta, and yellow. Bundles of threads will also mix visually to create impressions of a full range of colors.

Secondary colors (also known as the *subtractive secondaries*) are those colors about midway between a pair of primaries on the color wheel: blue, red, and green (09-08).

These names for primary and secondary colors may vary from the simpler red-yellow-blue color wheel you learned in elementary school, but they are the terms used by professional colorists and manufacturers. They also produce more accurate coloration in dyes, pigments, printing inks, paints, *and threads,* because they are more predictable and controllable.

When you draw or stitch, you inevitably place hues in relationship with other hues. The simplest relationship is *monochromatic*: tints, tones, and shades of a single hue (for example, light green, bright green, olive green, dark green). (See 09-09.) This relationship tends to "hum a single note," and results in an expressive effect that is simple, gentle, subtle, flat, and focused.

While monochromes (09-09) are a reliable choice, they can feel "safe," predictable, or lacking in variety, especially if used alone over substantial areas of stitch work. Whether the medium is dye, paint, or thread, I recommend that you avoid settling for the color names and types pre-packaged by manufacturers. Be more adventurous in your exploration of available mixtures and nuances. The next time you think of "green," remember that there are many thousands of greens from which to choose—and that they will always be enlivened if contrasted, for example, with some complementary magenta. Mix and use colors freely to achieve subtler and more interesting effects; use value and intensity (discussed below) to temper and control *which* greens you use; and always remember to consider their context.

Temperature is the relative warmth or coolness of a hue. We associate warm colors (red, yellow, orange) with fire. They tend to convey more energy, movement, and activity. We associate cool colors (blue, green, violet) with ice, snow, water, or vegetation. They tend to remain more serene, calm, and still. Choosing an overall color temperature at the beginning of a project will automatically infuse it with emotional undertones and shade the meaning in your drawing. (See also 12-32.)

09-07 Hand-stitched primary colors: cyan, magenta, yellow. Stitch: satin. Cotton floss on silk noil.

09-08 Hand-stitched secondary colors: blue, red, green. Stitch: satin. Cotton floss on silk noil.

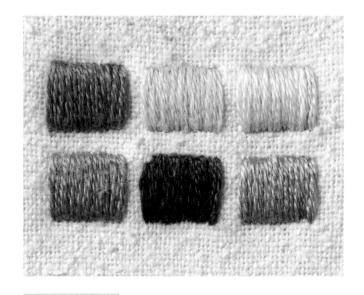

09-09 Hand-stitched monochromatic colors: tints, tones, and shades of green. Stitch: satin. Cotton floss on silk noil.

Value

Value is the relative lightness or darkness of any color or hue—or its relationship to steps in a value scale from white to black.

High value hues are light or closer to white (for example, as in 09-10, light violet, light green, and pink).

Low value hues are dark or closer to black (for example, as in 09-11, navy blue, forest green, and dark purple).

The degree of value *contrast* between the lines and shapes in a drawing will make them either clear or obscured. The highest possible value contrast is black and white, which is why we typically print book text in black on white pages: it is the easiest to see and to read. The lowest value contrast exists when the marks and the surface match in hue and value, so that only variations in texture reveal the presence of the marks. All other value relationships lie in between, yielding different levels of clarity. Colors that are all one value tend to blend together, even when the hues vary.

A combination of light, medium, and dark values in a composition creates a powerful and interesting *dynamic range*, nuancing the color palette, expressively shading and grading shapes and spaces, and creating unusual or special effects. Value contrasts, when coupled with line weight variations, give you a double-edged tool *both* to shade and slightly alter thread colors *and* to make certain colors stand out and others recede. The appearance of each colored mark you make will shift significantly with the addition of a second color next to it, moving it forward or backward in *implied* space while also changing its apparent hue. (See 09-12 and 09-13.) Line weight contrasts and the *close proximity* of the marks assist in controlling this effect.

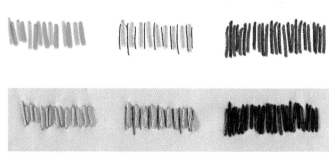

TOP 09-12 Left: *similar* values (and line weights) barely differentiate the colors. Center: highly *contrasting* values (and line weights) "pop" the darker color forward. Right: two *hues* of similar *low* value "vibrate" in alternation *despite* similar line weights. Digital drawing with Corel *Painter*™.

BOTTOM 09-13 Hand-stitched interpretations of value and line weight variations in 09-12. Stitch: straight. Cotton and wool threads on cotton.

09-10 Hand-stitched high value (light) colors. Stitch: satin. Cotton floss on silk noil.

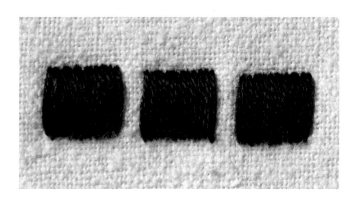

09-11 Hand-stitched low value (dark) colors. Stitch: satin. Cotton floss on silk noil.

IDENTIFYING VALUES

If you are having trouble identifying the values present in a color palette or a drawing, make a photocopy of it. Black and white photocopiers immediately reduce the colors to a gray scale, revealing the values present. This may also help you to visually separate the effects of value and intensity in any color palette.

In a representational drawing, value contrasts can define recognizable shapes and indicate their positions in space. High values (light hues) tend to recede, while low values (dark hues) tend to advance. Including shapes in medium values creates a full range of spatial positions.

09-14 Hand-stitched interpretation of a Monet sketchbook drawing detail. Dramatic value contrasts define the space of a town square. Stitches: straight, self-couching, cross, couching, hatching, detached chain. Cotton threads on cotton. Scale: 2" × 2".

Intensity/Saturation

Intensity—also known as "saturation" or "chroma"—is the relative purity or concentration of color described by adjectives such as bright or dull, pure or muddy, garish or drab. High intensity/saturation hues are bright and pure (for example, as in 09-15, hot pink, lime green, or sunny yellow).

Low intensity/saturation hues are dull or muddy (for example, as in 09-16, slate blue, beige, or olive green).

High intensity colors seem to advance toward the viewer, while low intensity colors seem to recede. Adding the color effects of intensity to the three-dimensional effects of value provides a powerful means to express the illusion of depth. (See 09-17 and 09-18.)

Among all the color "tools" available to you for expression, *contrasts of intensity* have the most power to make a color palette richer and more interesting. While colors of *similar* intensity tend to strike a uniform "note" or emotional tone, *contrasting* intensity interactions create a fuller and more robust spectrum for the eye to blend, and a more complex atmosphere. Placing bright and dull colors adjacent to each other provides each with an effective balance or "color partner." The result can range from electric or highly visible to shadowy or softly ghost-like. Varying the *proportions* of high and low intensity extends the possibilities even further.

09-15 Hand-stitched high intensity (bright) colors.
Stitch: satin. Cotton floss on silk noil.

09-16 Hand-stitched low intensity (dull) colors.
Stitch: satin. Cotton floss on silk noil.

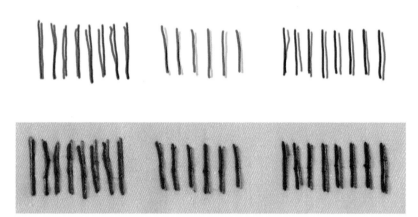

TIPS ON COMBINING VALUE AND INTENSITY

Confused? Not to worry. Because the concepts of value and intensity operate *simultaneously* in all colors, many people have trouble visually separating the two concepts. But try to think of them as two *cooperating* attributes that lend each color its unique personality, making it distinguishable from all other colors.

Some confusion arises with the terms themselves. To describe the lightness or darkness of hues we use only the word "value" in order to describe how nearly white or black it is. "Value" says it all. But for intensity, multiple words are used interchangeably, although having exactly the same meaning: "saturation," "chroma," "intensity," "purity." This attribute is the amount of *pure color* present, without the interference of other colors mixed with it in the dye pot, paint palette, or printing press.

The best way to work your way through these issues is to practice the following exercise to analyze a single color, using a gray scale and a graded color wheel as aids. This will help to train your eye to visually separate these linked characteristics.

First: Identify the color's value. Hold a value scale next to the color you are analyzing and slide it along until you find the step in the scale that matches the color in relative lightness or darkness. Which step in the scale does it match? Is it near white (high value), black (low value), or somewhere in the middle (medium value)? Describe the color's value using those terms: high, medium, or low *value.*

Second: Identify the color's intensity or saturation. Hold a graded color wheel near the color. Rotate and slide to find the correct hue first, and *then* find its degree of purity. Where is it on the color wheel? Near full strength (high intensity), near a color that you can't quite describe or name (low intensity), or somewhere in-between (medium intensity)? Describe the color's intensity using those terms: high, medium, or low *intensity.*

Third: Combine them. Use the value and intensity modifiers together in a phrase to describe the color's characteristics fully. It may help if you remember that a color may be dull (*low* intensity) even though light (*high* value) *or* bright (*high* intensity) even though dark (*low* value). This may be the most confusing part, but once you wrap your mind around the idea of two attributes working together to form a color, it will make sense and will allow you to "read" the formative characters of any color.

Practice in identifying value and intensity of single colors will dramatically expand your ability to move beyond notions that certain colors only "go" with other colors, and will allow more adventurous color palettes in your stitch work.

Contrast: Color contrasts call attention to certain places in a composition. Depending on the context, even small amounts of certain color, in certain places, can generate dramatic impact. For example, in a composition composed mainly of pastel washes (high values), a small amount of dark blue instantly calls attention to itself and the viewer's eye immediately gravitates toward it.

Proportion: The proportion of colors in a composition places emphasis on one color or another and conveys the sense of one mood or another. For example, if you use 80% grays and 20% reds in your composition, it will "read" as relatively subdued but with spots of bright color. If, on the other hand, the composition is 80% reds and 20% grays, it will "read" as relatively more dynamic but with some tempering. The colors are the same in either case, but proportion affects the visual result.

Reducing color intensity but *not* value: To *reduce* the saturation/intensity of a color (make it duller) *without changing* its value (lightness/darkness), *add its complementary color to it.* Example: If you have a green thread you wish to make a bit more dull, add a magenta thread of similar value next to it, or mix them in the same needle.

Reducing color intensity *and* increasing *or* decreasing value: To *reduce* the saturation/intensity of a color (make it duller) *and* change its value, *add black or white* (the "value changers") *before you also add the complementary color.*

The importance of your surroundings: Color matching should be done in a working environment that is neutral. If, for example, you work in a blue room, this will affect your color perception of everything you make (or photograph) there. Try to minimize color and pattern around you. White is the ideal wall color for your workspace because it least influences color perception of objects and materials in the room.

"Managing" your eyes and color perception in the studio: When your eyes feel tired and you begin to see color after-images, you should probably "take the hint" and stop working for a while! But as an alternative, stare at a neutral gray for three to five minutes. A gray card (available from camera sellers) is useful for this purpose. If, on the other hand, you leave the work for long periods of time, allow your eyes to adapt to the environment again for about 10 minutes before resuming.

Optical Mixing with Thread

When you mix colored threads, beads, or small bits of fabric, the tiny scale of the interacting colored elements insures a high degree of optical mixing. That is, your eye actually does the work of combining the colors into a "composite" color. To get the visual mixes you want, do some test samples to play with proportions and placement of colors. Stand back and view them from a distance to test the mix. Large blocks of color—groups of marks, gestures, or shapes—may be necessary to visually "carry" a color the distance you want.

Marks of differing colors placed side by side optically mix along their lengths. Each color retains its own presence while it tempers adjacent colors (context, again!). Whether the lines are thick or thin, long or short, densely or sparsely placed, the colors will interact. The heavier the thread, the coarser the blending; the thinner the thread, the subtler the blending. (See 09-20 and 09-22.) When close together, colors which individually don't seem especially "interesting" can nevertheless blend nicely into an appealing composite color. This is especially helpful to transform crude or uninterestingly colored materials—for example, when working with limited, recycled, scrap, or discarded supplies.

Stitching *across* a mark and using more open spacing mimics gestures that are transparent, delicate, or hazy, and adds a soft blending at higher values. Where the lines cross, overlapping transparencies also form composite colors. (See 09-24.)

OPTICAL MIXING TO CREATE "COMPOSITE" COLORS

If you want to use a particular color but don't have quite the "right" one, use optical mixing to create the impression of it. Place two or more colors closely adjacent, or mix them in the needle, allowing them to blend optically, until you have the right proportions to form the color you want.

TOP 09-21 Color mixing with adjacent *fine* marks. Digital drawing with Corel *Painter*™ acrylic tool.

BOTTOM 09-22 Hand-stitched interpretation of 09-21. Delicate and thin threads more easily blend in the viewer's eye. Stitch: straight. Cotton floss (2 color strands mixed in needle).

TOP 09-19 Color mixing with adjacent *heavy* marks. Digital drawing with Corel *Painter*™ acrylic tool.

BOTTOM 09-20 Hand-stitched interpretation of 09-19. Bold and coarse threads retain more of their individual color identities, as in the drawing. Stitch: straight. Cotton floss (6 strands of each color).

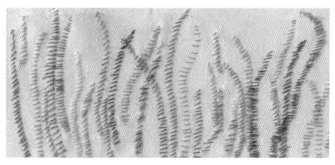

TOP 09-23 Soft, hazy, broad marks. Digital drawing with Corel *Painter*™ acrylic tool.

BOTTOM 09-24 Hand-stitched interpretation of 09-23. Stitching across the marks. Stitch: straight. Cotton floss (single strand).

Complementary Colors

When placed together, complementary colors (those directly opposite each other on the color wheel) tend to "sing." (See 09-25.) At all values and intensities, they infuse compositions with more interaction, excitement, energy, and contrast. Use a complementary palette to evoke visual vibrations and make more adventurous or powerful statements.

Split complements—any hue combined with *both* of the colors to either side of its complement on the color wheel—can be equally energetic. (See 09-26.) (These can be located by striking a long, isosceles triangle inside the color wheel with the sharpest point indicating the first hue. The other two points will indicate the other two hues.)

09-26 Split complements, horizontal triplets.
A: magenta, blue-green, yellow-green. B: blue, yellow-orange, yellow-green. Hand stitch: satin. Cotton floss on silk noil.

09-25 Complementary colors, vertically paired.
A: cyan, red. B: purple, yellow-green. C: green, magenta. Hand stitching: satin. Cotton floss on silk noil.

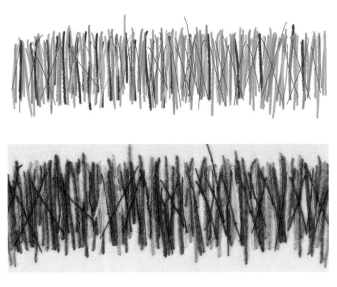

TOP 09-27 Complements *and* split complements. Digital drawing with Corel *Painter*™.

BOTTOM 09-28 Hand-stitched interpretation of 09-27. The lacing introduces the idea of plying or twisting the colors and holds down the long floats. Stitches: laced back, chain. Cotton floss (1 strand) on cotton.

Analogous Colors

Analogous colors are those next to each other on the color wheel. (See 09-29 and 09-32.) Used together in a composition, they tend to "murmur" or "whisper," and the resulting work will be serene, harmonious, and subtle. Use an analogous palette to convey softer emotions and quiet thoughts.

Changing the value of paired analogous colors also changes their visual presence and emphasis. They remain harmonious and gentle in effect, but gain visual power as they become darker.

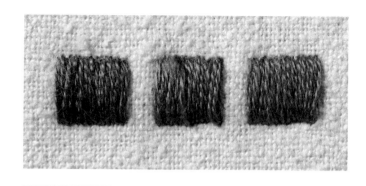

09-32 Analogous colors: cool. Hand stitching: satin. Cotton floss on silk noil.

09-29 Analogous colors: warm. Hand stitch: satin. Cotton floss on silk noil.

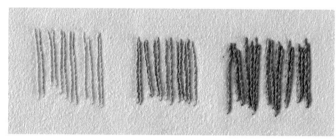

TOP 09-33 Analogous colored marks in three values. Digital drawing with Corel *Painter*™.

BOTTOM 09-34 Hand-stitched interpretation of 09-33. Stitch: laced stem. Cotton floss on silk noil.

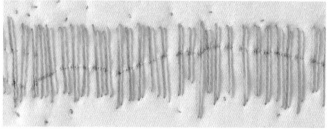

TOP 09-30 High value analogous colors. Digital drawing with Corel *Painter*™.

BOTTOM 09-31 Hand-stitched interpretation of 09-30. Tacking stitch locations change on adjacent marks, forming an implied curved line. Stitch: couching. Lightweight tapestry wool on cotton.

Color Mixing
in the Needle

For centuries, embroiderers have mixed strands of different colors in the needle to create the illusion of a new, rich "composite" color that is created in the human eye. Color fills provide the dual opportunities to mix colors in the needle *and* to set colors side-by-side to create highly idiosyncratic and individualized color palettes.

Most manufactured stitching threads are available in a limited range of colors, and most people don't routinely dye their own thread. But there is a way to circumvent these limitations. By combining multiple strands of different colors in the needle—and then using them as one—you can still achieve nuances through a more intimate and smaller scale of optical blending. The more colors you place together in the needle, the more complex the composite color. Even when similar colors are paired, this technique creates richer composite colors—and allows you to expand your color inventory without having to buy more thread!

With multiple threads in the needle, the colors rotate around each other and change their relationships during the stitching process itself. The real magic lies in *allowing* them to cross, twist, and ply—and then discovering the interesting and sometimes random results. Use of variegated threads—those which have "built-in" color changes already manufactured into the thread—causes additional color changes as they mix in the needle and therefore further enhances the element of delightful randomness.

TOP RIGHT 09-35 Mixed colors in the needle.
Hand stitching: cross, straight, seeding, couching.
Valdani 35 wt. variegated cotton on dyed cotton.

RIGHT 09-36 Mixed colors in the needle.
Hand stitching: satin. Cotton floss on cotton.
(Collection: Carole Baker, Cincinnati, Ohio, USA.)
Photo credit: Marc Brandeis.

Color Mixing with Overlaid or Crossed Threads

You can layer stitches that *cross* to build color atmospheres, create complex backgrounds, fill shapes, or grade colors. This technique is well-suited, for example, to rendering the complex colors of landscapes. The color effects will be as individual as the colors used to create them.

In contrast to the adjacent linear marks discussed above, the interaction of *crossed* marks is quite different. Crossed marks leave many tiny spaces for the fabric to intervene and mix with the threads, approximating, although reversing, the issues encountered in stippling (discussed in Chapter 12). The interaction of crossed marks *at the point of the crossings* causes more "work" for the eye, and, as a result, the visual blending is dynamic. Even if individual marks themselves are already dynamic—for example, diagonal or raised—crossing them introduces a counter-direction tending toward balance.

When layering crossed marks, the *order* of the color layers is *very* important in establishing the overall color effect—but not necessarily in a way you may have predicted.

Despite the differing impressions of the two images in 09-37, each of them used exactly the same *palette* of colors in the same *proportions*. However, on the left, the warm colors were stitched first and then progressively overlaid with stitching in the cooler colors, while on the right, the colors were stitched in the opposite sequence. In both, however, the colors laid down *first* dominate the visual impression, and the colors laid down last resemble visual accents.

09-37 Color mixing with crossed threads. Left: colors added from the palette row in left-to-right sequence. Right: colors added from the palette row in right-to-left sequence. Hand stitching: straight. Cotton floss on cotton-linen blend.

09-38 Color mixing with crossed threads in tints and shades of blue. Left: Values stitched in light-to-dark sequence. Right: Values stitched from dark-to-light sequence. Hand stitching: straight. Cotton floss on linen.

The lesson: Color sequence makes a difference, but don't automatically assume that "what's on top"—the color closest to the viewer—will dominate a composition.

Let's look at another example, but instead of color *temperature,* this time focusing on monochromatic colors (tints and shades of blue) in gradating *values.*

The two images in 09-38 use exactly the same *palette* of blues in the same *proportions.* However, on the left, the lighter blues were stitched first and then progressively overlaid with stitching in the darker blues, while on the right, the color values were stitched in the opposite sequence. In both, however, unlike the result in 09-37, the color values

laid down last—"what's on top"—really *did* dominate the visual impression.

The lesson: As in 09-37, value sequence made a difference, but with the opposite result. Sometimes "what's on top" dominates—but sometimes it doesn't.

Bigger lesson: The outcome depends on your particular choices and combinations of colors, values, intensity, and sequence.

Really Big Lesson: Before you embark on a large composition, it's a good idea to make a sample, to prevent unpleasant surprises—or perhaps to discover delightful ones.

TIPS FOR LAYERING STITCHES

• Crossing marks to build color requires large numbers of stitches in close proximity on the fabric. Therefore, the fabric needs to be stretched tightly to prevent rippling. Physically speaking, the stitches begin to "fill" the fabric, making it increasingly harder to insert the needle, so using a more openly woven fabric increases the potential *room* for stitches *and* makes stitching *easier*.

• Layering stitches to build color is a version of "rhythmic stitching." (See the "Try this!" project in Chapter 10.) The effect can be soft and complex in high value/low intensity colors or quite bold in contrasting complementary colors. Even with frequent color changes, layered stitching quickly defines space, without necessarily filling it completely, and allows shape edges to remain soft or blurred.

• Variegated thread increases color movement without the need to re-thread the needle, plot color changes, or work in multiple layers, but requires you to accept the "timing" of the color changes already contained in the threads, or—difficult but not impossible—to anticipate their sequences in order to control their placement.

• Establish a steady stitching rhythm and continue it. To minimize interruptions in your rhythm, keep several needles threaded up in advance.

• Use your intuition and watch the color interactions with each stitch so that you can plot your strategies without slowing the rhythm or speed of stitching. In some ways, this kind of hand stitching approximates use of a sewing machine, but the speed is slower, internally driven, slightly meditative, and completely individual.

Crossed colors of similar value and intensity blend easily into a rich composite. Larger proportions of one color will tend to dominate the effect, enriched and shaded by all other colors present.

Pairs of complements or split complements double the dynamism and create strong visual vibration, especially at high intensities. At moderate intensity and high value, they tend to neutralize (de-intensify) themselves when viewed at even a slight distance. Remember this to achieve the appearance of blends tending toward "gray" but doing so with richness and visual interest.

TOP 09-39 Variety of hues with similar values and intensities. In this case, there is a larger amount of green than of the other colors, and therefore green dominates, but a rich blended effect is still created by all the colors in proximity to each other. Digital drawing with Corel *Painter*™.

BOTTOM 09-40 Hand-stitched interpretation of 09-39. Stitches: laced stem (bottom layer); stem (middle layer); couching (top layer). Cotton floss (2 strands) on cotton.

TOP 09-41 Crossed split complements (yellow/green, blue/green, red/violet) of moderate intensity and high value de-saturate when overlaid. Digital drawing with Corel *Painter*™.

BOTTOM 09-42 Hand-stitched interpretation of 09-41. Stitch: cross. Cotton floss (3 strands) on cotton.

Choosing colors from around the entire color wheel forms a "complete" and satisfying visual balance, enlivened by varying the values and intensities.

At *high* intensity, the result will likewise appear "intense," like a cross-mark rainbow.

At *low* intensity, on the other hand, the colors chosen from the entire color wheel tend to merge into a complex gray.

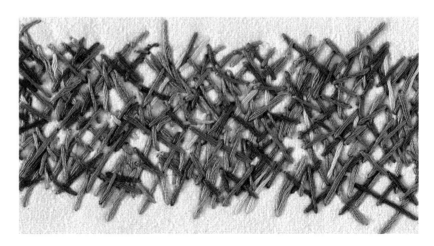

TOP 09-43 Crossed *high* intensity colors from every area of the color wheel. Digital drawing with Corel *Painter*™.

CENTER 09-44 Hand-stitched interpretation of 09-43. Stitch: straight. Cotton floss (6 strands) on cotton.

BOTTOM 09-45 Hand-stitched reinterpretation of 09-43, but using *low* intensity colors from every area of the color wheel. Stitch: straight. Cotton floss (6 strands) on silk noil.

Changing the weight of the lines in crossed marks will shift the resulting effect between dynamic and subtle. In 09-46, the colors used in the upper and lower portions are the same, but the upper portion uses three strands (resulting in a bold projection of marking) while the lower portion uses one strand (resulting in a calm and delicate blended effect).

Crossed stitches, orchestrated in overlapping "bands," create blended gradations across the surface. Choose the sequence of colors you want to use, place them in order, and then begin stitching with the first one. Work in an openly spaced "wave" across the surface from one side to another. As you approach each transition point from one color to another, *overlay* some of the first color *with* the second color, then overlay the second *with* the third, and so on. Alternatively, work with *pairs* of colors in the needle, then *remove* one thread and *add* the next thread in the color sequence as you move across the composition with each desired color change.

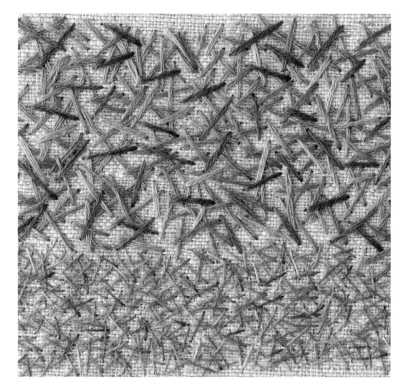

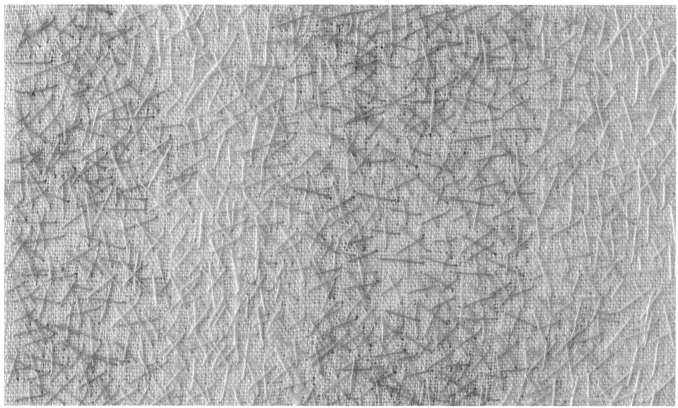

TOP RIGHT 09-46 Differences of impression created by differing line weights in the same palette of low intensity colors. Hand stitching: straight. Cotton floss on linen.

ABOVE 09-47 Blended gradations in overlapping bands. Hand stitching: cross. Cotton floss on softened linen.

Try this!

9.1 / Stitch a value scale

Mark out a sequence of seven to nine 1" × 1" squares on white fabric. Using any stitches or combination of stitches you like, fill each square with stitches in *even steps* from white, through a series of grays, to black. Keep this as a reference for *value* in future work.

9.2 / Stitch a color wheel

Find a good color wheel from a book or art supply source. Using a pencil (the color doesn't matter), draw the outlines of the color wheel in sections of equal size (so as not to "favor" any color over another) on a piece of white fabric (any size you choose). Referring to the color wheel, choose colors of the thread which match each section of the wheel, and fill in the corresponding outlines you have drawn. (You can begin with any color as long as you fill the rest of your outlines with the entire wheel in proper color *sequence*.) See 09-06 for an example. I chose there to use French knots for the primary colors, chain stitch for the secondary colors, and satin stitch for the rest, but you need not do the same. Keep your wheel as a reference for *color* in future work.

9.3 / Optical blending

Create a composition of any kind: for example, a portrait, still life, or landscape; an abstract version of any of these; or a grouping of picturesque marks and expressive gestures. Use optical color blending to shade shapes and/or gradate colors across a background area. Goal: develop and practice approaches to combining thread colors for lush and controlled results. This is an open-ended exercise. You make all the choices, and you can do it as many times as you wish.

9.4 / Inspiration from historic textiles

Historic textiles can provide rich inspiration for color palettes in your work. Find some examples, in books or online, of individual textiles whose color inspires you. Choose several to analyze. Carefully make note of the specific color palette and the proportions of the colors for each example. Choose, combine, or even dye your own threads to match one of these historic works. Use this color palette of threads in your own stitched composition in approximately the color proportions as in the historical piece. Note: This is not an exercise in rendering your own stitched *duplicate* of the *imagery* or *techniques* used in historic textiles. Make something new using any image you want and any stitches you like, but practice mindful stitch and color choices to approximate the palette of your chosen historical source.

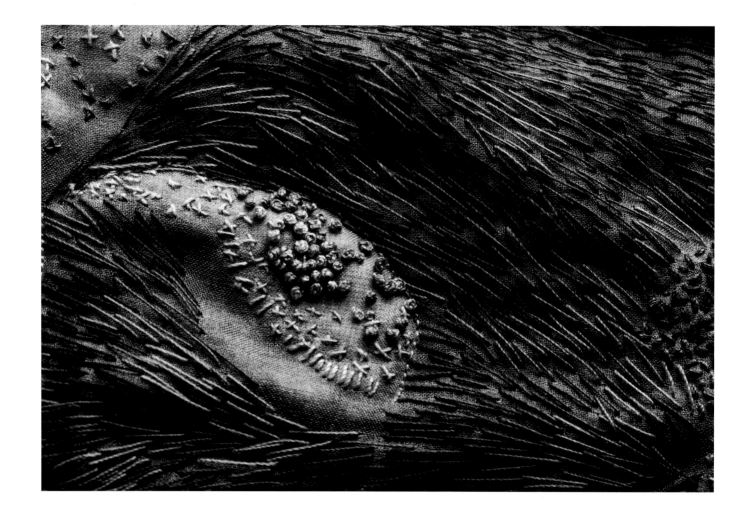

A previous chapter discussed ways of achieving translucent and transparent effects through choices of background fabrics which themselves can (in various degrees) be seen through. But this is, after all, a book focused on stitching, and the stitched fills you place on a background fabric can also be "transparent" to whatever degree they allow the background fabric to be seen and therefore to contribute to a composition's effect.

This is mainly the result of where and how the stitched fills are placed, or not placed. Experiment with turning the direction of the stitches, working them more erratically, setting them in sections of opposing directions, or layering and combining them.

10-01 Hand stitching: straight, cross, seeding, French knots. Cotton thread on digitally printed linen.

Transparent Fills: "Rhythmic" Stitching

Filling or defining *larger spaces* is most effectively achieved with what I call "rhythmic" stitching, in which you set a personal pace using stitches you can work quickly and spontaneously, without "overthinking" or belaboring the exact placement of each individual stitch, in order to achieve an effect often described in other media as "painterly." This effect is further influenced, of course, if the background fabric bears imagery or pronounced colorings of its own. (See "Try this!" project 10.3 at the end of the chapter.) Worked in this manner, the stitches may leave relatively long floats, which have the potential to wrinkle or draw up the cloth, which can be an asset or a liability, *depending on your intent.*

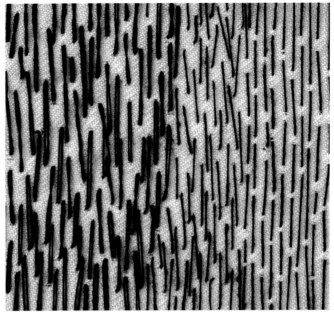

10-03 Hand stitching (moderate speed of fill). Horizontal, vertical, or diagonal placement directs the eye accordingly. Stitch: straight (double and single threads). Cotton thread (1 and 2 strands) on cotton sateen. Scale: 2.5" × 2.5".

10-02 Hand stitching (rapid rate of fill). Cross hatching is well-suited to shading and creating a sense of dimension. The speed of this fill construction also left long floats on the surface. Single strands stitched in several densities with irregular intersections and angles. Stitch: straight. Cotton thread on cotton sateen. Scale: 2.5" × 2.5".

HANDLING LONG FLOATS

When long floats are not properly tensioned, they result in drooping or floppy lines which *may* mar the look of the finished piece or spoil your intent. The solution to this problem is twofold: First, make sure your fabric is tightly and evenly stretched in a hoop or frame during the *entire* stitching process. Second, with each stitch, make sure that you pull gently on the thread to sufficiently "set it" in the fabric. Avoid pulling so hard that the fabric intersections become holes or that puckers are raised, but make sure all the looseness is gone and the stitch is firm before moving to the next stitch. Consider keeping the finished work under tension (frame or display it permanently stretched) to maintain the stability of very long floats.

10-04 Hand stitching (slower speed of fill). Unlike 10-03, this fill is even and neutral, incorporating marks in all directions, and therefore does not lead the eye in any particular direction. Stitch: large-scale seeding (some single, some double). Cotton thread (1 and 2 strands) on cotton sateen. Scale: 2.5" x 2.5".

10-06 Hand stitching (rapid speed of fill). Quickly-done, large-scale stitches, layered or touching each other. Balanced, non-directional, but energetic. Stitch: cross. Cotton thread (single strand) on cotton sateen. Scale: 2.5" x 2.5".

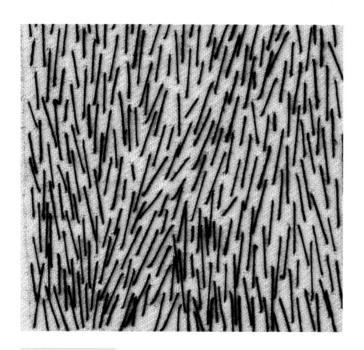

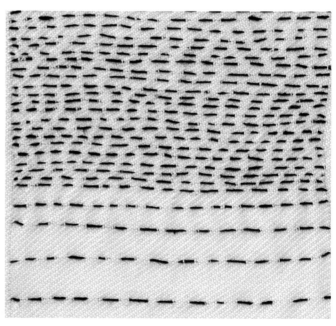

10-05 Hand stitching (rapid speed of fill). Directional placement, but random and fluid. Stitch: straight. Cotton thread (single strand) on cotton sateen. Scale: 2.5" x 2.5".

10-07 Hand stitching (slower speed of fill). Light to dark gradations. Can be stitched in any direction. Subtle and gentle. Stitch: running, but changing densities. Cotton thread (single strand) on cotton sateen. Scale: 2.5" x 2.5".

In 10-08, rhythmic stitching (of the type in 10-05), applied to a digitally printed image, delineates the shapes (rocks) by concentrating the stitching *around* them.

In 10-09 (overleaf), internal fill marks, quickly stitched, indicate the edges of a shape *without* the presence of an explicit solid *outline*.

10-08 Hand-stitched transparent fill: straight, cross, seeding, French knots. Cotton threads on linen, surrounding digitally printed photographs of rocks.

10-09 Hand-stitched transparent fill: straight, seeding, back.
Cotton floss on cotton and silk organza fabrics with added glass
beads. Scale: 9" × 11".

Transparent fills can be used to highlight certain areas of a composition. Tiny stitches worked on printed or painted cloth images accentuate lines or shapes, add detail, and enliven surface textures. In 10-10, seeding suggests the tiny leaves of fern foliage, simultaneously advancing the foliage to the foreground.

Small stitches with more intense thread colors can brighten a printed color palette to increase its drama, while adding both texture and dimension to the shapes. Colors that are a bit lackluster can shine with the addition of higher intensity colors, as in 10-11. Conversely, using duller or less intense colors calms the palette and quiets the effect. A printed background fabric that is too garish can be tamed by the application of quieter, lower-intensity stitching.

You can enhance any area of a composition on fabric with fills to add subtle undertones to selected areas, to change the color hierarchy with shots of bright color, or to heighten or subdue specific colors and textures. These alterations enliven the original print, highlight certain areas, and emphasize the mood of the image.

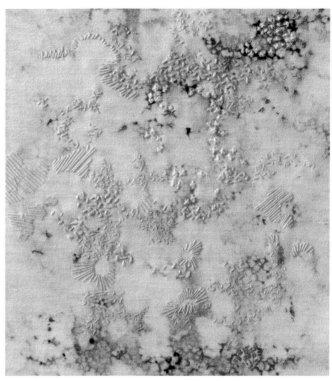

10-11 Filling in higher intensity thread colors enlivens and defines printed areas. Constants: materials. Variables: color, orientation, density, placement on image, stitch type. Hand stitching: straight, seeding, cross. Cotton floss on digitally printed heavy cotton twill. Scale: 8" × 10".

10-10 Scattered seeding defines the tiny budding leaves and adds texture and dimension to both cloth and image. Constants: materials, hand stitch type. Variables: color, orientation, density, placement on image. Cotton floss on digitally printed layered cotton and silk organza. Scale: 9" × 11".

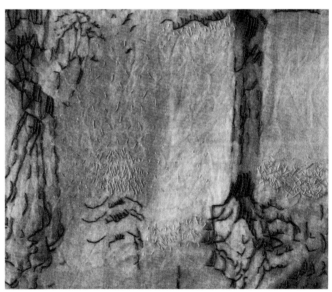

10-12 Enhancing color areas with transparent fills. Constants: materials. Variables: color, orientation, density, placement on image, stitch type. Hand stitching: straight, seeding, blanket. Cotton floss on digitally printed cotton.

Transparent Fills: Beads

Glass beads, both opaque and transparent, cut in rounded shapes, cylinders, or facets, are available in a wide variety of colors and sizes and are easily added to the stitching process. Stitching with beads lends each stitch a kind of playfulness with light reflection and physical dimension.

The amount of reflected light from each individual bead depends on its shape and the material from which it was made. For example, glass beads, faceted beads, crystals, and transparent seed beads all tend to reflect a lot of light, whereas plastic, rubber, wood, and bone beads add color, but tend to be opaque and to absorb rather than reflect light. All beads will add texture and dimension to cloth. The size of the beads determines the subtlety or drama of the effect.

ABOVE 10-13 Highlights with transparent glass seed beads and fly stitches. Sewing thread (to fasten beads) and cotton floss (for stitches) on digitally printed, then layered and pieced silk organza and cotton. (Collection: Duke University Medical Center, Durham, North Carolina, USA.) *Photo credit: Marc Brandeis.*

RIGHT 10-14 Detail of 10-13. *Photo credit: Marc Brandeis.*

High contrast between widely scattered bead or stitch colors and background fabric color will make the surface sparkle or dance visually. Every stitch will be clear and visible, which requires thoughtful placement. *Low* contrast between the bead or stitch colors and background color creates subtle textures or highlights that wash across a surface, or fade in and out. Their blending with the ground allows you to apply the stitches more spontaneously.

In 10-13, the individual beads are of approximately the same size throughout the composition, but their scattering across a wide surface area infuses the image with radiant light and the suggestion of water droplets.

TECHNICAL TIPS: SEEDING

Seeding (seed stitch) is a clustering or distribution of tiny straight stitches oriented at differing angles or opposing directions to each other but visually balanced. It is especially useful for filling shapes or background areas with color or texture. The stitches can be worked singly, in pairs, in triplets, or in other groupings, depending on the density or color effects desired. The spacing between stitches can be regular, gradating, or irregular for alternative effects.

• To make straight stitches look more like dots, keep the width of the thread and the length of the stitch nearly equal in measurement. For example, combine several strands of floss (a low-twist thread) in the needle and then make very short stitches.

• Even when your aim is to keep the width and length of the stitches roughly even, many individual stitches may well be longer than they are wide, thus expressing direction and moving the eye. This can be counteracted by turning the angles of the stitches perpendicular, or nearly perpendicular, to each other.

• The larger the thread, the larger the needle and amount of force required to pull the thread through the fabric. The stab method of stitching (see the Glossary) works best.

• Openly woven fabrics ease densely spaced stitching, but may allow dark threads to show through as "shadows" on the front of lighter fabrics.

Transparent Fills:
Small Stitches (Seeding, Detached Chain, French Knots)

When seeding is stitched across a surface or shape with *regular* density and a *constant* stitch size, the space appears *flatter* or more even. In 10-15, variegated lightweight wool threads are stitched evenly across the space using long stitches and large, even intervals, creating a calm, stable surface while introducing subtle color variations, visual texture, and spatial fill. The combined effect is open and even (from the even density) and fuzzy (from the wool yarn and the nubby silk noil fabric).

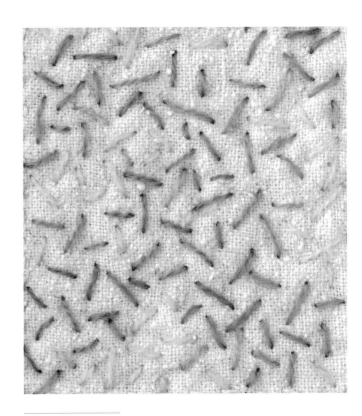

10-15 Flat and even seeding. Constants: stitch size, density, hand stitch type. Variable: color (hue). Variegated wool thread on silk noil.

Although detached chain stitches naturally make elongated dots—ovals, teardrops, seed shapes— their directional effect can be counterbalanced by alternating their orientations. Lightweight thread makes delicate dots which, when evenly spaced, yield an even background texture.

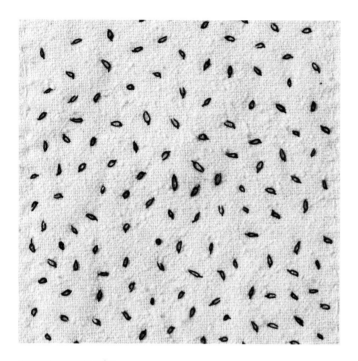

10-16 Evenly distributed and counterbalanced detached chain stitches. Constants: materials, thread/line weight, color, stitch size, stitch spacing (roughly equal between stitches), stitch type. Variables: orientation. Cotton sewing thread (50 wt.) on silk noil. Scale: 2.5' × 3".

Filling stitches can be evenly distributed, yet color changes can create the impression of shapes *without* the presence of defined contours. For example, in 10-17 a single hue of red thread was worked in double seeding (constant stitch size) across the *entire* square. The impression of shapes was created entirely by changing choices of a *third* stitch added to the center of each pair of red: light green in the small central core; steadily darker greens in the ring around the core; and orange at the top and corners. The added colors optically blended with the pairs of red—the technical name for this visual phenomenon is *simultaneous contrast*—to change our perception and to create the illusion of circular shapes, even though the composition contains no actual circular lines.

TOP 10-17 Transparent fill with simultaneous contrast. Hand stitching: double and triple seeding. Cotton floss (3 strands) on silk noil. Scale: 3" × 3".

ABOVE 10-18 Detail of 10-17.

French knots, round and dot-like in appearance, add considerable real dimension and texture to fills. The color and placement of the knots can be planned and sketched in advance with colored pencils, markers, paints, or digital drawing tools to coordinate color juxtapositions before the slower process of stitching begins.

In 10-20, French knots capture the *feeling* of the dotted drawing without reproducing each individual dot. You can control the spacing of the dots (regular or irregular, sparse or dense) to vary their filling effects.

Watercolor wash effects, digitally produced and printed on fabric, can be enhanced with color seeding to shade, emphasize, or texture the printed color areas. (See 10-21.) Low contrast stitches "sink into" the surface and blend with the printed color, adding emphasis or highlights to selected areas. Clusters of stitches aligned into larger gestures will create color washes *even without the underlying print.* Washes fill larger areas or gestures with directional movement of color.

To achieve the look of brushstrokes, pencil shading, or strokes of chalk or pastels, align and cluster the filling stitches in bands or swaths across the surface. (See 10-22.) Adjust the relative contrast between the stitch colors and the background color to make the gestures appear strong and dramatic, or subtle and gentle.

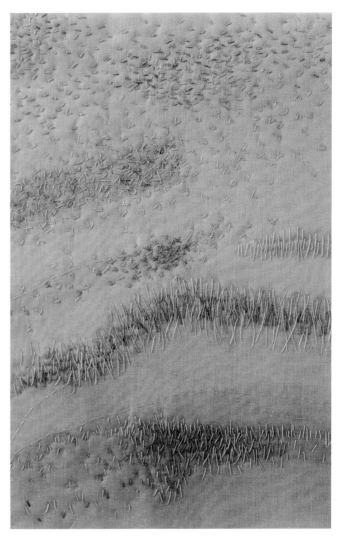

10-21 Color washes. Constants: materials. Variables: color, orientation, density, placement, stitch type. Hand stitching: straight, fly, detached chain, running. Cotton threads on digitally printed cotton cloth. Scale 8" × 10".

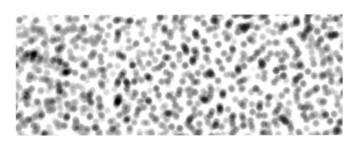

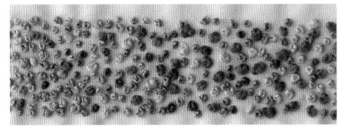

TOP 10-19 Very small dots, rounded and well-delineated, graded (left to right) from cool to warm. Digital drawing of color stippling with Corel *Painter*™ pencil tool.

BOTTOM 10-20 Hand-stitched interpretation of 10-19. French knots add color and surface texture to transparent fills. Cotton floss on cotton.

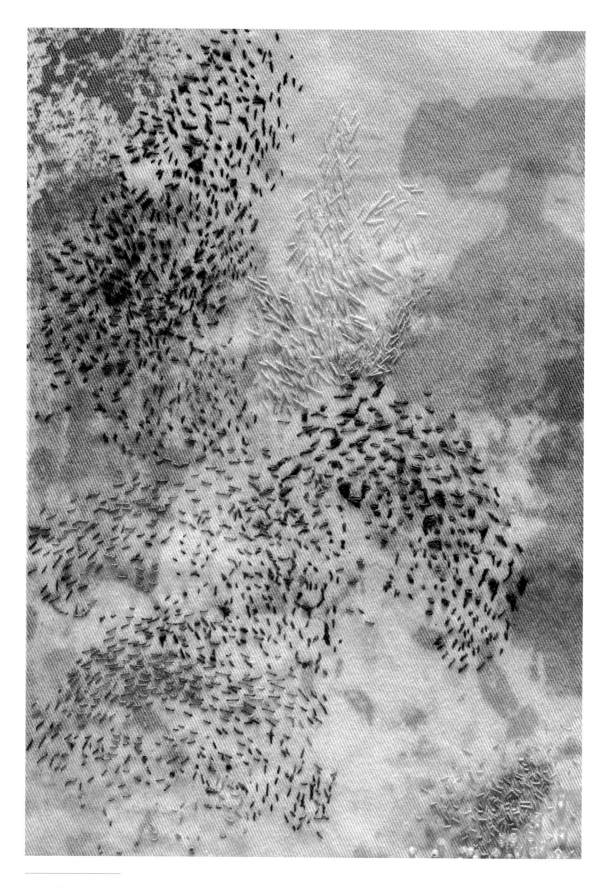

10-22 Gestures and washes of color. Constants: thread type, hand stitch type. Variables: stitch size (slight variation), color, density, orientation. Variegated cotton thread on cotton twill.

Try this!

10.1 / Overlapping shapes

Create a stitched composition using transparent fills in which some shapes are separate, some touch, and some overlap to give the impression of three-dimensional physical space around them. Practice using color to accentuate the overlapping of shapes and enhance the illusion of depth.

10.2 / Transparent fill
with small stitches and beads

Create a stitched composition that combines curved, bent, and broken lines but "transparently" leaves the background fabric exposed in ways that enhance the overall effect when stitching and background work as a "team." Embellish it with transparent beads placed at strategic points, or along stitched lines, or in the exposed background fabric spaces themselves, in ways that enhance the feeling of movement across the surface.

10.3 / "Rhythmic" transparent stitching

This *timed* exercise is intended to help you to master the skill I call "rhythmic" stitching, a useful technique for quickly and spontaneously creating fill. (This skill also provides a comfortable foundation for Chapter 5's large-scale "Try this!" project 5.3.)

Directions: In order to minimize the distracting effect of color choices, you'll use only white fabric and only black thread. Using pencil, mark a 6" square or rectangle on the fabric. (6" of fabric may not sound like much, but the goal is to mark an area slightly larger than you *think* you can *easily* fill.) Stretch the fabric in a hoop or frame with the rectangle in the center—within easy reach, but not obscured by the hoop.

Because your goal is to find a comfortable, steady, but quick internal "stitch rhythm" without the distraction of stitch variety, you'll be placing stitches of a *single* type across the entire marked square. Therefore, choose straight *or* cross stitch, but *not* both. Then thread and knot 6 to 10 identical needles with thread, perhaps 18" per needle, and have them ready and waiting.

Here's the goal: You're going to "cover" that penciled square with stitched fill. But, because this is an exercise in creating *transparent* fill, "covering" the square means that your stitches should completely "populate" the square so that no area looks obviously "empty" of stitching, but also means that no area is so full of stitching that the background fabric can't be seen.

Set a timer for 20 minutes—or if you feel brave, or are trying this project for the second or third time, 15 minutes. Start the timer—and start stitching! But this is not a race. Stitch steadily and repeatedly, *finding an internal rhythm and making each stitch on the beat of that rhythm.* Don't "overthink" this. Don't stop to make "compositional" decisions. Don't worry if the stitches vary somewhat in size, placement, or craftsmanship. Try to ignore the busy "meddling" part of your mind that wants to analyze and comment. (*Well, now, that one didn't look very good, did it?*) Just find a comfortable pace, and *keep stitching.* If you run out of thread, leave a tail on the back, pick up another threaded needle, and *keep stitching until the timer sounds* (unless your personal rhythm turns out to be so fast that you're on the verge of going beyond "transparent" fill all the way to "opaque").

Time is up? *Now* look at the extent of the coverage, and think about *how you felt while doing it.*

In many years of teaching, I have found that students don't initially understand the nature of this exercise, even after I myself have just demonstrated it and described what they're about to do. But then they try it for themselves, perhaps more than once, stitching without interruption, trying to silence the analytical and fearful parts of the mind— and they experience the liberating sense of a personal "rhythm" of paced stitching. This goes to the very heart of what I call the "meditative" nature of repetitive hand work.

Although the colors and stitches varied, I myself used this kind of "rhythmic" stitching to make illustrations 10-01 through 10-08.

Very dense stitch placement can completely cover a fabric. If there are enough of them, stitches of any type and individual size create an opaque fill for spaces and shapes.

Choose stitches based on the texture you want to create: smooth and quiet, rough and energetic. Some stitches simply take longer to fill space than others. To achieve more complex results, stitches may also be turned, re-oriented, worked more erratically, set in sections of opposing directions, layered, or combined. Whatever your choices, expect the needle to become progressively more difficult to push through the cloth as an area's stitching density increases.

11-01 Opaque fill. Hand stitching: French knots. Cotton floss on silk noil.

Opaque Fills in Satin Stitch: The Standard Choice

Traditionally, the most common choice for opaque fill is densely worked satin stitch, which creates flat and even opaque shapes easily and directly. It can be worked with single or multiple threads in the needle, covering small or large areas. By nature, satin stitch leaves a float on the fabric surface, ranging from dot-like (in very small stitches) to line-like (in longer ones).

11-03 Hand stitching (moderate speed of fill). Dense and flat surface, but oriented in multiple directions to maximize textural effect. Stitch: satin (multiple directions). Cotton floss (3 strands) on linen. Scale: 1.5" × 1.5".

11-02 Hand stitching (slow speed of fill). Very dense, flat, even surface. Easy to shape into any outline. Stitch: satin. Cotton floss (2 strands) on cotton. Scale: 2" × 2".

The direction of the satin stitch can be changed to break up an area into smaller facets, each of which will appear slightly different in color. In 11-03, only one solid (*not* variegated) thread color was used. Perceived color differences result entirely from thread direction and angle of light reflection.

Long and short stitch, also widely used as an opaque fill, offers the added advantage of incorporating shading and grading naturally into its structure. When each row is a different hue, alternating thread colors lie adjacent and blend optically.

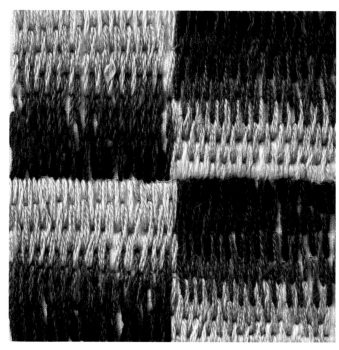

11-04 Hand stitching (slower speed of fill). Excellent grading and shading stitch, but slower than satin stitch, and somewhat hard to fit into certain shapes. Stitch: long and short (a variation on satin). Cotton floss (2 strands) on cotton. Scale: 2" × 2".

Opaque Fills:
Stitches Other Than Satin

If you venture beyond tradition, you'll find that many other stitches pack densely or layer well to create both opacity and texture simultaneously. Each stitch brings a bit of its own character to the texture created and distinguishes one area from another.

In 11-05, *chain* stitch (on the left, in rows) is linear and faster, while *detached chain* (on the right, clustered and packed) is slower and more highly textured.

11-06 Hand stitching (moderate fill speed). Stitch: stem. Cotton floss (3 strands) on linen. Scale: 1.5" × 1.5".

11-05 Hand stitching (slow to moderate fill speed). Stitches: chain (left), detached chain (right). Cotton floss (3 strands) on linen. Scale: 1.5" × 1.5".

In 11-06, tightly packed *stem* stitch becomes gestural, directional, textured, and visually active. This can be done with varying weights of thread for different effects from delicate to chunky.

In 11-07, tightly packed and layered *cross* stitch is very textured but balanced, and creates both perceived and—because the stitches are in fact layered—actual physical depth.

11-07 Hand stitching (rapid fill speed). Stitch: cross. Cotton floss (3 strands) on linen. Scale: 1.5" × 1.5".

French knots can be densely placed to fill any shape, as in 11-08. Varying their size will produce not only the fill itself but also additional surface texture.

Whip stitch is typically used to make diagonal marks separated by spaces. However, in 11-09, *densely* placed diagonal whip stitches at changing but balanced angles produce an effect almost like weaving or plaiting. This composition could also have incorporated more complex combinations of color.

Seed stitch, like whip stitch, is often dispersed across the surface. In 11-10, however, closely packed seeding becomes an opaque fill in which changes of color also lead to changes of direction but remain balanced. This composition could also have incorporated more complex combinations of color.

11-09 Hand stitching (very rapid fill speed). Stitch: whip. Cotton floss (3 strands) on linen. Scale: 1.5" × 1.5".

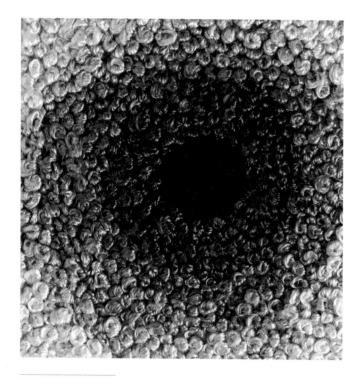

11-08 Hand stitching (*very* slow fill speed). Stitch: French knots. Cotton floss (3 strands) on linen. Scale: 1.5" × 1.5".

11-10 Hand stitching (slow fill speed). Stitch: seeding. Cotton floss (black: 6 strands, gray: 2 strands) on linen. Scale: 1.5" × 1.5".

TECHNICAL TIPS ON FRENCH KNOTS

Working French knots is easier when the fabric is stretched on a hoop or frame, and then secured in a floor stand or table clamp. This provides a "third hand," leaving both of *your* hands free to manipulate the needle and hold tension on the thread.

Densely packed French knots gently "sculpt" the fabric, adding texture, bulk, and loft. Keeping the fabric very tightly stretched in a hoop or frame will minimize the sculpting. Conversely, working on un-stretched fabric will allow you to control the sculpting and to add physical dimension to the color or textured effects achieved.

Blanket stitch, true to its name, is typically used to protect the edges of blankets and other fabrics. In 11-11, it is layered to form a highly textured, dimensional, almost lumpy surface, but one which retains strong and clearly identifiable lines.

Tightly placed *couching* makes a smooth surface, as in 11-12. The tacking threads inherent in couching can be placed randomly or arranged in patterns. In either case, the placement of the tacking threads will become more visible if they differ in color from the laid thread itself. Because multiple tack stitches would be needed to force the softness of couching into a sharp corner, it is best suited to fill round or oval shapes.

11-12 Hand stitching (moderate fill speed). Stitch: couching. Cotton floss on linen. Scale: 1.5" × 1.5".

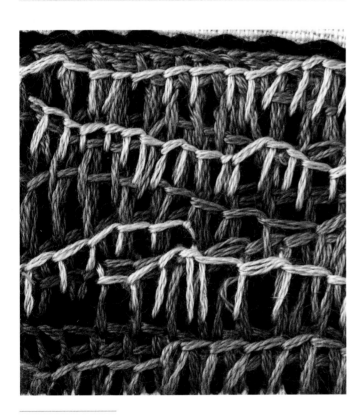

11-11 Hand stitching (moderate fill speed). Stitch: blanket. Cotton floss on linen. Scale: 1.5" × 1.5".

Opaque Fills: Introducing Color

Adding color to opaquely stitched shapes enlivens them and offers opportunities to compose, create dimensional effects, and convey meaning.

When various *small* stitched colors are placed in great density to touch one another and cover the surface, they can produce multiple effects, dependent on the viewer's vantage point. Seen close-up, the surface is subtle, lush, and intense, its separately colored stitches individually visible, as in 11-01, the photograph which introduces this chapter. That close view clearly reveals the blue stitches *within* the "orange" areas. But seen from a distance, the eye and brain mix a "composite" color of "orange"—although one tempered and influenced by the differing oranges and the blues among them—as can *also* be seen in 11-01. (Try it: Put down the book and back away.)

The dramatic effect of the viewer's distance can be seen in 11-13 (of which 11-01 was a *detail*). The knots add both optical blending and texture to the surface, and the result resembles a small carpet. Complementary colors define the primary shape (the circle within the square). Although all of the knots in the composition are approximately the same size, the many variations of color value and intensity create variety, richness, and depth.

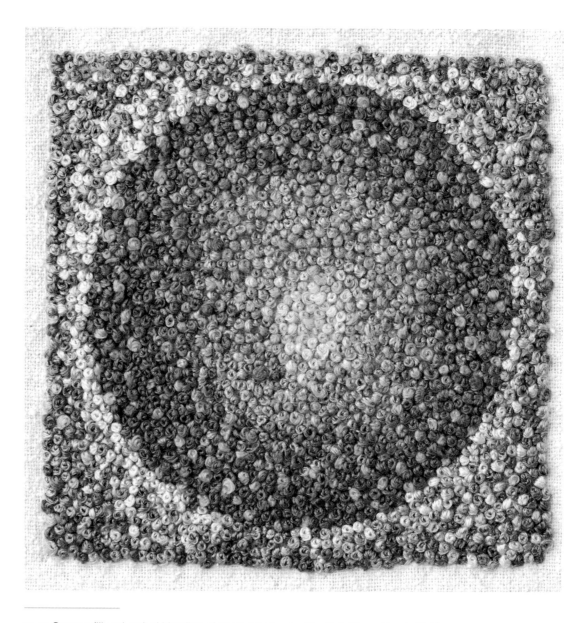

11-13 Opaque fill and optical blending of small dots inspired by Pointillism. Hand stitching: French knots (2 strands, 3 or 4 wraps around the needle). Cotton floss on silk noil. Scale: 3" × 3".

Compositional frames completely filled with geometric shapes of the same type and size can likewise appear truly grid-like, as in 11-14.

But rounding selected geometric edges, or varying their sizes, or placing them slightly off-balance to one another can make a composition appear less formal and more fluid—literally so in 11-15, an aerial view of river valley farmland rendered in delicious "fantasy" colors. The white "river" shapes are actually portions of the background fabric left completely unstitched but then defined by the fill of softened geometric shapes.

TOP RIGHT 11-14 Hand-stitched geometric shapes. Stitches: satin, back. Cotton floss on cotton fabric. Scale: 5" × 5".

BELOW RIGHT 11-15 Hand stitching: satin. Cotton floss on cotton. Scale: 4" × 4". (Collection: Renwick Gallery of the Smithsonian Institution, Washington, DC, USA.) *Photo credit: Marc Brandeis.*

COMBINING STIPPLING WITH OPTICAL COLOR MIXING

Clustering a variety of differently colored dots is even more time-consuming than working the dots in a single color, whether you are using colored pencils, drawing software, or needle and thread. The work requires focus and patience, many hours to complete to satisfaction, and especially good lighting and sharp eyesight. The technique is effective for small areas of optical blending, texture, or smooth color transitions, but impractical for filling large spaces because of the time and materials required.

Alternatively, fill can be used selectively to highlight areas of a printed composition while leaving other areas open, as in 11-16, 11-17, and 11-18.

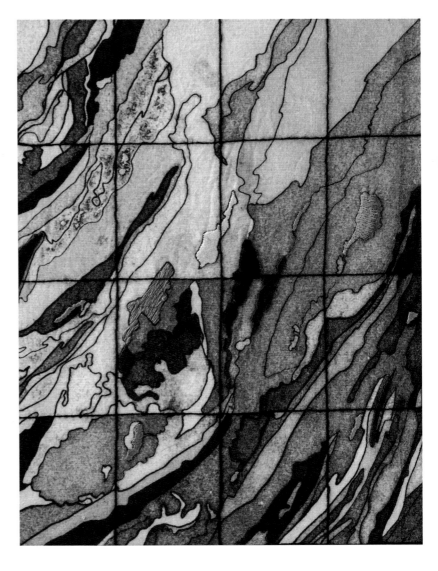

RIGHT 11-16 Hand-stitched fills to highlight selected shapes. Stitches: satin, padded satin, couched satin, back, long and short. Cotton floss on digitally printed cotton fabric. Scale: 7" × 9.5".

BELOW LEFT 11-17 Detail of 11-16.

BELOW RIGHT 11-18 Detail of 11-16.

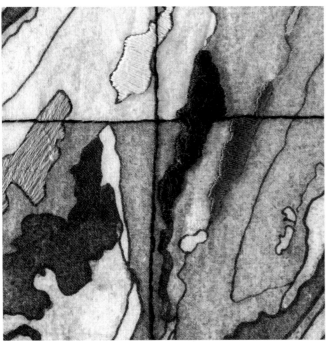

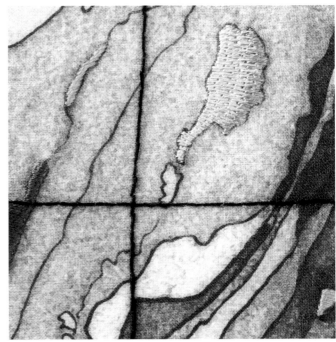

Opaque Fills: Gestural ("Painterly") Effects

In preparation for 11-19, 11-20, and 11-21, a sampler was produced for each image using direct-application textile pigment techniques. The sampler was then photographically scanned and digitally printed on the background fabric to guide the hand-stitched opaque fills interpreting the sampler in thread.

TOP LEFT 11-19 Opaque fill on a digitally printed sampler originally done with sgraffito, stamping, and found tools. Stitches: stem, straight, cross, satin, running, back, French knots. Valdani 35 wt. cotton thread on silk noil. Scale: 4" × 4".

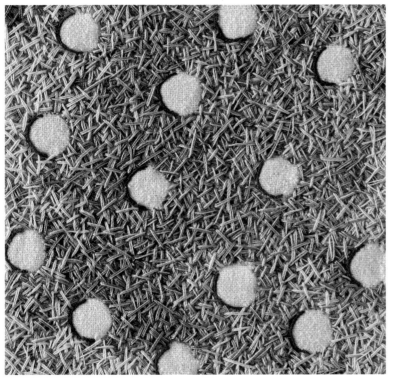

ABOVE 11-20 Opaque fill on a digitally printed sampler originally done with sponging, mechanical block-outs, and stamping. The circles are areas left unstitched. Stitches: straight, cross, laced back. Valdani 35 wt. cotton thread on white silk noil. Scale: 4" × 4".

DIGITAL PRINT? OR HAND PRINT ALONE?

Scanning an image which has already been created by dyes or pigments hand-applied to fabric is a convenient way of saving the image digitally for possible future reuse. Of course, it also then allows the image to be machine-printed digitally on cloth, whether once or many times. But if you don't have access to this technology, or prefer to work only by hand, you can directly apply colors and marks to your cloth using textile paints or thinned textile pigments. In either case, *before* stitching your lines and fills directly over your hand printing or painting, allow the liquid marks to air-cure for at least a day, and then heat-set them using a press cloth and dry, hot iron, or in a clothes dryer set to maximum heat.

ABOVE LEFT 11-21 Opaque fill on a digitally printed sampler originally done with sgraffito, sponging, stamping, fork marks. All printed marks and shapes covered in stitch but portions of background fabric left exposed. Stitches: laced back, cross, straight, seeding, French knots. Valdani 35 wt. cotton thread on silk noil. Scale: 4" × 4".

ABOVE RIGHT 11-22 Stitches: straight, zigzag. Cotton thread on cotton. Scale: 8.75" × 5.25".

Opaque Fills: Thread Painting

Opaque fills can also be created with free-motion machine stitching using a technique called *thread painting*.

Basic thread painting involves moving stretched fabric back and forth under the needle, again and again, allowing the stitches to pile up, crowd together, and cover a shape or area of the design. This is most easily accomplished by dropping the machine's feed dogs so that you have free control of the fabric. This technique is well-suited for mixing thread colors and building up complex, even photo-realistic, images on cloth. (For in-depth information on this technique,

see Carol Shinn: *Freestyle Machine Embroidery* in the Bibliography.)

Thread painting creates a directional effect when straight stitch is used, and a more energetic, but less directional effect when zigzag stitch is used. Begin with an ink or pencil sketch, a quick acrylic painting, or an image printed directly on the fabric, to serve as an "under-painting" of areas to be covered with stitches. Alternatively, you can stitch spontaneously, as you would draw with pastels on paper. Thread painting allows great flexibility in color mixing and optical blending to build precise color nuances and diverse textures, but also stiffens the fabric considerably. (See "Try this!" project 11.3.)

The thread painting sampler in 11-22 followed a guide image made from direct-application techniques (stamping, painting, sponging, sgraffito) which were then photographically scanned and digitally printed.

Add deeper texture to thread painting by using the *tacking stitch* on your sewing machine. The texture is unusual and dimensional—sometimes slightly humorous if the stitch rows turn out looking like little "worms" or corkscrews, or a child's Slinky® toy—but can be very effective or dramatic in the right context, especially when stitched on a large-scale piece.

FREE-MOTION MACHINE TACKING

If your machine has a tacking stitch function, you can exploit it for highly textural stitching. Set the machine's stitch length very short (as you might for satin stitch). Choose the tacking stitch setting. Stitch along a line, creating a long tunnel of tacking stitches one after the other. When you have enough stitches, reverse direction, change the machine setting to straight stitch, and stitch along one side of the line of tacks (which would otherwise pull out easily) in order to anchor them.

11-23 Free-motion machine tacking stitch (manipulated). Cotton thread on hand printed cotton.

Try this!

11.1 / Creating shapes with voids

Create a composition in which stitches are used to create one or more voids (shapes composed of unstitched cloth). (See examples in 11-15 and 11-20.) Use any stitch type. Choose densities of placement to define the void(s).

11.2 / Play with opacity and transparency of shapes

Create a composition in which stitches are used only to outline some of the shapes but to define and fill others. For example: experiment with making the same shape appear transparent, three-dimensional, or opaque, according to the way you outline or fill (or don't fill) it.

11.3 / Thread painting with free-motion machine stitching

Start this project with a photograph you have taken or found in a magazine of a subject you find appealing to interpret. Choose images with complex color palettes, or in which color has been blended and built up on the surface. Consider photos of landscapes, textured nature scenes, travel destinations, food, plants, close-up images of animals (fur, feathers, scales), or the paintings of the Impressionists or Abstract Expressionists.

(Note: Commercial use of all, or major portions of, *someone else's* photography or artwork may raise copyright considerations, and even a less extensive use of someone else's imagery requires, at the least, acknowledgment of its source. Therefore, select *a small section of the photograph* to interpret in thread painting.)

As a stitching guide, sketch an image on the center of a small piece of heavier weight, stable cloth (about 8" square)—or use an image transfer—or digitally print the image on the fabric. Use machine embroidery thread and free-motion machine stitching to "thread paint" the image, building color through layering threads for maximum detail, texture, and color nuance, completely covering your guiding sketch *and* the ground fabric. Follow-up: Try inserting tiny bits of fabrics in collage fashion as you stitch to help build the surface and add extra color in the background where necessary. Or allow the technique to distort the fabric three-dimensionally into a low relief surface or a completely three-dimensional form. Develop your own approach and gestures.

11.4 / "Rhythmic" opaque stitching

Refresh your memory by reading Chapter 10's "Try this!" exercise 10.3, which involved using "rhythmic" stitching to selectively "populate" (but not completely hide) a 6" square of fabric and create a "transparent" stitched fill.

This time you'll be going for an opaque fill, completely covering the marked area of a background cloth so that *none* of the cloth remains visible.

To support the density of the stitching, choose a stable fabric such as a cotton twill or tightly woven linen. Stretch the fabric in a hoop or frame with the rectangle in the center—within easy reach, but not obscured by the hoop. Because your goal is to find a comfortable, steady, but quick internal "stitch rhythm" without the distraction of stitch variety, you'll be placing stitches of a *single* type across the entire marked square. Therefore, choose straight *or* cross but *not* both.

To keep your goal manageable (remember: this is a *timed* exercise!), mark a smaller square on the cloth, such as 3". Prepare 6 to 10 needles, again with about 18" of thread per needle, but (unlike 10.3, which used only black) this time you can choose up to three colors.

Set a timer for 30 minutes—or if you feel brave, or are trying this project for the second or third time, 20 minutes. Start the timer—and start stitching! But this is not a race. Stitch steadily and repeatedly, *finding an internal rhythm and making each stitch on the beat of that rhythm.* Don't "overthink" this. Don't stop to make "compositional" decisions. Don't worry if the stitches vary somewhat in size, placement, or craftsmanship. Try to ignore the busy "meddling" part of your mind that wants to analyze and comment (*Well, now, that one didn't look very good, did it?*). Just find a comfortable pace and *keep stitching.* If you run out of thread, leave a tail on the back, pick up another threaded needle and *keep stitching.* If you run out of one of your three thread colors, change colors and *keep stitching* until the timer sounds or you've completely filled the square.

Although the colors and stitches varied, I myself used this kind of "rhythmic" stitching to make illustrations 09-37, 09-38, 11-07, and 11-20.

You can control many *degrees* of transparency and opacity through the range of densities in your stitching. Shading—the technique of grading from opaque to transparent by revealing increasingly larger bits of cloth between marks—can suggest the visual illusion of *three*-dimensional space or volume on a *two*-dimensional surface.

We will borrow several indispensable tools from the world of drawing on paper and adapt them for stitched drawing: *hatching* (a sequence of parallel lines), *cross hatching* (intersecting sets of lines which form a grid), and *stippling* (masses or clusters of tiny dots or marks). These techniques depend on *gradation* to create shading, which translates easily from drawing to stitching.

Gradations can vary in their *type* of change as they spread across the surface (changes of stitch, thread type, density, or scale); the *speed* with which they change (the number of steps, slow or fast, used to make those changes of stitch, thread type, or scale); and the *direction* of change (up, down, across, parallel, concentric, zigzag, or other). Each of these variables, whether used alone or in combination, contributes to the overall effect.

ABOVE 12-01 Interpretation of architectural detail from Giorgio Morandi sketchbook drawing. Hand-stitched cross hatching in straight stitch. Cotton floss on cotton. Scale: 2" × 2".

12-02 Interpretation of Edgar Degas sketchbook drawing detail. Hand-stitched hatching in straight stitch and couching. Other stitches: seeding, French knots. Cotton floss on cotton. Scale: 2" × 2".

Shading with Hatching

Hatching, the use of repeated parallel lines to shade and define, uniquely allows *directional placement* of lines to lead the eye over and along the surfaces of shapes—defining edges, indicating directions and amounts of curvature, and separating objects from each other. The closer the lines, the darker the shading.

Hatching techniques are by no means foreign to the textile arts. For centuries, both tapestry weavers and embroiders have used the technique—weavers through placement of alternating shots (weft rows) and embroiderers through alternating long and short stitches—to blend colors in ways that create new "composite" colors or imply three-dimensionality.

In color, and at a very delicate scale, repeated hatch marks coalesce into color fields and behave like color washes. In the following sequence of steps from photograph to digital print to finished embroidery (12-03, 12-04, and 12-05), you can see how hatching transforms the look and style of the stitched drawing.

TOP 12-03 Photograph of Nandina shrub foliage. *Photo credit: Susan Brandeis.*

ABOVE 12-04 Hand-stitched interpretation of 12-03, in progress. Note the pale version of the photograph first digitally printed on the silk noil fabric to guide the hatching.

12-05 Hand-stitched interpretation of 12-03, completed work. Leaves: color hatching in straight stitch. Stems: back and stem stitches. Cotton sewing threads and machine embroidery threads on digitally printed silk noil. Scale: 4" × 4".

Shading with Cross Hatching

In traditional drawing on paper, artists use cross hatching—often in black pen and ink, pencil, or marker—to shade areas and change values. In the viewer's eye, gradations of line weights and spacing produce the effect of differing shades from black to very light gray, which heighten the volume and physical presence of shapes.

Cross hatching uses *crossed* lines (or grids) for shading. Although the lines may intersect at varying angles, cross hatching is visually stable (rather than directional) in effect. The size, scale, character, density, proximity, irregularity, and angles of line intersections all contribute to the amount of shading or sense of dimension created.

When the lines of cross hatching are stitched in contrasting hues, they also create the illusion of new composite colors through optical blending and chromatically tinted shadows around objects in the composition. (See overleaf.)

12-07 Hand-stitched interpretation of 12-06.
Cross hatching in *fine* cotton threads on cotton fabric.
Stitch: straight. Scale: 1" × 2.5".

12-08 Hand-stitched interpretation of 12-06.
Cross hatching in *heavy* cotton threads on cotton fabric.
Stitches: straight, couching. Scale: 2.5" × 4.5".

12-06 Digital drawing of cross hatching, various sizes, with Corel *Painter*™ pencil tool.

12-10B Hand-stitched interpretation of 12-09b. Value contrast. Stitch: straight, couching. Cotton threads on cotton fabric.

12-09 Digital drawing of cross hatching, various color combinations and sizes, with Corel *Painter*™ pencil tool.

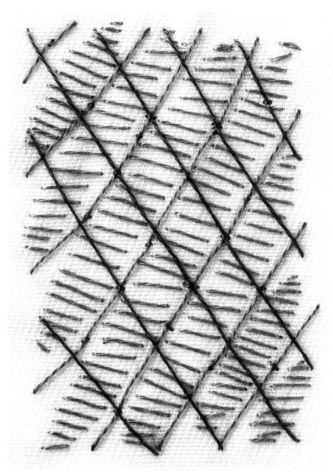

12-10A Hand-stitched interpretation of 12-09a. Single color. Stitch: straight. Cotton threads on cotton fabric.

12-10C Hand-stitched interpretation of 12-09c. Subtle hue contrasts. Stitch: straight, couching. Cotton threads on cotton fabric.

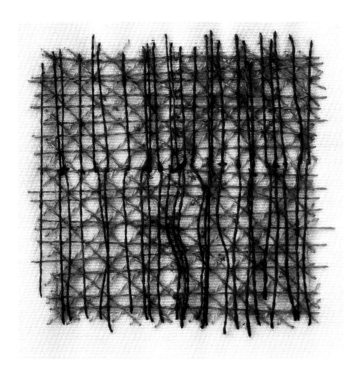

12-10D Hand-stitched interpretation of 12-09d. Value and temperature contrasts. Stitch: straight, couching. Cotton threads on cotton fabric.

12-10E Hand-stitched interpretation of 12-09e. Value and intensity contrasts. Stitch: straight. Cotton threads on cotton fabric.

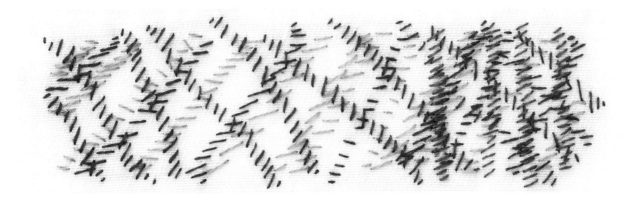

12-10F Hand-stitched interpretation of 12-09f. Complementary contrast. Stitch: straight, whip. Cotton threads on cotton fabric.

Applying a combination of hatching and cross hatching fills to a printed image enhances three-dimensionality while adding shading, texture, and shape definition. In 12-11, straight stitching defines the edges of the building and the sidewalk bricks. Cross hatching in a variety of colors shades the walls, steps, and street. Cross hatching in black creates shadows, which increase the sense of perspective.

12-11 Hatching and cross hatching as fills on hand-stitched image of a European building and sidewalk. Stitches: straight, cross, fly. Cotton threads on digitally printed silk noil. Scale: 8" × 10.5".

Shading with Stippling

Stippling is the use of masses or clusters of tiny dots or marks, in any medium, to shade, define, emphasize, or fill in backgrounds, surfaces, or shapes. In this classic drawing and rendering technique, pens, pencils, or chalks are used to make punctuated or staccato touches on paper surfaces, brushes are used to apply dabs on painted surfaces, or a stylus is used to tap dots or marks on a graphics tablet. Each change of tool, or change of angle or pressure, also changes the scale, style, and character of the individual dots or marks.

Gradations in stippling, achieved through changes in dot or mark size, density, value, color, or line weight, tend to *move* the eye through a composition or to create the illusion of volume or space. As a shading tool, stippling has the advantage of producing *very fine-grained gradations*, thus increasing your ability to achieve delicacy and nuance.

Stippled dots or marks can be placed on a surface with mathematical precision, thoughtful scattering, or carefree randomness. In whatever way it is composed, stippling provides a useful tool for moving the eye and creating the illusion of space or volume.

12-13 Stippling with black marker on paper.

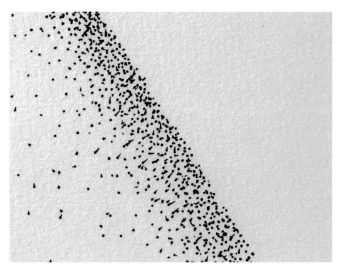

12-14 Stippling with black marker on paper.

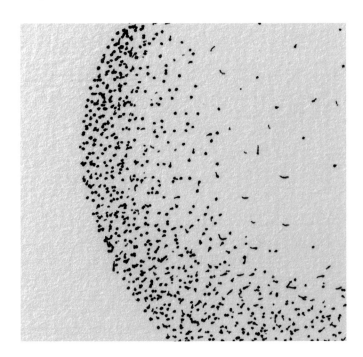

12-12 Stippling with black marker on paper.

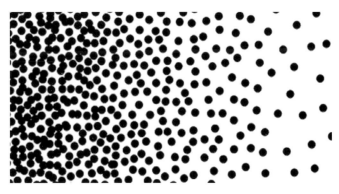

12-15 Stippling with Adobe *Photoshop*™ brush tool.

Like hatching and cross hatching, stippling is easy to translate into stitching. As little as a single stitch can visually read as a round "dot" or—if even slightly elongated—as a tiny linear "dash." Almost any small stitch can be employed for stippling. The exact type of stitch—straight, seed, French knot, cross, detached chain, or fly—matters less than its *small size*. But whether in individual stitches or tiny clusters, whether scattered across a surface or gathered in tiny masses, each *type* of stitch will still contribute its own contour characteristics to the textural feel of the shading.

With pencil or pen, with graphics tablet, or with needle and thread (!), stippling is a pleasantly slow and meditative technique of repeated and controlled hand motions.

Stippling: Density

A classic use of stippling shades objects to give them the illusion of *volume*. In a simple example (12-16), stippling grades from the outside edge of a curve, creating the sensation that we are looking at the surface of a ball or sphere. (If you are unsure about how to place shaded areas on a drawn object, such as a ball, aim a strong light on a ball and then take a black-and-white photograph of it. The photograph quickly reveals areas of highlight and shadow on the ball's surface.)

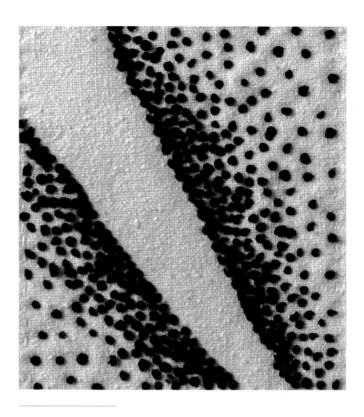

12-17 Stippling with French knots in changing densities. Constants: color, thread/line weight, hand stitch type. Variables: density. Cotton floss (2 strands, in 2 to 3 wraps around the needle) on silk noil. Scale: 2.5" × 3".

In stippling, a visual gradation is created when the dots are placed progressively closer together so that dense concentrations (darker areas) gradually disperse into sparse concentrations (lighter areas) in other locations.

In 12-17, even though black is the only thread color used, the gradation of density along and away from the two diagonal lines frames the unstitched center and generates the illusion of deeply receding distance (perspective) or the changing depth of a white "crevice."

A *single* color of thread will appear to *grade* the color of the fabric if the stippling density decreases or increases. In 12-18, stitches concentrate densely in the center, creating a darker vertical band, then disperse as they move outward, thus lightening the color as the background fabric assumes greater prominence. The stippling effectively changes our perception of the color of the cloth.

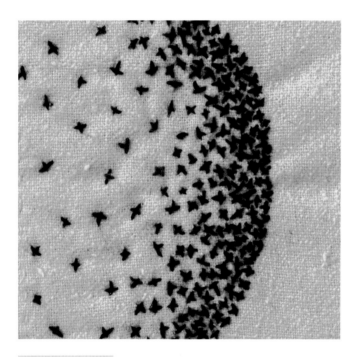

12-16 Shading with stippling. The change of density creates the illusion of volume. Constants: color, thread and line weight, hand stitch type. Variables: orientation, density, stitch size (slight differences), density. Cotton floss (2 strands) on silk noil. Scale: 2.5" × 3".

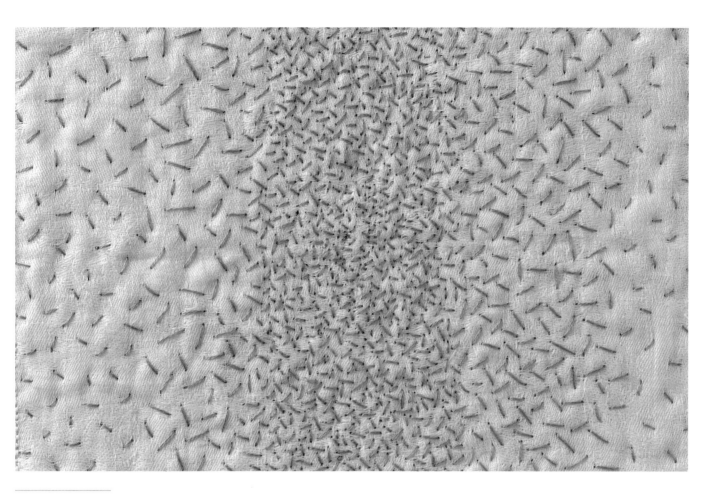

12-18 Gradation of seeding. Isolated stitches at the sides blend more with the fabric and appear lighter. Constants: color, material, and stitch type. Variations: density, stitch size. Cotton floss on heirloom linen. Scale: 7" × 8".

A dense concentration of small straight stitches at a central point focuses our attention on that spot. In illustrations 12-19, 12-20, and 12-21, the layout of marks begins at a clearly defined center, but differing effects are created by choices of density and materials.

Black thread on a white cloth (12-19) mimics the traditional appearance of black ink on white paper. White thread on black cloth would be equally effective. Either combination maximizes *value contrast* between the fabric and thread colors, clearly revealing the locations of the individual stitches. The impression is that of a concentrated center from which less dense particles are "escaping."

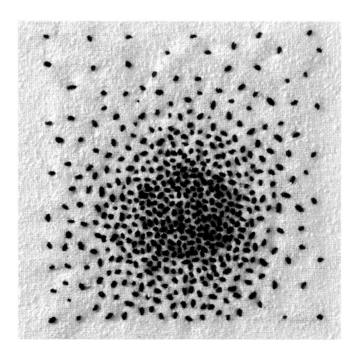

RIGHT 12-19 Seeding in black and white. Constants: color, material, stitch size, hand stitch type. Variable: density. Cotton floss (6 strands) on silk noil. Scale: 3.5" × 3.5".

In 12-20, the same stippling layout, stitched with bugle beads (tiny glass cylinders), scatters regular and evenly-sized marks across the surface and carries a lot of visual "punch." The combination of hard and soft materials (glass and fabric) adds contrast to accentuate the added dimension and central focus. The central spot is now raised off the surface, and the changing orientation of the surrounding beads gives the impression that they are "in orbit" around the center.

In 12-21, cut pieces of *gold purl* (a "thread" essentially made of a gold wire wound very tightly like a tiny spring) were used to stipple. The gold reflects light, especially where the bits are closely packed, and clearly conveys the precious metal from which they are made. The central spot now glows.

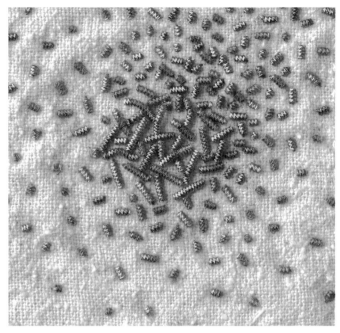

12-21 Chipping. Preciousness is conveyed by the gold metal material. Constants: materials, color, hand stitch type (seed). Variables: orientation, direction, density Gold purl and cotton thread on silk noil. Scale: 2.5" × 3".

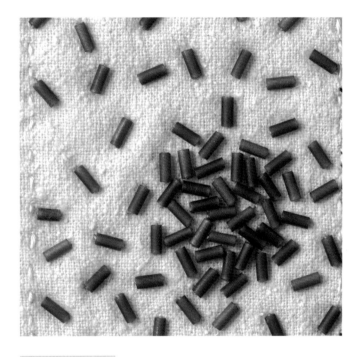

12-20 Stippling with bugle beads. Gradation of spacing outward from a central cluster. Constants: materials, color, stitch type (seed). Variables: orientation, density. Glass beads and cotton thread on silk noil. Scale: 2.5" × 3".

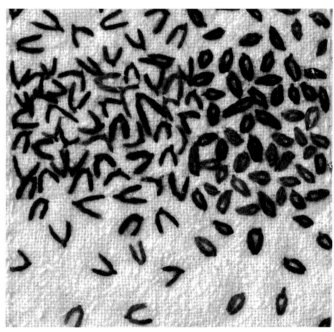

12-22 Stippling with combined fly and detached chain stitches. Constants: color, stitch types. Variables: number of strands, direction, density. Cotton floss on silk noil. Scale: 2.5" × 3".

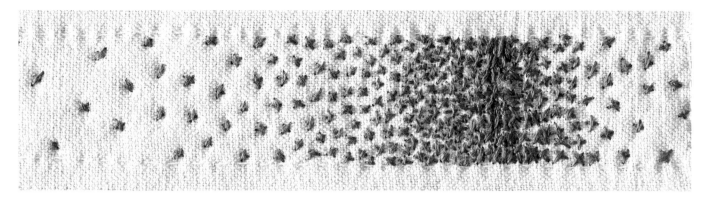

12-23 Gradation of density changes in cross stitch. Constants: thread color, line/thread weight (3 strands cotton floss), stitch (cross stitch), and materials. Variables: density. Hand stitching: cross. Cotton thread on linen. Scale: 1.5" × 6.5".

Areas or bands of very dense stippling will make the fabric seem to curve or bend.

In 12-22, the area of heaviest concentration gives the impression that the fabric *flexes* in the middle. The combined characters of fly and detached chain stitches add visual movement and weight to their angles and relationships.

When the spacing between cross stitches grades from sparse to *very dense* and back again to sparse, as in 12-23, the expansive nature of crossed stitches causes them to overlap and merge at the place of their densest concentration, and the illusion of flex in the fabric itself is even further increased along the line of greatest density.

CHIPPING WITH GOLD PURL

Among the several types of precious metals thread stitching known generally as goldwork, *chipping* is the name given to seeding with gold purl. In traditional goldwork, the purl, which is hollow, is cut into small pieces of identical length and then sewn down, threaded like beads. *Untraditionally*, the purl bits in 12-21 have been cut into varying *lengths* to explore some dynamic possibilities.

Stippling: Value

Using multiple *values* of thread expands shading possibilities further. A very delicate gradation, fading into background color, can be achieved by changing the color of the thread gradually. In 12-24 (overleaf), the lighter dots and dashes on the left are more difficult to distinguish from the background because of their low value contrast with the fabric color, and therefore contribute to the gradation gathering toward the right, where bold marks in darker values clearly contrast with the fabric. Careful planning of changes in thread colors, stitch choices, and stitch orientations can maintain the liveliness of a composition even when the value changes are gradual.

In 12-25 (overleaf), a similar value gradation in a range of blues shades the cloth from light to dark, but threads of similar value are clustered in almost column-like groupings and, despite some blending across the edges of the three groupings, the transition from one value to another is bolder and more obvious. The density and color create an illusion of three-dimensional space deeper than the more grayscale example in 12-24. Different stitch types are *evenly* dispersed and maintain a sense of visual vibration across the surface.

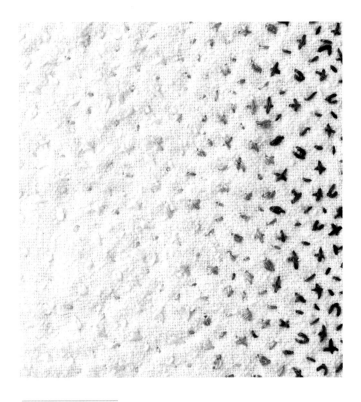

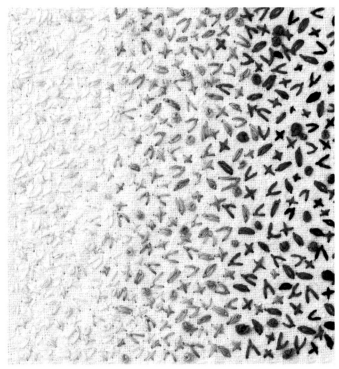

12-24 Value gradation with combined stitches. Constants: thread and line weight (2 strands floss), density, stitch sizes. Variables: color (whites, grays, and black), stitch types scattered and intermingled. Hand stitching: straight, cross, fly, detached chain. Cotton floss on silk noil. Scale: 3" × 3".

12-25 Gradational seeding with changing thread colors. Constants: density. Variables: color, orientation, stitch type. Hand stitching: fly, detached chain, cross, French knot. Cotton floss (2 strands) on silk noil. Scale: 3" × 3".

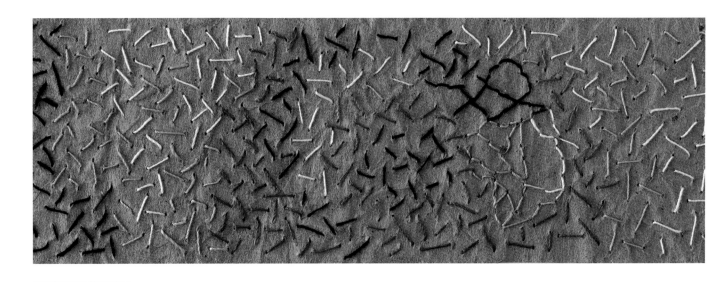

12-26 Stippling with seed stitch in black, gray, and white cotton floss on crumpled brown wrapping paper. (Too many needle holes in paper can make it fall apart. Don't over-perforate!) Constants: density, materials, stitch type. Variables: color, stitch sizes.

For a very different effect, try using a range of black, white, and gray threads on a medium-value ground. As a reminder that the ground need not always be cloth, 12-26 uses brown paper. The value gradation moves swiftly (speed), hopping from white to black in only four value steps. On this tan ground, the medium grays tend to sink into the ground (low contrast with background) while the whites and blacks *both* advance visually (higher contrast). Choosing the color of the ground fabric together with the colors of the threads is important in achieving the desired value gradation effects.

Stippling: Line Weight

More subtle gradations result from changing line weights. Seed stitching may be worked with single, double, or triple sets of parallel straight stitches or varying line weights using single or multiple strands of thread in the needle.

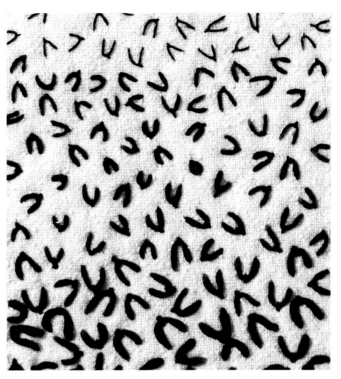

12-28 Line weight gradation in fly stitches. Constants: color, density, stitch size, stitch type. Variable: line weight. Cotton floss (2 to 6 strands) on silk noil. Scale: 2.5" × 3".

12-27 Single, double, and triple seeding in differing line weights. Constants: material, hand stitch type. Variables: density, thread color (variegated). Valdani 35 wt. cotton thread on silk noil. Scale: 2.5" × 3".

More strands of floss in the needle will *increase* line weight (heavier) and the visual presence of a stitch. In 12-28, the number of strands increases slowly and incrementally from the top to the bottom, which creates a gentle and subtle gradation. Fly stitches have a pleasant visual motion and dynamic quality caused by two diagonal lines held at an acute angle, and add a fluttery, active quality to stippling. The stitches with the heaviest line weight seem closest to us in space, and seem to "tip" the surface plane.

Mixing and intermingling a variety of different small stitches creates more visually complex gradation whose effects can be further enhanced by contrasting thread weights and stitch sizes. In 12-29 (overleaf), several stitches combine for an active, dance-like quality. Changes of size and weight create the impression of "flow" toward the right.

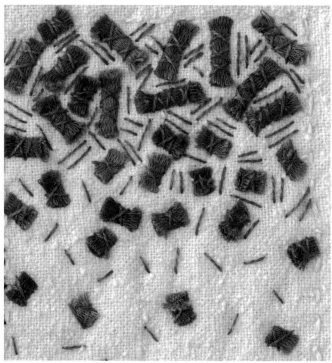

12-29 Stippling with French knots, detached chain, fly, cross stitches. Constant: color. Variables: thread and line weights, stitch sizes, types, orientations, density. Cotton sewing thread and floss (2–6 strands) on silk noil. Scale: 3" × 3".

12-30 Stippling in marks of contrasting sizes. Constant: color. Variables: scale, orientation, and density of marks; hand stitch types (couching, straight, cross, seed). Cotton floss and cotton braided tape (both naturally dyed with cutch) on silk noil. Scale: 2.5" × 3".

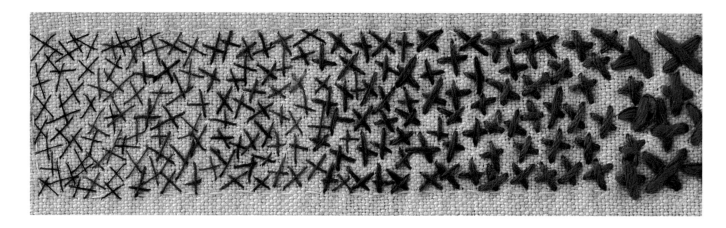

In 12-30, stippling marks of differing sizes establish a hierarchy and abrupt gradation that renders the larger marks visually more important. The smaller stitches worked in the open spaces counterbalance the larger marks, providing a vibrant contrast of scale and a visual blending of the single color.

In 12-31, a *single color* of increasingly thicker threads stitched in succession creates shading that also adds increasing physical dimension.

12-31 Gradation with line weight and material changes. Constants: color (hue, value, intensity), density, stitch (interlocking cross stitches). Variables: materials, fiber content, thread weight, stitch size. Hand stitching. Cotton, wool, and rayon on linen. Scale: 1.5" × 6".

Stippling: Color

Stippling offers a sophisticated tool for grading or shading with colors in a shape or on a surface. The composition in 12-32 grades color *temperature* from warm to cool with dots worked in tiny cross stitches. The effect requires extra time, planning, and attention during stitching to mix the complementary colors smoothly where their paths cross in the gradation. Where the two colors overlap and optically blend, a rich, calm, and interesting composite color materializes.

BELOW 12-32 Gradation from warm to cool. Hand stitching: cross. Cotton floss (2 strands) on silk noil. Colors: 6 warm hues and 7 cool hues in even values and intensities. Scale: 3" × 3".

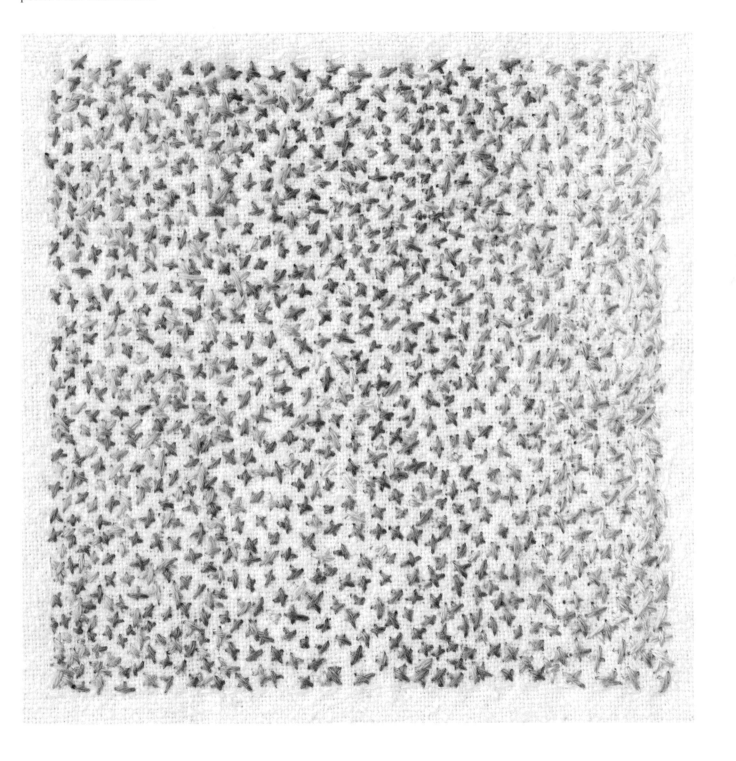

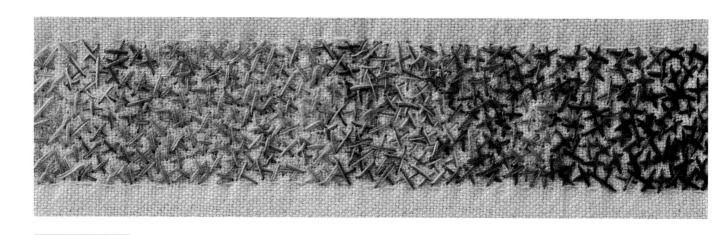

12-33 Complex color combinations using pairs of variegated threads. The gradation flows smoothly, while individual stitches have contrasting personalities. Constants: thread type and weight, density, stitch type. Variables: color (hues, values, intensities all change in the thread variegations). Hand stitching: cross. Cotton threads on linen.

Variegated threads, used in combination, offer exciting ways to create complex color gradations. Try using two different colors of variegated thread together in the needle (as in 12-33). The colors will optically blend as you stitch and create automatic color changes. You can make these changes even more complex by *changing out one of the threads* periodically. The thread changes can be random, sequenced, or more intricately orchestrated. Because all variegated threads change differently, some of them will surprise you even when you have planned the combinations.

SHAPING HALOS

Haloing requires working in a circular fashion around a central point or the contour of a shape. Stretching the fabric in a hoop that can be *rotated* during stitching facilitates the ease of stitch placement.

Stippling: Halos

A gradation of marks, from dense around a shape's outline to sparse at the edges, creates a "halo" effect that highlights the edge and can cause the shape to "glow."

In 12-34, the radiating color rings of tie-dyeing on the cloth establishes an underlying set of colors to which seeding responds. The stitched marks in the white ring create a dynamic halo through high intensity color contrasts.

Conversely, in 12-35 (see overleaf), haloing with low contrast seed stitch (seeding) is quiet and subtle, and the halo itself lies close to the surface while still adding slight texture. The dimensional contrast and visual flash are heightened by adding beads to the seeding stitches. When stitches and beads are used *in combination*, the stitches provide an intermediary step or "bridge" between the surface of the fabric and the dimension of the beads.

In 12-36, a halo incorporating transparent (rather than opaque) beads reflects light and makes the shape glisten.

A contrast of opaque, blended, and transparent shapes will energize and vary a composition. Choose which shapes you fill according to their relative importance in your composition. Ask yourself: What do I want to emphasize?

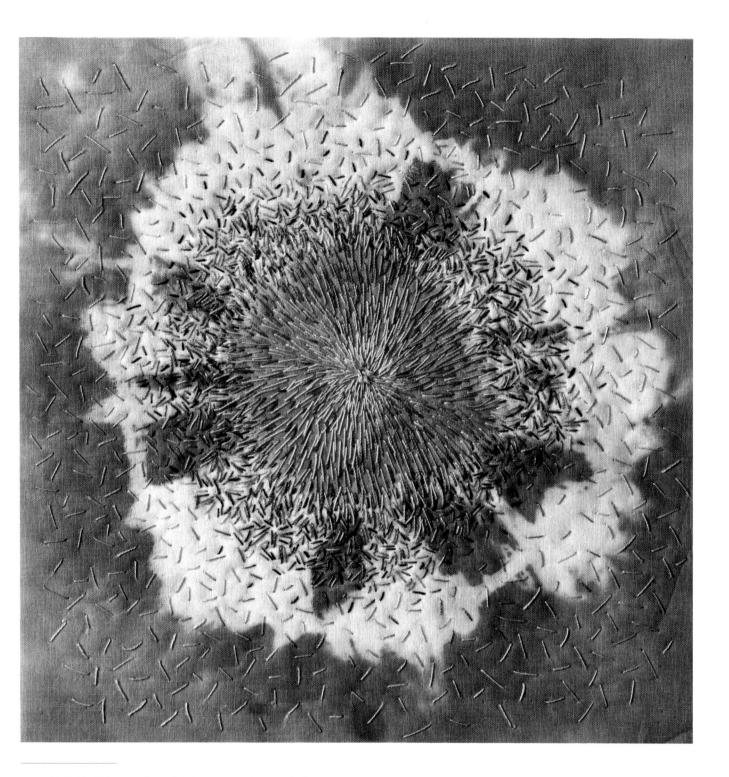

12-34 Straight stitches and seeding to create a dynamic halo.
Valdani 35 wt. cotton thread on tie-dyed cotton print cloth. Scale: 7" × 7".

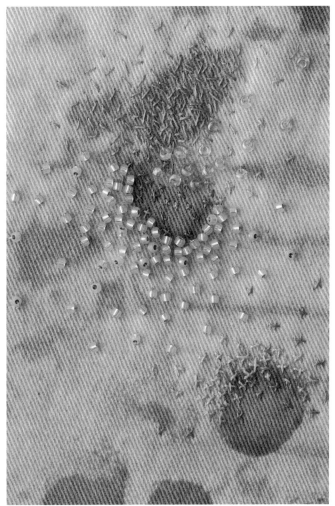

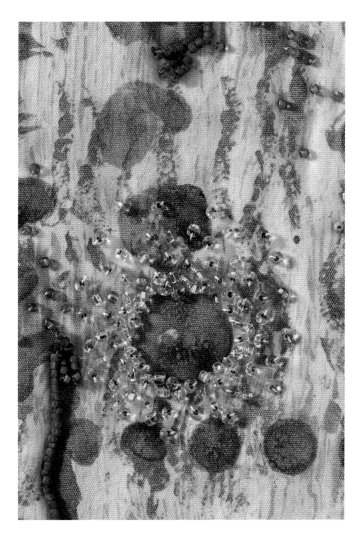

12-35 Haloing with a combination of stitched seeding and cross stitches (both low texture) and glass bead seeding (high texture and light reflection). Cotton floss (for seeding and cross stitches), quilting thread (to fasten glass beads) on hand screen-printed cotton twill.

12-36 Haloing with transparent glass bead seeding for a subtle glistening effect. Cotton thread on hand-stamped and hand-painted cotton.

Try this!

12.1 / Create the illusion of depth

With a pencil, draw a circle on your fabric. Use hatching, cross hatching, or stippling with any stitches. Shade the circle to appear like a three-dimensional ball. (If you are unsure about the areas that should be shaded, set a ball in a strong light on your work table and note where the areas of light and dark fall; or make a black-and-white photograph to reduce the image to gray scale.)

Alternative exercise: Do the same exercise with a cube or rectangular solid (like a box). Shade the sides to make it appear solid and three-dimensional.

12.2 / Direct application of pigments and stippling

This project requires you to get your hands dirty to prepare the fabric for later stitching. Directly apply pigment, fabric paint, or dye to the surface of the ground cloth by stamping, painting, sponging, mechanical resists, stencils, sgraffito, mono-printing, drawing, rubbings on relief surfaces, or drawing with found objects. Play with making marks, creating patterns or images, and combining colors.

Before stitching, allow the fabric to air-cure for at least a day, and then heat-set it using a press cloth and a dry, hot iron or in a clothes dryer set to maximum heat.

Shade and texture the printed fabric in response to the marks you made, enhancing, subduing, and completing the effects.

Follow up exercise: Shade the fabric in any way you like, in any color combinations. *Then* apply the pigments or fabric paint on top of the stippling (yes, *after* stitching) for more unexpected and exciting effects.

12.3 / Transform an ugly commercial fabric

Choose commercial fabrics with added patterns, images, or dyed effects (rather than solidly colored cloth). To give yourself a challenge, select prints that, in your view, are lackluster or downright ugly. Using any wash-fast threads, beads, sequins, or bangles you wish, stitch in response to the surface color and pattern already on the fabric and try to improve its looks or expressive potential. (You may think that an ugly fabric is irredeemable, but I've used this project in workshops and university classes across many years, and people come up with some very inventive—and fun—"cures.") Enhance or obscure details, change colors, or highlight desirable areas to transform this "ugly duckling" into a swan. Or at least a more attractive duck.

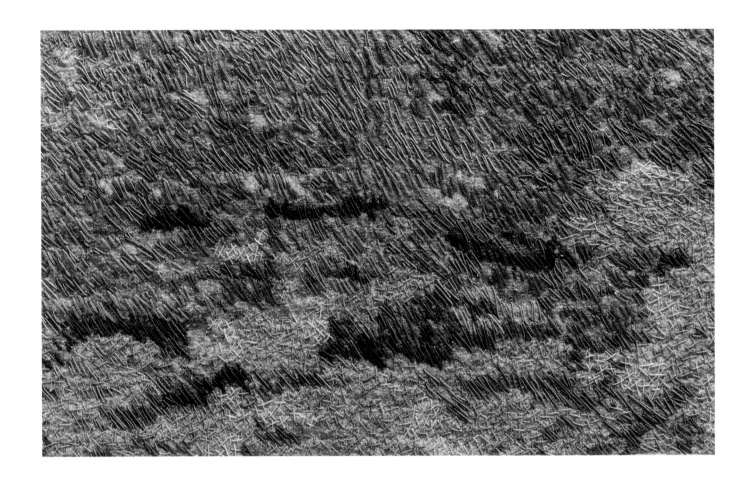

Stitching produces marks whose inherent three-dimensionality creates *actual* texture, further accentuated by the choice of materials used. In fact, the opaque, transparent, and shaded fills discussed in previous chapters all resulted in different kinds of surface texture.

Some individual stitches have their own textures—especially those that are "raised" such as knots, twists, or pile stitches. But the textured effects of flatter stitches can also be expanded with layering, lacing, padding, and the addition of other materials such as beads, bangles, and sequins. You can combine thread choices and stitch choices to build textures that intentionally emphasize or differentiate shapes, add visual interest or complexity, populate and fill larger background areas, or convey the experience of touching objects in the real world.

Whether thread or fabric, each different material you use contributes its own unique tactile characteristics. For instance, wool will usually look fuzzier and more matte, while rayon will usually look smoother and more reflective. Depending on its processing, cotton can assume many different textures, from smooth to rough. Combinations of different thread types will contrast either dramatically or subtly, with each other or with the background fabric. Sensitive use of materials can temper, enhance, transform, or exploit the specific textured effects of your stitches.

ABOVE 13-01 Textured fill over a larger surface area. Hand stitching: straight, cross. Cotton threads on digitally printed silk noil.

Viewers often respond to texture by coming closer to the work, or even reaching out to touch it. A delicious textile composition does almost "beg" to be touched, and the *feel* of cloth and thread in our own hands is one of the reasons so many of us choose to work in fiber.

In the following examples, I began with photographs of various natural forms taken in a variety of places, and then chose the stitches and materials to convey the predominant texture—the "feel."

In 13-02, the "organic" feel of lichen and shiny moss on small rocks, photographed at the Oregon coast near sunset, is interpreted in colors which, although not entirely "realistic," recall my memories of how I *felt* in that place at that time. Repeated raised small marks almost fill the entire surface area of the cloth, which was printed with the photographic image before stitching began.

13-03 Hand stitching: detached chain, fly, straight, back, seeding. Cotton floss on digitally printed linen. Detail from a larger composition in varying colors.

In 13-03, short stitches, with fat bundles of dull, matte threads, create a lumpy textured surface with an aged look— a textured semi-transparent fill—appropriate to a close-up view of rock wall textures photographed at abandoned ancient cliff dwellings in the American Southwest.

13-02 Hand stitching: fly, cross, detached chain, seeding, French knots. Cotton threads and floss on digitally printed silk noil. Scale: about 7.5" × 10".

When I was a child, our family vacationed regularly in coastal Florida, and I loved to look for live sand dollars and to feel their soft, fuzzy edges. The photograph in 13-04 (taken not in Florida, or in my childhood, but in a natural history museum) brings out those furry qualities, and the interpretation in 13-05 positions the viewer almost as if miniaturized and closely *among* them.

13-04 Fossilized sand dollars with "furry" edges still intact. *Photo credit: Susan Brandeis.*

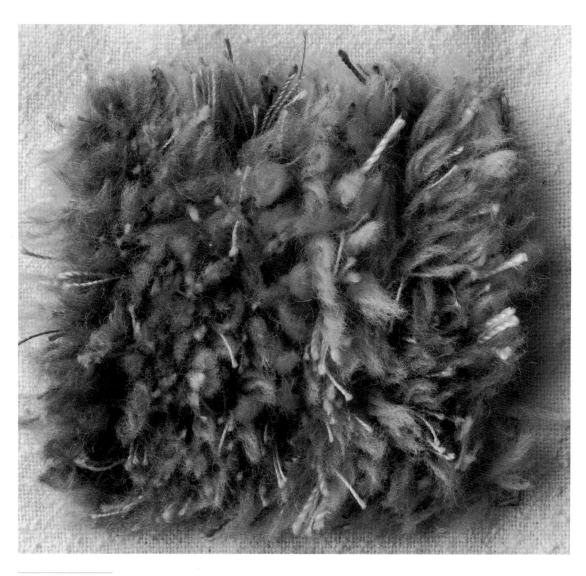

13-05 Hand-stitched interpretation of 13-04. Ghiordes knots ("Turkey work"). Wool tapestry yarn, cotton and silk thread on silk noil. Scale: 2" × 2".

To imitate 13-06's "gritty" textures of eroded rock and embedded bits of fossil, I combined a variety of fiber fills in 13-07. The French knots are not only used expressively to suggest the feel of the clumped forms in the photograph, but also used structurally to fasten down the netting I "bunched" by hand between them.

13-06 "Gritty" textures: dirt, sand, rock, and fossil bits.
Photo credit: Susan Brandeis.

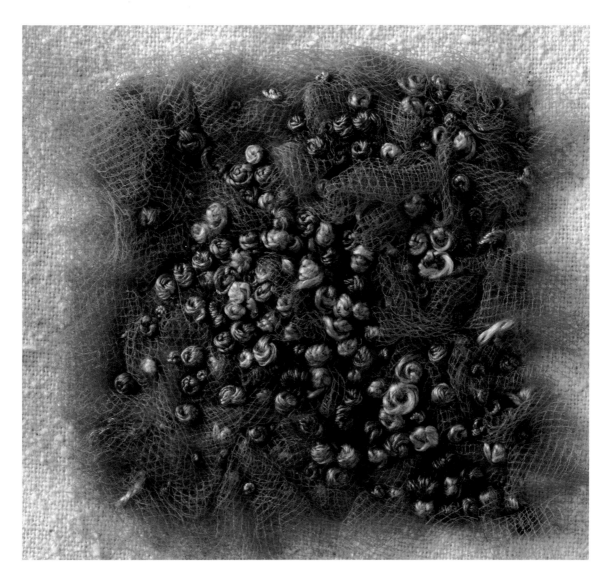

13-07 Hand-stitched interpretation of textures in 13-06.
French knots. Linen, cotton, silk, and synthetic threads on nylon
netting and silk noil. Scale: 2" × 2".

Another natural texture is captured in 13-08: a view, photographed during a seaside stroll, looking straight down at sand and hundreds of multicolored bits of shell. The stitched interpretation in 13-09 adopts an even closer point of view than the photograph. I used multiple *kinds* of stitching materials, all relatively rough in texture, to suggest the "gritty" feel of the sand and shells within my gaze (and beneath my bare feet). The fill is predominantly French knots, with seeding between them to add still-smaller dots of color.

13-08 Sand and tiny shell fragments.
Photo credit: Susan Brandeis.

13-09 Hand-stitched interpretation of 13-08. French knots, back, straight, seeding. Paper, wool, alpaca, cotton, linen, raffia on silk noil. Scale: 2" × 2".

Although the cactus thorns in 13-10, photographed in the American Southwest, look quite stiff and vicious from a distance, on this relatively young plant they were actually quite flexible when carefully touched. As with the sand dollar edges rendered in 13-05, the fiber interpretation in 13-11 adopts a miniaturized viewpoint from *within* the overlapping and crossing thorn structures.

13-10 Cactus thorns. *Photo credit: Susan Brandeis.*

13-11 Hand-stitched interpretation of 13-10. Straight, cross, Ghiordes knots ("Turkey work"). Cotton, rayon, and hand-twisted ramie threads on silk noil. Scale: 2" × 2".

Many areas of the coast of California are arid, like much of the state's interior, despite their proximity to the ocean. The softness of cloth and thread aren't naturally suited to making sharp edges, but I interpreted the deeply eroded seaside cliffs of 13-12 by using stiff threads in a gruff, cord-like way—without using actual cords—by making high-relief stitches around other stitches. (But I should have worked in just a few little orange and pale green stitches to give "credit" to the succulent plants stubbornly clinging to the smallest patches of soil in this otherwise inhospitable terrain.)

13-12 Jagged, eroded cliffsides. *Photo credit: Susan Brandeis.*

13-13 Hand-stitched interpretation of 13-12. Double-laced chain, laced stem, stem, blanket/buttonhole. Linen, hand-twisted ramie, handspun hemp on silk noil. Scale: 2" × 2".

On a long-ago trip to Italy, I was fascinated by all the textures and colors of roof tiles—terra-cottas within other shades of terra-cotta, all further changed over the years by weathering and bits of lichen. In 13-15, unlike 13-13, I *did* use actual cord as a base structure corresponding to the very defined and linear rows of the tiles. Then I used overcasting to completely wrap and hide the underlying cords. Finally, I used very short straight and back stitches in variegated threads to suggest the sprinkling of the tiles' lichen "companions."

13-14 Italian roof tiles.
Photo credit: Marc Brandeis.

13-15 Hand-stitched interpretation of 13-14. Overcasting, back, straight.
Heavy cotton cord (core), Valdani 35 wt. cotton on silk noil. Scale: 2" × 2".

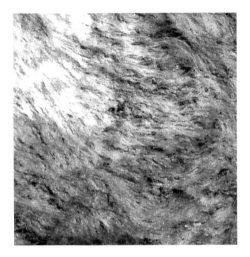

In 13-16, seaweed undulating in the back-and-forth currents of ocean tidal wash was photographed at the coast of Oregon. The fiber interpretation called for elongated stitches in frequently changing directions to suggest the swaying plants. Some stitch materials were chosen for their shiny ("wet") impression, while the exposed sides of twisted threads suggest the textures of the seaweed's very fine and soft blades.

13-16 Seaweed, sand, and water.
Photo credit: Susan Brandeis.

13-17 Hand-stitched interpretation of 13-16. Straight, stem. Rayon floss (loosely spun), rayon thread, cotton floss on silk noil. Scale: 2" × 2".

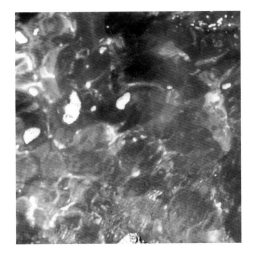

An ocean tide pool in Oregon (13-18), gently rippling and sun-sparkled water above coarse rock sediment, called for an even more literally "wet"-looking assortment of fills. I stitched all of the dark threads first. I used even shinier whites and pale grays and blues, optically blending to form shades of "silver," to stitch over the darks until the composition approached the balance of light and dark, reflection and absorption, water and rock, in the photographic inspiration.

13-18 Tide pool waters. *Photo credit: Susan Brandeis.*

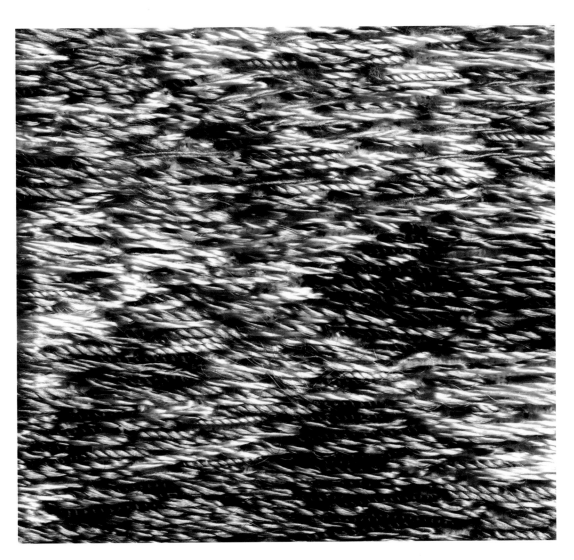

13-19 Hand-stitched interpretation of 13-18. Satin, straight, long and short. Shiny rayon thread and floss, nylon thread, silk floss on silk noil. Scale: 2" × 2".

Try this!

13.1 / Describe a part of your physical world

Take some photographs of indoor objects or details of outdoor places, or use some photos you already have. The photo should be a close-up view or a detail of a larger view, something small enough (or—as in the example of the seaside cliffs shown above—large enough) to suggest an overall "readable" *texture* that can be rendered in stitched fill.

Write down some words to verbally describe the photographed texture.

Now try to render a stitched impression of the image. To minimize the possibility of feeling overwhelmed, mark off a small area of your fabric ground, just two or three inches across. Don't worry about literally reproducing the details of the photograph, and don't worry about making stitches "correctly."

Your goal is to approximate the *feel* of that texture and the *words* you wrote down to describe it through your choices of fill materials (thread types) and fill structures (direction, sequence of stitching, arrangement of colors).

Feel free to distort, alter, compress, stretch, and manipulate the materials and stitches in whatever way you think will accomplish the goal. ("Incorrect" stitches can actually accomplish wonderful things *if* they contribute to the purpose of the composition!)

Try it again, and again (and again?) with other interpretations of the same image, or choose different images.

13.2 / Texture embellishment

Start with a printed or handwoven cloth (hand or commercially produced). Using a variety of repeated small stitched marks, add textures to the surface that enhance the marks, patterns, or images already on the cloth. Choose colors and materials for their characteristics and expressive effects.

13.3 / "Time Travel"
in stitched texture

If project 13.1 captured your interest, try this more open-ended follow-up exercise: Stitch a series of panels, all of the same size, which visually describe the *sequence* of textures you found while peeling an onion, or dissecting a flower, or cutting open a pomegranate, or breaking open the contents of a small *piñata*, or . . . use your imagination.

And I mean that you can *really* use your imagination when thinking about source imagery here. I myself first imagined this time sequence project while my husband and I were cleaning out the interestingly *textured* lint from beneath our refrigerator. As I watched the changing patterns made by the "dust bunnies" scattering across the floor on tiny air currents, an idea popped into my mind, and I told him: "Leave that stuff there for a minute. I need to photograph it. And *don't move.*"

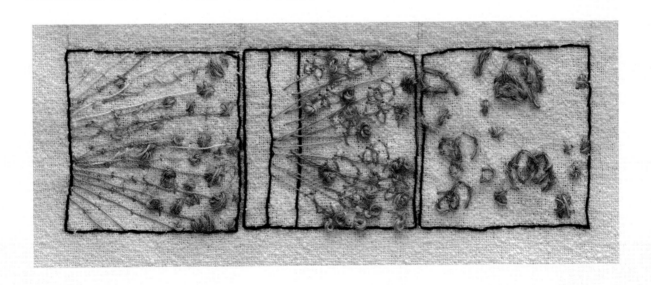

13-20 Hand-stitched interpretation, in differing perspectives, of refrigerator "dust bunnies" blowing across the kitchen floor. Straight, couching, back, cross, fly, loose French knots. Cotton and wool on silk noil. Scale: each square 2" × 2".

Getting Started: A Guide to Stitching

This is a convenient but basic guide to common stitches mentioned elsewhere in the book. For more complete guidance on stitchery techniques, see the Bibliography.

General Tips for Successful Stitching

- Use the best quality threads, fabrics, needles, and scissors that you can afford, even when you make samples. Good tools and materials make needlework a joy; the frustrations of using poor quality tools and materials can discourage you from stitching. Store and handle your tools with care.

- Use washfast and lightfast threads to preserve the longevity of your work.

- Choose a needle of approximately the same diameter as your thread. The needle's size should open a hole in the cloth that is large enough for the thread to traverse easily. If you find yourself tugging at the thread to pull it through the fabric, the needle may be too small. If the needle leaves holes in the fabric that are larger than the thread, the needle is too large.

- Cut and use pieces of thread about 18" to 20" long. Longer threads may twist, tangle, fray, knot, or break, making the stitching a chore rather than a pleasure. Shorter threads require re-threading the needle too frequently.

- Separate the strands of embroidery floss and use only the number of strands you need. To separate the strands without tangling them: Using your thumb and forefinger, pinch the strands together near one end and let them hang from your fingers. The upper ends of the threads should extend above the pinch. While you hold the strands firmly, at the top, select a single strand and pull it upward and out of the bundle. If you need more than one strand, pull each one out individually in this same way.

- Stitching is "eye intensive" work, so work in good light. I recommend using both overhead *and* focused lighting to eliminate interfering shadows. Ideally, the focused light (such as an angle arm lamp) should come from your *non-dominant* side so that your own hand won't cast a shadow across the work.

- To keep the fabric clean, stop frequently during stitch sessions to wash your hands.

- Hold the threaded needle in your dominant hand and hold the hoop with the stretched fabric in your other hand. Alternatively, clamp the hoop onto a floor stand or tabletop stand to free up both hands for stitching. Occasionally you may need to use the fingers of your non-dominant hand to manipulate the fabric (from either the top or the bottom) and to more easily draw the needle through the cloth.

- To begin stitching, do one of the following: 1) Make a quilter's knot in the end of the thread and push the needle up and through from the back of the fabric, or 2) On the face of the fabric, take two or three tiny running stitches toward the starting point, then a tiny back stitch, and hide these with your first intentional stitches.

- Set your stitches in the cloth with even amounts of tension on the thread. Pulling *too tightly* will pucker the fabric, deforming a design that is intended to be flat. Pulling *too loosely* leaves either loose threads or long floats, both of which look sloppy or unresolved. (You *can* pull too much or too little *intentionally* to create special three-dimensional or textural effects.)

- To add stability to any fabric before stitching, back the fabric with thin cotton batting. Or, to create a stable surface for *heavy* accumulations of stitching, try stacking two fabrics. The top fabric should be squared and oriented with the straight of the grain vertical and horizontal (as would be usual). Rotate the bottom fabric 45° to place its grain *on the bias*. Trim the excess fabric away from the bottom layer and baste the two layers together until your stitching is completed. Then remove the basting stitches. Both the batting and stacked fabric methods help to prevent the stitches from pulling holes in the fabric and to prevent the backs of the stitches from showing through to the front.

- To remove stitches but avoid slitting the fabric, run the *eye* end of the needle under the stitches and then cut them with small sharp-pointed scissors that are pressed tightly against the needle.

- Don't rush. Work slowly and savor the quiet.

Stitch Types

Back Stitch:

Connected stitches that create solid lines. Used for outlines, text, contour drawing.

Directions: Bring the thread to the front of the cloth, *near* the end of the proposed stitch line. Then take a small stitch back down exactly at the end of the line, and back up again, a bit *farther* along the line. For each successive stitch, insert the needle back down into the same hole where the last stitch emerged, and then up again a stitch-length ahead.

Back stitch, left-handed.

Back stitch.

Back stitch, right-handed.

Blanket Stitch:

(also called Buttonhole Stitch): A looped stitch used for edge binding or beaded edges. Distort to work in curves or angles.

Directions: Mark (or imagine) two parallel lines on the fabric. Bring the thread up from the back at the end of the top line. Stitch down on the bottom line a short distance to the side, and up again directly above that on the top line, keeping the thread looped under the needle tip so it will catch in place. Pull the thread to set the stitch tension. Repeat down the row

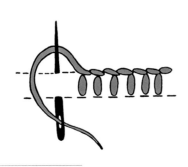

Blanket stitch, left-handed.

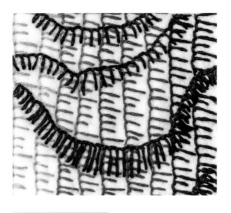

Blanket stitch.

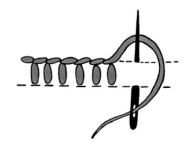

Blanket stitch, right-handed.

Chain Stitch:
Interlocking loops used for heavy outlines or dense filling.

Directions: Bring the thread up from the back of the fabric. Then holding a loop to the side with your thumb, insert the needle again *in the same hole*. Bring the needle up again a short distance away, *inside and catching the loop*. Interlock the stitches by consistently starting each stitch *inside* the last loop.

Chain stitch, left-handed.

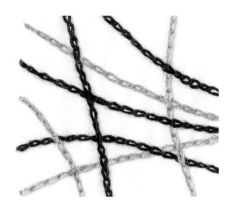

Chain stitch.

Chain stitch, right-handed.

Couching:
Attaching threads with a series of small stitches. Used for prominent outlines, borders, edges, text, and fills.

Directions: Couching uses two threads—a *laid* thread and a *tacking* thread—and a separate needle for each thread. Bring the *laid thread* (the one being couched down) up from the back at the starting point (or simply lay it on the fabric surface). As you move the laid thread along the desired line, use a second needle with the *tacking* thread to stitch over and across the laid thread at intervals. To finish, either pull both threads to the back and secure them; or stitch over the end of the laid thread to cover the raw end and integrate it into the work.

Couching, left-handed.

Couching.

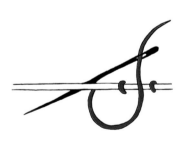

Couching, right-handed.

In *self-couching*, the laid thread and tacking thread are *one in the same*. The laid thread tacks itself down as you construct the line in shorter joined segments. Used for meandering lines, text, and decorative fill.

Directions: Bring the thread to the front at the beginning of a line, and then back down further along the line, leaving enough loose thread to follow the curves in this segment of the line. Next, bring the needle back up alongside the loose thread and take a series of tacking stitches over it to hold the curves in place. After this first segment is tacked down, come up in the same hole as the last segment ended and take another stitch farther along the line. Then again, return to tack it down. Proceed along the line in this way until the whole line is stitched and tacked into place.

Cross Stitch:

Two straight stitches overlapped at an angle. Used for textures, shading, transparent or opaque fills; also used in counted thread embroidery.

Directions: To make an *individual* cross stitch, bring the thread up from the back and make a straight stitch down, then come up again to the side and make a second straight stitch angled across the first one. To make a *row* of cross stitches, bring the thread up from the back and make a row of diagonal stitches using the whip stitch, and then work back in the other direction with whip stitch to cross each stitch in the first row (illustrated). Traditionally, cross stitch "arms" are the same length and the angle of crossing is perpendicular, but you can vary both (see photo).

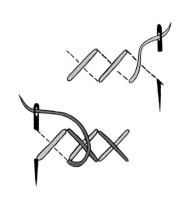

Cross stitch, left-handed.

Cross stitch.

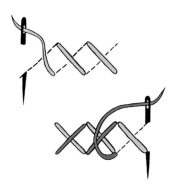

Cross stitch, right-handed.

Detached Chain Stitch:

A single loop that makes a teardrop shape. Used for textures, shading, loops, transparent and opaque fills.

Directions: Bring the thread up from the back of the cloth and form a loop. Re-insert the needle into the *same hole*, then back up again *inside the loop*. Catch the loop with the needle before you tighten the thread. Take a tacking stitch back down around the thread to secure the loop in place.

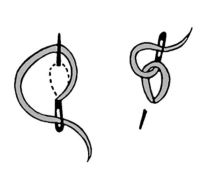

Detached chain, left-handed.

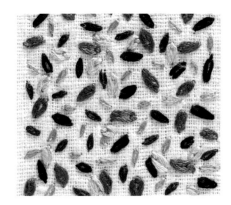

Detached chain.

Detached chain, right-handed.

Double Running Stitch: see Running Stitch.

Fly Stitch:
A stitch made with a caught loop that is shaped like the wings of a fly. Used for flickering textures, shading, transparent or opaque fills. Fly stitches can be joined (illustrated) or separated (in the photo).

Directions: Working with a triangle of three needle insertion points, bring the thread up from the back of the cloth at the first point. Take a stitch down at the second point and back up again at the third point (which should be about midway between the first and second points). Catch the loop under the needle and make a tacking stitch over the thread to anchor the angle in place.

Fly stitch, left-handed.

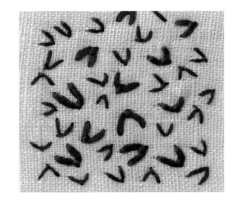

Fly stitch.

Fly stitch, right-handed.

French Knots:
Small (deliberate) knots that resemble dots or beads. Used for textures, fills, shading, and color blending.

Directions: Bring the thread up to the front of the fabric. With the needle pointing *away from* the fabric, wrap the thread around the needle two, three, or more times (depending on desired knot size). Pull the wrapped thread firmly against the needle near the point and hold that tension in place. Insert the needle back down very *close* to where it emerged (*but not in the same hole*). Continue to hold tension on the wrapped thread as you pull the needle through the wraps and the cloth to the back. Secure before moving to the next knot.

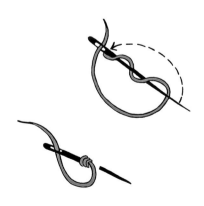

French knot, left-handed.

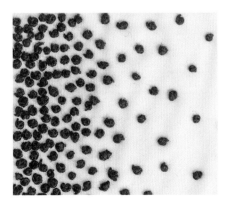

French knot.

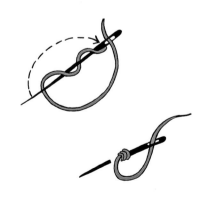

French knot, right-handed.

Ghiordes Knot: see Turkey Work

Lacing (of running, chain, or back stitches): A non-structural element threaded through a base stitch. Used to smooth or waver lines, to contrast or blend colors.

Directions: Make a line of running, back, chain (or other) stitch in the desired direction. Then, using a blunt needle and the lacing thread, work from the bottom toward the top (as illustrated) to lace your way back through each stitch *without going through the fabric*. To *smooth* the stitched line, lace repeatedly from the same side (in a kind of spiral). To make the line *waver*, alternate the lacing back and forth: first from one side, then from the other side.

Lacing, left-handed.

Lacing.

Lacing, right-handed.

Long and Short Stitch:
A variation on the satin stitch. Used for fills, shading, gradations, or color blending.

Directions: Make a row of closely-spaced satin stitches that *alternate in length*—one short, one long—repeating across. In all succeeding rows, make all satin stitches the *same length*, connecting them to the previous row by inserting the needle in the same holes. Each row will create a sort of dovetail that allows the two colors to alternate and blend. Rows can be straight (as illustrated) or curved.

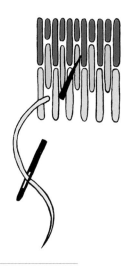

Long and short, left-handed.

Long and short stitch.

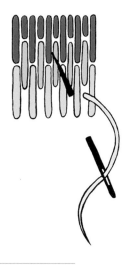

Long and short, right-handed.

Overcasting:

A variation on couching which is essentially a satin stitch over cording. Used for very heavy, stiff lines, borders, bold contours, and long dimensional lines.

Directions: Like couching, overcasting uses two threads (or groups of threads)—a *laid* cord (or large thread bundle) and a *tacking* thread. Bring the laid cord up from the back of the cloth at the beginning of the line (or lay it on the surface). Arrange it along the desired pathway, and stitch over it with the tacking thread with stitches so close that they touch each other and completely cover the laid cord. Pull the laid cord back down through the cloth at the end of the line. (See *couching* for more tips.)

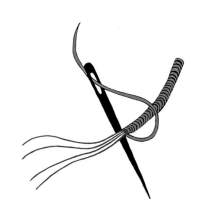

Overcasting, left-handed.

Overcasting.

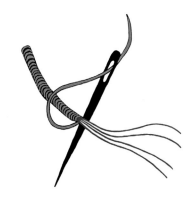

Overcasting, right-handed.

Quilter's Knot:

A simple knot made with a threaded needle.

Directions: To start, hold the needle in your dominant hand and the end of the thread in the other, *pointing* the thread end and the tip of the needle *toward each other*. Pinch the end of the thread underneath the needle with your thumb and press both (needle and thread) against the forefinger of your dominant hand. Hold the pinched thread in place, while you wrap the thread around the needle several times. Hold the wraps in place with the thumb and forefinger of your non-dominant hand and pull the needle through the wraps with your dominant hand. Pull the knot to the end of the thread. The knot should be small, neat and have no loops or kinks.

Running Stitch:

A simple universal stitch.
Used for basting, joining, broken lines, and transparent fills.

Directions: Bring the needle up from the back of the fabric. Then, with a rocking motion, repeatedly push the needle up and down through the fabric along a line. After taking two or three passes through the fabric, pull the thread through these stitches. Continue stitching along the line in this manner. To make very precise and evenly-spaced running stitches, use the *stab method* to make each individual stitch, one at a time.

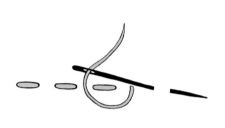

Running stitch, left-handed.

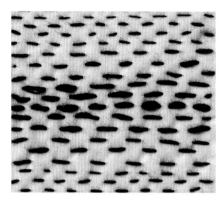

Running stitch.

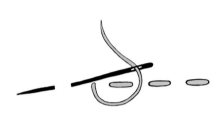

Running stitch, right-handed.

The *double running stitch* visually resembles the back stitch, although it lies flatter against the fabric. It is composed of *two passes* of running stitches (one pass in each direction along the *same* line). The second pass fills in the gaps left by the first pass, allowing open spaces to be filled with another color. (See AP2-02, bottom center segment.)

Satin Stitch:

Closely-worked parallel straight stitches that completely cover a shape. Used for opaque fills, shape definition, and color blending.

Directions: Determine the outline of a shape: draw it with a pencil or, for greater precision and contour stability, stitch it with a line of small back stitches. Bring the thread up from the back of the fabric at one edge of the shape, outside the outline, and down again directly across on the opposite side, inserting the needle to *enclose* the outline again. Take the next stitch directly beside, parallel to, and touching the first one. Repeat these parallel stitches until they completely fill the shape. (Use the *stab method* of stitching to increase the precision needle entry and exit points and achieve very accurate shape outlines.

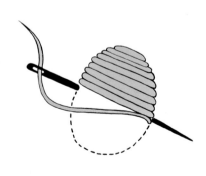

Satin stitch, left-handed.

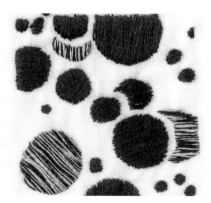

Satin stitch.

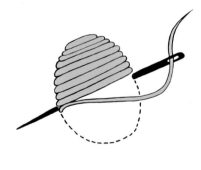

Satin stitch, right-handed.

Sewing Method of Stitching: Making stitches with a single "rocking" needle action up and down through the cloth. This method is the one most often used to illustrate stitches in books (and in this guide) for its visual brevity. The sewing method is quick, less precise, and most successful on loosely stretched fabric. (See also the stab method of stitching below.)

Stab Method of Stitching:

Making each stitch with two complete motions—one up and one down—through the fabric. The stab method is slow, produces more precise stitches, and is the only type of method that can be used on very tightly stretched fabric. (See also, the sewing method of stitching above.)

Directions: Plunge the needle directly down through the fabric in one motion. Then move your hand underneath the fabric to grip the needle, and push it straight back up through the fabric in a second and separate motion. (A faster alternative is to pass the needle back and forth from one hand positioned on the top of the fabric to the other hand positioned underneath.) This method of stitching produces precisely placed stitches and can also ease thicker threads through fabrics. To facilitate the method further, use a floor stand to hold the hoop and to free both hands to stitch.

Stem Stitch:

Variation on back stitch. Used for curves, thick outlines, transparent or opaque fills.

Directions: Bring the thread up from the back of the fabric at one end of a marked or imagined line. Pointing the needle back toward that end of the line, insert the needle down to begin the first stitch, then bring it back up alongside the middle of the stitch and tighten the thread. Keeping the *thread* held out of the way *below* the needle, make the downward needle insertions slightly *below* the line, and the upward insertions slightly *above* the line. (The stitches will slant slightly and lie partially alongside each other along the line.)

Stem stitch, left-handed.

Stem stitch.

Stem stitch, right-handed.

Straight Stitch (and seeding):

The simplest stitch. Used for straight lines and single marks. Groups of tiny straight stitches (worked singly, in pairs, or in triplets, as in the photo) scattered across a surface are called seeding. Used for fills, textures.

Directions: Bring the needle up from the back of the cloth, and then down through again at another point at any distance away. Repeat for each stitch desired. For seeding, scatter very small straight stitches across the surface in *contrasting orientations*.

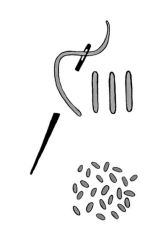

Straight stitch, left-handed.   Straight/seeding.   Straight stitch, right-handed.

Turkey Work:

A pile stitch with long thread ends protruding from a series of knots (also known in weaving as a Ghiordes knot or rya stitch; and in macramé as a lark's head knot). Used for heavy textures, rug-like pile surfaces, and three-dimensional effects.

Directions: Start with an *unknotted* loose thread end laid on the *face* of the cloth. Take a very small horizontal stitch to the side, leaving the *tail* of loose thread hanging down. Hold the thread above the stitch and out of the way. Insert the needle to the side and take a second small horizontal stitch, coming up in the same hole as the first stitch went down. Tighten the stitch to secure the knot (it will have the loose tail and the longer thread coming out from under it). Leave a loop of thread (long enough to make two cut ends) as you move on to make the next horizontal stitch beside the first one. Every two horizontal stitches in the row will form a knot. The loops that connect the stitches in the row create the pile. After the row is completed, the loops can be left in place (looped pile) or clipped in half (cut pile).

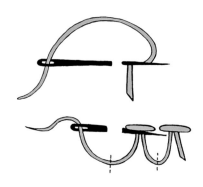

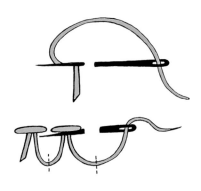

Turkey work, left-handed.   Turkey work (cut).   Turkey work, right-handed.

Whip Stitch:

A straight stitch variation that produces rows of diagonal marks. Used for gathering, lines of diagonal marks, transparent and opaque fills.

Directions: Bring the thread up from the back of the cloth at the bottom of the desired line. Insert the needle back down on the opposite side of the line and just a little above (at a diagonal). Thereafter, make a series of stitches straight across and perpendicular to the desired line. This will leave a trail of roughly parallel diagonal stitches on the *face* of the fabric, and a row of parallel vertical or horizontal bars on the *back*.

Whip stitch, left-handed.

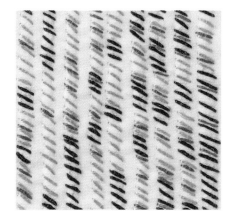

Whip stitch.

Whip stitch, right-handed.

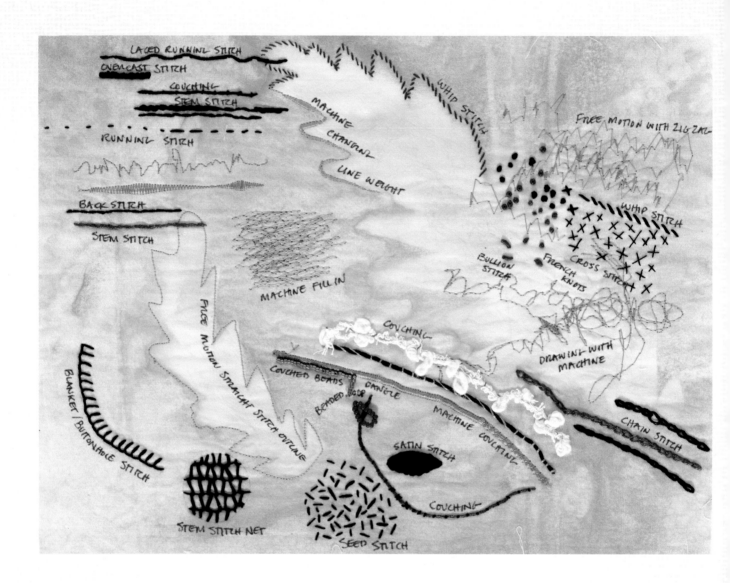

Getting Started: Help from Samplers

Set aside mental images of formal and intricately stitched *historical* embroidery samplers. The kinds of stitched samplers I want to discuss here are simpler, smaller, and more informal. They let you test ideas and materials, practicing stitches and stitch combinations without the pressure of making a finished piece.

You can treat these samplers as "sketchbooks" in thread (although, as the book makes clear, I also recommend keeping an actual sketchbook of drawings which can even precede any stitching). They're places to try out ideas and techniques, working at whatever speed you want, stitching with serious intent or just "playing" to see what happens when you try something new.

However you make your samplers, they're for your eyes only, a way of "talking to yourself" with a needle and thread.

Try a sampler whenever you're wondering how to proceed before starting a larger piece, or feeling the urge to experiment with something new. Try to analyze what worked, what didn't, and why.

Save your samples, perhaps organized in a notebook as a sort of "reference library" of things you've tried or things you may use in the future. Many of the illustrations in this book document my own decades of pleasurable time spent making useful samplers.

Although I make many types of samplers, I often return to a simple layout of square segments marked on the fabric and then individually filled with stitching. For me, the empty squares invite fill and spur invention. When I stitch in multiple squares on one piece of cloth, I can make instant comparisons among the alternatives. (See AP2-01 through AP2-05.) This works for *me*, but I encourage you to develop *your own* approach and format (which might change from one project to the next).

For example: You can create large individual samples for specific purposes, or mix smaller samples together on one cloth. You can stitch on a long strip or "scroll" of fabric, adding new sections with each new idea, and rolling up your scroll at storage time. You can stitch directly on the printed or dyed fabrics you routinely use in your work, adding to the pattern or image, stacking or piecing multiple cloths to test effects (as in the sampler on the facing page). Choose the methods that best serve what you want to accomplish.

"Catalog" Sampler of *Multiple* Stitch Types

This is a way to compare the things you can do with *multiple* kinds of stitches, and to test and compare them all in one place.

The need to make color choices can often "get in the way" when your main purpose is to practice stitches, so I usually recommend restricting sampler thread colors to black, white, and gray on a background fabric that is white or some other solid color. (The fabric color could, for example, be black, if your goal was to practice stitches in white or gray.) Contrasting colors, if introduced at all, should be used sparingly for accents.

You'll be stretching the fabric across a hoop before stitching begins, so choose a size of fabric large enough to leave at least 2" of space on all sides where the fabric will be clamped in the hoop.

With the fabric still on a table or other flat surface, mark small rectangular (or, if you prefer, oval or circular) segments (1.5" to 3") separated from each other by at least ½". Then take the time to plan or sketch a tiny composition which will fully use each space.

Fasten the marked fabric in a hoop, and then "populate" each square with a *different* stitch type. In AP2-01, some of my own compositions are quite simple, but others more complex. Some cover most of the square, but others only a small part. However, *all* were *composed*, either by drawing on the fabric itself or by having an actual small drawing at my side to serve as a guide to my stitching.

AP2-01 "Catalog" sampler of multiple stitch *types*. From top left: Seeding, satin, long and short, back, couching, overcasting, chain, cross, whip, stem, blanket, French knots. Cotton floss on cotton. Scale: 7.5" × 9.5"; each segment 2" × 2".

Sampler of *Multiple* Effects Using a *Single* Stitch Type

For more intensive experimentation with a stitch type you find especially appealing, focus on using just that *one* kind of stitch to achieve a variety of effects. This is also a very organized way to practice and "play" with a new stitch type that you haven't used before.

As described in the sections above, you'll mark segmented shapes on a fabric which will then be stretched in a hoop, and I recommend choosing a solid-color background cloth and then restricting thread color choices in order to focus on the stitched effects themselves.

In AP2-02, for example, the entire sampler used only running stitch.

AP2-02 Single stitch sampler: patterns and effects of *running stitch.* From top left: spacing changes, opposing orientations, concentric circles, gradation of line weights, leaving voids to form shapes, irregular undulating lines, lacing alternatives, contrast of color lacing vs. double running, fills with contrasting line weight and orientation. Cotton floss on cotton.

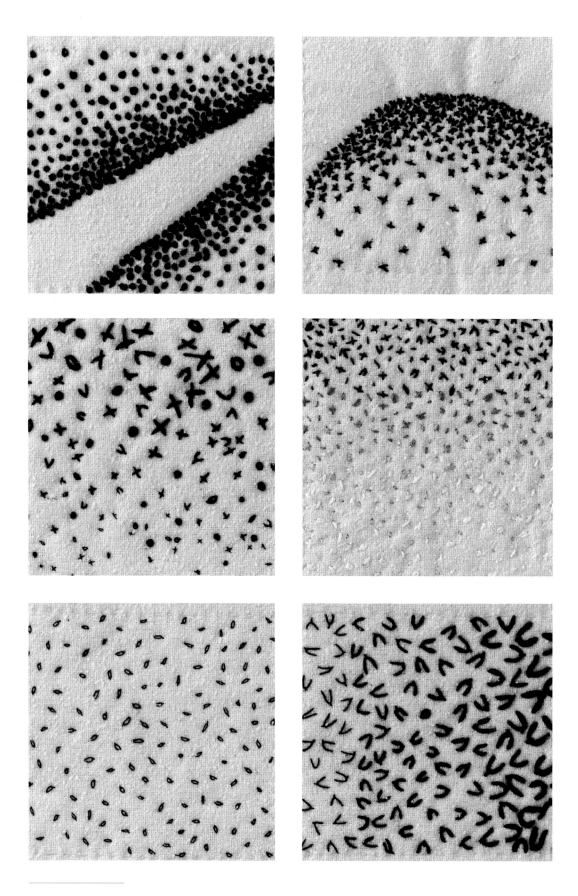

AP2-03 Sampler of effects in *black and white shading.* Hand stitching: French knots, cross, fly, detached chain, seeding. Cotton floss on silk noil.

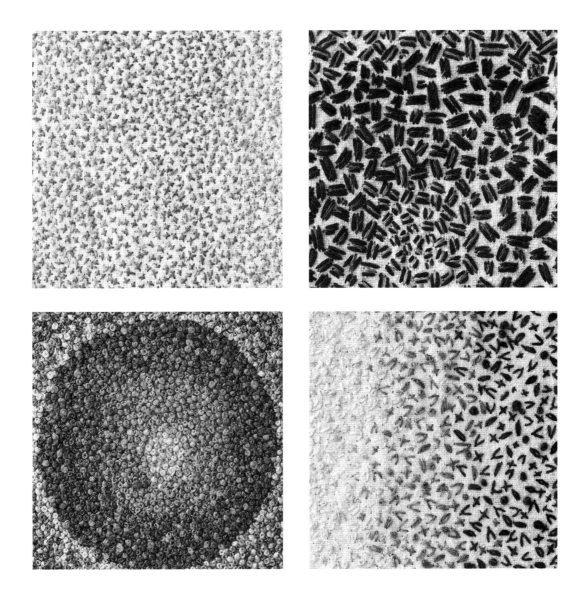

Sampler of *Multiple* Effects Using *Multiple* Stitch Types

Begin as described in the sections above by marking a fabric to be hooped for stitching and creating a tiny drawn composition for each marked segment. But this time, play with *appropriately* matching different stitch types to different *intended* effects. Whether you confine your thread colors to monochromes (as in AP2-03) or choose to experiment with color (as in AP2-04), or with combinations of color, materials, *and* stitch texture (as in AP2-05), use a single *solid* color of background fabric in order to focus on the effect of the stitching alone.

AP2-04 Sampler of effects in *color shading.* Hand stitching: cross, seeding, triple seeding, French knots, fly, detached chain. Cotton floss on silk noil.

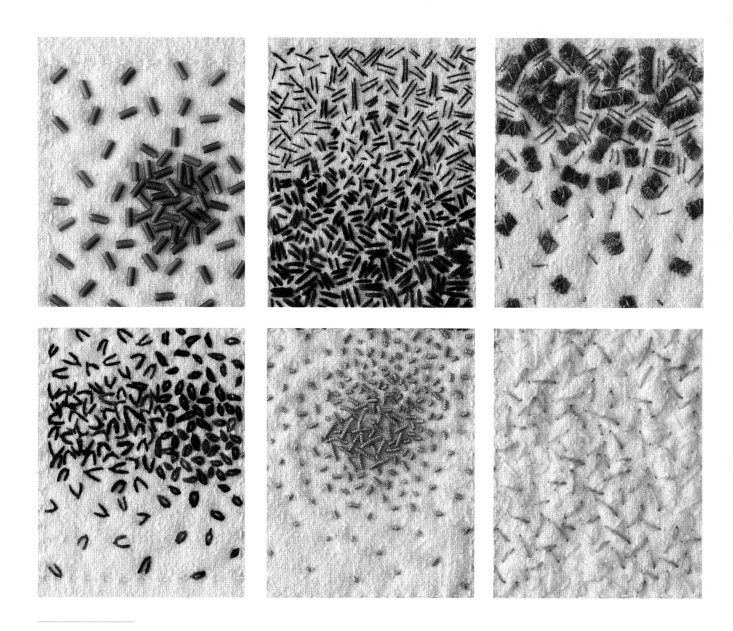

AP2-05 Sampler of effects in *seeding with various fiber and fill types.* Overlapping and contrasting effects of diverse materials, densities, scales, and line weights. Hand stitching with cotton floss and tape, wool, gold purl, glass bugle beads on silk noil.

Hand-stitched interpretation of Vincent van Gogh drawing detail in cotton threads on cotton cloth.
Stitches: running, back, French knots, straight, seeding, detached chain, satin, stem. Scale: 2" x 2".

Getting Started:
Matching Expression and Technique

This book seeks to lead you through a lyrical but logical journey of skill building and creative imagining—to demonstrate ways you can stitch *intentionally* to capture your perceptions, experiences, moods, feelings, and emotions.

While the book provides many examples of my own interpretations of ideas, the illustrations are not meant to be copied, but rather to spark your interest. Every person working in stitch, or any other medium, needs to find her (or his) own way toward "what works."

There is nothing "wrong" with stitching spontaneously "just to see where it goes." Various exercises in the book actually encourage you to "play" with stitch types and effects, especially those still outside your comfort zone, or others you've never tried before.

But when the time arrives to make a finished composition—to display in your home, to give to a friend, to sell—then you need to have some kind of vision of "where it's going" before you start on the stitched journey to go there. In decades of university and workshop teaching, I've found it useful to students of many ages—as it has always proven useful to me—to put *concept* first, to think about what the maker wants to express, and then fit the techniques to the desired expression, the *intended* outcome.

Most of us conceive expression, even in non-verbal media, with *words*. We describe (with words) the effect an image has on us, or (with words) the effect we'd like to result from an image we are making or plan to make.

My own technique, before beginning any textile piece, even if I'm starting with imagery from my own photographs, is to think of a descriptive word, or group of words, that summarize what I want to express. I actually go beyond just "thinking" of the words. I *write* them in my sketchbook. I write down other words which describe the characteristics of the "main" words. *What does it feel like?* I brainstorm about connections to some other words. And, next to the written words, I make little sketches—*many* of them—of images that might depict the words. The words themselves are mental and creative "prompts." They might, for example describe the physical characteristics of an object, or the way I myself felt when I was in a particular physical place or emotional "place."

I find it especially important to sketch or make small samples—and that is a place where I routinely astonish students. I tell them: "Make at least 25 thumbnail drawings, or small fabric collages, or small stitched samplers, expressing [concept X]."

AP3-01 Free-motion machine stitching: zigzag, satin.
Cotton thread on layered hand-dyed cotton and silk organza.

Their eyes bulge. "25? 25??! How is that even possible?" The answer is: It's not only possible, but nearly always necessary and helpful—because the first one, or two, or three things that you draw or collage will almost always be *the easiest and most obvious.* The real brainstorming begins when you *feel* that you might already (and quickly) have run out of ideas, but you keep pushing yourself. This is often challenging, but it's also how you get *past* the obvious. This is when—and how—you can get to the moments you experience as "Aha!"

I've been keeping sketchbooks and sample swatches for years. They fill a *long* shelf. I had fun doing them. And I didn't just fill them and file them away, never to be opened again. I *look* at them periodically, and even though most of them will never become larger finished pieces, all of those sketches and quick samples keep feeding new ideas and stimulation into my current work. You may find it helpful to do the same.

Here are some ways I think about concepts, what they mean, and what kinds of marks, gestures, and colors can be appropriate to expressing them. Keep in mind that this collection of images is the very opposite of exhaustive. Not a single one of these examples is the *only* way—and maybe not even the "best" way—to express the concept. (Remember that classroom exercise of "at least 25.") And the same general type of imagery can also be used to express more than one concept.

I know that you can find your own way.

Some Word Prompts about the External (Physical) World

BLUNT

Thick, dense, advancing, powerful. Like rips in a window screen. Hard edges. Dense, flat stitches in gradually widening strokes that suggest force and pressure.

BLURRED

Indistinct, faded, smudged, unclear. Like smeared wet ink, or streaked paint. Perhaps squinting, or motions the eye can't focus, or even "floaters" inside the eye itself. High contrast marks (crisp, clear) alongside low contrast marks (vague, faint, hazy).

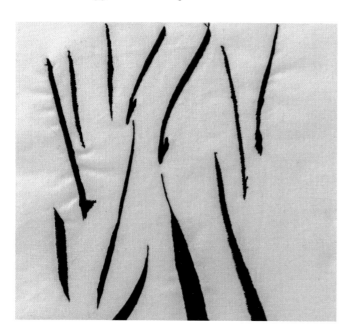

ABOVE AP3-02 "Blunt." Hand and machine stitching: satin, back, long and short, machine satin. Cotton threads on cotton.

RIGHT AP3-03 "Blurred." Hand stitching: detached chain, straight, fly. Cotton floss (black and a range of grays, *not* variegated) on cotton kettle cloth.

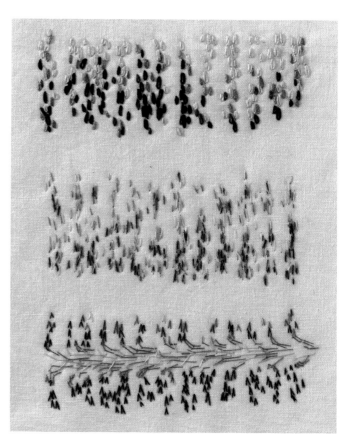

BOLD

Strong, heavy, prominent, solid, vivid, eye-catching, pronounced. Like bars on a window or graffiti on a building. Wide even line weight; strong color contrast; dense and dimensional stitching.

AP3-04 "Bold." Hand (couching, straight, back, satin, padded satin) and machine (satin) stitching. Cotton floss and threads on digitally printed silk noil.

BROKEN

Discontinuous, fragmented, interrupted, uneven, disjointed. Like lane markings on a highway. Short spaces between marks; linear placement; the eye completes the lines suggested by the segments.

BUMPY

Lumpy, rough, rutted, jerky. Like the surface of corrugated cardboard, or uneven cracks in pavement. Active, lively, wiggly lines in continual motion; small hills and valleys; regular *or* irregular rhythms.

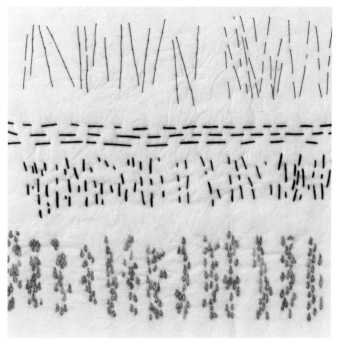

AP3-05 "Broken." Hand stitching: couching, straight stitches, running, chain, detached chain. Cotton sewing thread and floss, wool thread on natural combed cotton.

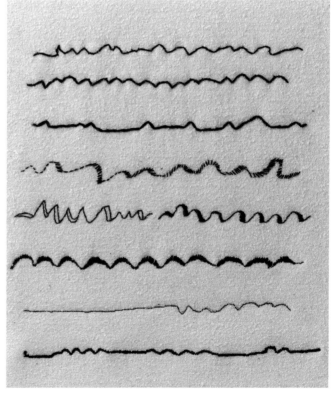

AP3-06 "Bumpy." Hand stitching (couching, self-couching, back, whip, satin) and machine (straight, satin) stitching. Cotton and cotton/polyester threads on silk noil.

COMPRESSED

Squeezed, squashed, tensed, compacted, stuffed, jammed, constricted. Like a spring pushed down and poised to release. Tension: deep and closely-spaced lines with undulating hills and valleys. Release: gentle curves to straightening line.

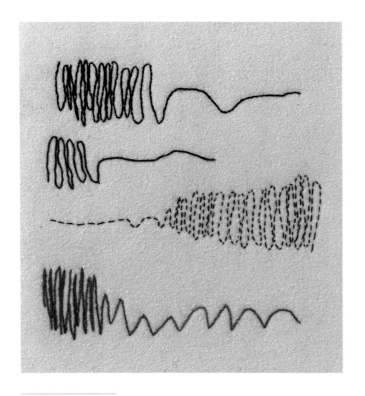

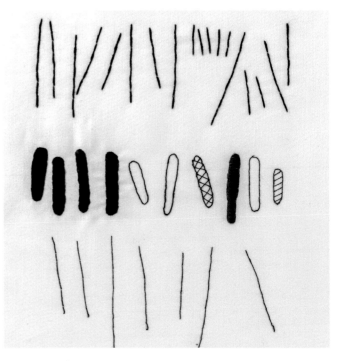

AP3-08 "Crisp." Hand stitching: double running, back, satin, cross, whip. Cotton floss and threads on cotton broadcloth.

AP3-07 "Compressed." Hand stitching: back, running, couching, laced back. Cotton floss and threads on silk noil.

CRISP

Sharp, brittle, firm, snappy. Like the edges between black and white stripes. Smooth edges; long straight lines; high contrast; clear and concise; undecorated, unembellished.

CURLED

Curved, meandering, coiled, twined. Like plant seedlings growing or plant tendrils unfurling. Gentle curves; uneven, slow motions; suggestive of continued movement.

AP3-09 "Curled." Hand stitching: back, laced back. Cotton threads on softened linen.

FLUID

Graceful, smooth, continuous, liquid. Like gently flowing water. Similar color values; long soft seamless curves; gentle crossings or intertwinings; cool colors.

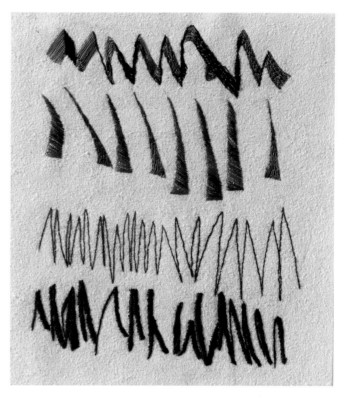

AP3-11 "Jagged." Hand stitching: back, satin, straight, and couching, laced back, couching, self-couching, back, stem, satin. Cotton threads on silk noil.

AP3-10 "Fluid." Hand stitching: stem, laced back, running, back. Cotton threads on cotton broadcloth.

JAGGED

Sharp, spiky, barbed, serrated, emphatic, abrupt, tough. Pointed things: icicles, thorns, mountain peaks. Clean firm edges; narrow angles; very sharp corners and turns (less than 45°); sharp jerky rhythms; strong color contrasts; dark and intense.

LOOPED

Coiled, twirled, circled, twisted. Lively energetic forward motion. Like scribbles. Smooth; continuous; sweeping and overlapping curves that change direction; circular rhythm; colors repeat in cycles.

AP3-12 "Looped." Hand stitching: satin, chain, laced back, buttonhole. Cotton thread on silk noil.

ORGANIC

Animated, biological, alive. Mimicking nature's shapes, contours, and variations. Like the living matter around us: leaves, vines, stems, veins, roots. Rounded, curved, irregular, tapering; colors as varied as those in nature.

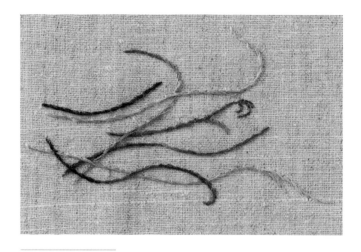

AP3-13 "Organic." Hand stitching: stem, back. Variegated cotton floss on linen.

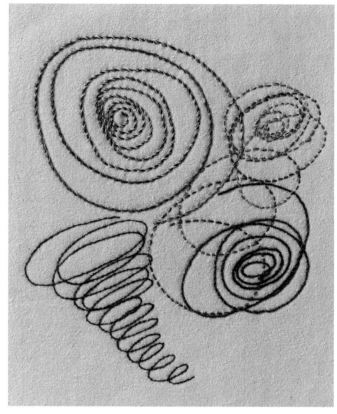

SWIRLING

Revolving, surging, spiraling. Like eddies, whirlpools, tornados, or swiftly draining water. Overlapping and continuous; irregular and dizzying rhythms; circling back repeatedly.

TOP RIGHT AP3-14 "Swirling" (in thin lines). Hand stitching: running, laced running, outline, back, laced back. Cotton threads on silk noil.

RIGHT AP3-15 "Swirling" (in thick lines). Hand stitching: chain, laced chain, couching. Cotton, pearl cotton, and rayon on silk noil.

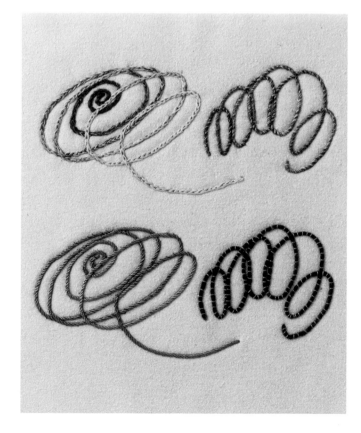

Some Word Prompts about
the Internal (Emotional) World

ANXIOUS

Uneasy, nervous, agitated, bothered, fretful, keyed up, jumpy. Like a hitch in the breath, or "butterflies" in the stomach. Discontinuity; irregular spacing; contrasting erratic rhythms; sharp peaks and valleys; intersecting lines; abrupt changes; misalignment. Low to medium values.

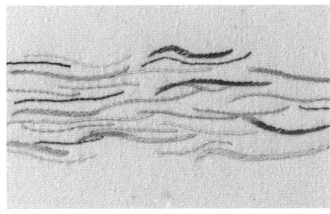

AP3-17 "Calm." Hand stitching: stem, laced back, laced running. Cotton on silk noil.

AP3-16 "Anxious." Hand stitching: straight, back. Cotton floss on silk noil.

CALM

Serene, tranquil, relaxed, cool, placid. Like floating, rolling, or gliding on undisturbed water; or lying on the ground to look at clouds moving slowly in the sky. Horizontal, elongated lines; gentle up and down curves; even spacing; minimal overlap; similar values and intensities of cool analogous colors.

CONFUSED

Tangled, convoluted, puzzled, mystified. Like being lost in an unfamiliar environment or whipping your head from side to side in bewilderment. Continually changing directions; looping, overlapping, and darting back and forth; unclear pathways; cacophony of colors to obscure the loopings; even distribution of color.

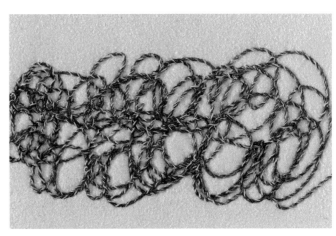

AP3-18 "Confused." Hand stitching: laced running. Variegated cotton threads on silk noil.

ELEGANT

Graceful, stylish, refined, beautiful, gracious. Like sophisticated signatures or finely-etched jewelry. Thin, long lines with smooth curves; low contrast, delicate, high value colors.

AP3-19 "Elegant." Hand stitching: stem, laced back, couching. Cotton threads on silk noil.

EMBARRASSED

Abashed, blushing, mortified, exposed. Like being caught in public underdressed or ill-prepared, or trying to suppress a painful truth. Vertical restraints; bright, indistinct form bursting forward; neutrals contrasting with high intensity colors.

FRENZIED

Frantic, wild, crazed, intense, fast. Like dashing around, or feeling overwhelmingly busy. Movement in all directions with abandon; repeated crossings; abrupt changes of direction; irregular rhythms and overlaps; neutral (or, alternatively, high intensity) colors.

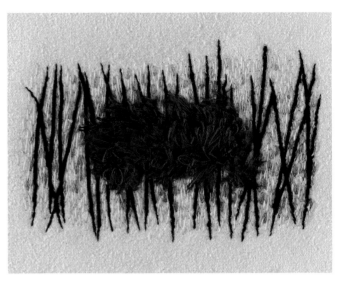

AP3-20 "Embarrassed." Hand stitching: detached chain, straight, Ghiordes knots ("Turkey work"). Cotton floss on silk noil.

AP3-21 "Frenzied." Hand stitching: stem. Cotton floss on silk noil.

GENTLE

Quiet, soft, light, slightly curved. Like the tops of clouds or cotton balls. Low color contrast; constant values; short, light marks; slow smooth rhythm.

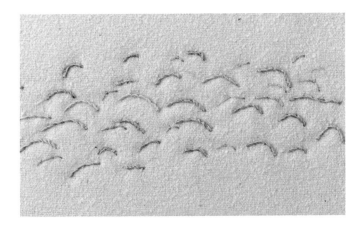

AP3-22 "Gentle." Hand stitching: laced back, stem. Cotton on silk noil.

LIGHTHEARTED

Airy, breezy, floating, playful, optimistic. Like a birthday celebration or thrown confetti. Vertical layout leads the eye upward; gentle curves; natural marks—dots, dashes, v's, and circles; light, pure pastel colors.

AP3-23 "Lighthearted." Hand stitching: back, chain, laced back, fly, detached chain, self-couching. Cotton thread on silk noil.

TIMID

Bashful, shy, unsure, retiring, faint-hearted. Like being afraid to speak or act. Short, thin, light lines; sparse spacing; uneven directions and orientations. Low contrast colors that recede.

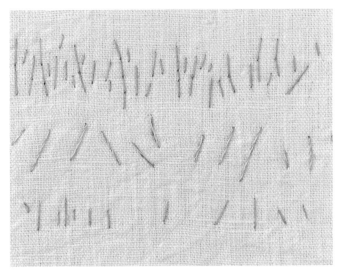

AP3-24 "Timid." Hand stitching: straight, back, couching, laced straight, straight. Cotton thread on softened linen.

WHIMSICAL

Quirky, unpredictable, joyful, silly, playful, jumpy, darting, dancing. Like party decorations, or toys piled in a playroom. Quick rhythms; tilted movements; frequent changes; bright colors, distributed unevenly, unexpectedly placed, or overlaid for high contrast.

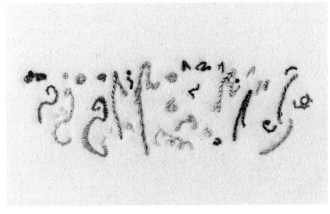

AP3-25 "Whimsical." Hand stitching: back, laced back, straight, French knots, self-couching, cross, stem. Cotton threads on silk noil.

Glossary

achromatics: White, black, and grays.

airbrush: A small, compressed-air-operated tool that blows paint, ink, or dye onto a surface. The airbrush allows finely and closely controlled spray painting.

analogous colors: Those colors next to each other on the color wheel. (See Chapter 9.)

blind contour drawing (see also *contour drawing*): A contour drawing made without looking at the paper in the process. That is, the artist imagines that her eyes and her pencil point are moving in tandem, the eyes seeing and the hands transcribing what is seen, without the aid of watching the drawing develop. The practice sharpens eye-to-hand coordination.

chipping: Seed stitch done with gold (metal) purl "thread," a hollow spring-like tightly coiled gold wire that can be cut into bits and sewn down like beads.

closure: The perceptual tendency for the eye to complete lines or shapes by filling in missing parts.

codex: A book constructed from multiple sheets of paper, papyrus, vellum, bark, or other material with hand-written contents and produced before the invention of the printing press and movable type.

color wheel: An abstract circular arrangement of colors that illustrates the visual and mixing relationships of the primary, secondary, and intermediary hues. Standardized color wheels (printed on card stock) are commonly used as a guide by artists, printers, dyers, craftsmen, designers, quilters, and other visual artists working with color.

complementary colors: Those colors directly opposite each other on the color wheel. (See Chapter 9.)

composition: The human hand organizing things. In visual art, the organization of elements (such as point, line, shape, plane, volume, texture, color) using guiding principles (balance, context, contrast, emphasis, focal point, gradation, illusion of space, pattern, placement, point of view, positive/negative space, proportion, repetition, rhythm, scale, space, uniqueness, unity, and variety) to form a coherent whole. These elements and principles provide powerful tools for expression and communication.

contour drawing: A drawing that captures only the essential outlines of an object or subject. The lines in the resulting drawing may be exact and descriptive or imprecise and lively. (See also blind contour drawing.)

cursive (also know as *longhand*): A system of handwriting in which the letters that form words are connected by a continuous line, only broken to indicate the beginnings and ends of words. The hand action is quick and fluid. The idiosyncratic aspects of an individual's handwriting emerge from the combination of the slope and connection of the letters, and how those attributes modify their shapes.

cutch: An ancient natural dyestuff from India made by soaking cutch wood in hot water, yielding a reddish-brown color.

de-intensified colors: Hues or colors that are lowered in intensity or dulled in effect. (See Chapter 9.)

dissolvable web: A film-like substance used to support insubstantial fabric or free-form lace-like stitching. The web subsequently dissolves when placed in hot water. It is also referred to as "wash-away embroidery stabilizer."

dovetail: Alternating the positions of stitches to interlock like the fingers of your two hands, with each stitch fitting in a space between a pair of other ones.

embroidery stand: A device with a clamp to hold an embroidery hoop or stretcher. Stands in many styles—made from metal, wood, or fiberglass—can rest on the floor, sit on a tabletop, or clamp to a table edge. Extremely useful for freeing up both hands for stitching.

floss: A shorthand reference to *embroidery floss*, a type of loosely twisted cotton, rayon, or silk thread that is specifically made for embroidery. Several individual floss strands (3 to 6) are normally loosely twined and packaged in a skein. The strands can be used in any number.

gradation: Gradual change across a surface in an orderly way. The characteristics of a gradation include: the *type* of change across a surface (for example, changes of color, shape, or position); the speed of the change (rapid steps give the viewer visual jerks, slow steps a smooth transition); and the direction of the change—up, down, across, parallel, concentric, zigzag, or other.

haloing: Placing stitches, beads, or dots in gradated densities—close together near a shape, and increasingly far apart moving outward from it. The gradation creates a radiating color effect that emphasizes and draws attention to the shape's edge. Using beads in a halo adds light reflection to the illusion.

hatching or cross hatching: In drawing, hatching is the use of repeated parallel lines to shade an area or shape in a composition. The related technique of cross hatching sets one series of repeated parallel lines at a nearly perpendicular angle across a second set of repeated parallel lines, resulting in a grid. Variations of line character, weight, proximity of placement, and angle of line intersection determine the resulting character and amount of shading.

hemp: The stem (bast) fiber of the cannabis plant. Hemp fibers are rather stiff and wiry in texture, and often used to make rope, stiff fabrics, papers, and fiberboards.

hue: The name of a color or its place on the color wheel. (See Chapter 9.)

intensity: The brightness or dullness of a color (also referred to as "saturation," "chroma," or "purity"). (See Chapter 9.)

lacing: Threading or weaving a separate thread back through a stitched line (such as running, stem, back, or chain stitch) either back and forth, or repeatedly from the same side. Lacing does not catch or pierce the underlying fabric, but simply gathers and links the line of individual stitches. (See Getting Started: A Guide to Stitching in Appendix 1 for illustrations and directions.)

long floats: Long stitches that are loose enough to droop away from the fabric surface. They often indicate insufficient tension on the thread during stitching and can make the product look poorly crafted or unfinished. (See Getting Started: A Guide to Stitching in Appendix 1.)

longhand: See *cursive*.

moiré pattern: A watery-looking interference effect created by the slight misalignment of two layered patterns or grids.

monochromatic: Tints, tones, and shades of a single hue or color.

needle (verb, *to needle*): Used by many needleworkers as a verb, *to needle* indicates the action of pushing a needle through cloth. The amount of resistance met depends on the type, twist, and density of the threads in the cloth's structure in relation to the size of the needle. For example, a cloth that firmly resists any needle is said to be "hard to needle."

optical blending or optical mixing: The results of combining colored dots, marks, lines, or small bits of material. The *tiny scale* of the interactions among the bits aids the human eye (and brain) to combine the separate colors and to perceive a single "composite" color. (See Chapter 9.)

palimpsest: Ancient manuscript or writing, often on vellum (calf skin), in which the earlier, original writing was scraped away imperfectly, and overlaid by newer writing. The older writing is still visible in a ghost-like image shimmering underneath the more modern text.

Phoenician: An ancient script from the Phoenician civilization in the eastern Mediterranean area called the Fertile Crescent. It is possibly the oldest verified alphabet and represents only consonant sounds. It is the historic root of Arabic, Hebrew, Latin, and Greek.

pointillism: A technique of painting with small dots of color applied in patterns to form shapes and images through the juxtaposition of colors and optical blending. The Pointillist art movement, an outgrowth of late-nineteenth-century impressionism, was spearheaded by the French painters Georges Seurat and Paul Signac.

primary colors: The basic colors from which all other colors are mixed. In pigments or dyes they are cyan, magenta, and yellow. In light they are red, blue, and green. (See Chapter 9.)

quilter's knot: A small, simple, tidy knot used to secure thread in cloth. (See Getting Started: A Guide to Stitching in Appendix 1 for instructions.)

raffia: The fibers produced by stripping the leaves of the raffia palm tree, a native of the African continent. The fiber is slightly slippery or waxy and quite flexible even when dry, and is traditionally used to make baskets, mats, and hats.

runes: Letters of ancient Germanic alphabets; precursors to the Roman alphabet.

sawtooth edge: A jagged or zigzag placement of stitches to create a ragged, pointed edge resembling the edge of a saw.

scale: The relative size of elements in a composition. Scale establishes a hierarchy of importance among the elements present.

secondary colors: Those colors about midway between a pair of primaries on the color wheel. In pigments and dyes: red, blue, and green; in light: cyan, magenta, and yellow. (See Chapter 9.)

shade: A color to which black has been added, which darkens and de-intensifies the original hue color. Shades can be achieved in paint, dye, pigment, colored pencil, pastels, or by combining threads.

simultaneous contrast: A visual phenomenon in which a single color is perceived differently each time it is set against a new background color. For example, the same yellow will *appear* different when surrounded by blue than when surrounded by orange or by purple. This concept was most ably described and documented by painter and educator Josef Albers in his paintings and book on color (see the Bibliography).

stab method of stitching: Plunging the needle directly down through the fabric in one motion and then pushing it directly straight back up through the fabric in a second and separate motion. (See also Getting Started: A Guide to Stitching in Appendix 1.)

stippling: In drawing or rendering, the use of many tiny dots or marks to create finely graded shading and softly molded illusions of volume.

temperature (of color): The relative warmth or coolness of a color. Warm colors are associated with fire (red, yellow, orange); cool colors with ice, snow, water, or plants (blue, green, violet).

tetradic: Any four colors on the color wheel connected by a square imposed inside it. Spin the square around for multiple options.

tint: A color of paint or pigment to which white has been added, yielding a lighter, chalky, opaque "pastel." Tints can be achieved in paint, dye, pigment, colored pencil, pastels, or by combining threads.

tone: A color to which gray or its complement has been added, resulting in slightly de-intensified mid-value colors.

triad: Any three colors on the color wheel connected by an equilateral triangle imposed inside it. Spin the triangle for multiple options. Triad color relationships seem complete and balanced. (See Chapter 9.)

value: The relative lightness or darkness of a color. High value colors are light; low value colors are dark. (See Chapter 9.)

value contrast: The relative positions of two or more colors on a value scale. Each color has a value that corresponds to a step on the value scale. The *closer* the values of two colors are on the scale, the lower the contrast between them. The *farther apart* the values of two colors are on the scale, the higher the contrast between them. The highest possible value contrast is between black and white, the two ends of the scale.

value scale: An achromatic sequence from white at one end, through incremental steps of gradating grays, to black at the other end. Standardized value scales (printed on card stock) are commonly used by photographers, artists, printers, dyers, quilters, and other visual artists to establish the relative lightness or darkness of colors they are assembling.

Bibliography

DESIGN

Albers, Anni. *On Designing.* Middletown, CT: Wesleyan University Press, 1961.

Albers, Josef. *Interaction of Color,* 4th ed. New Haven, CT: Yale University Press, 2013.

Bevlin, Marjorie Elliott. *Design through Discovery: An Introduction to Art and Design,* 6th ed. San Diego, CA: Harcourt Brace College, 1994.

Itten, Johannes. *The Elements of Color.* New York: Van Nostrand Reinhold, 1970.

Wong, Wucius. *Principles of Three-Dimensional Design.* New York: Van Nostrand Reinhold, 1977.

Wong, Wucius. *Principles of Two-Dimensional Design.* New York: Van Nostrand Reinhold, 1972.

DRAWING AND ILLUSTRATION: TECHNIQUE

Aimone, Steven. *Expressive Drawing: A Practical Guide to Freeing the Artist Within.* New York & London: Lark Books, 2009.

Borgeson, Bet. *The Colored Pencil.* Rev. ed. New York: Watson-Guptill, 1993.

Clayton, Elaine. *Making Marks: Discover the Art of Intuitive Drawing.* New York: Simon & Schuster, Atria paperback, 2014.

Dodson, Bert. *Keys to Drawing.* Cincinnati: North Light Books, 1985.

Edwards, Betty. *Drawing on the Right Side of the Brain: A Course in Enhancing Creativity and Artistic Confidence.* Los Angeles: J. P. Tarcher; New York: St. Martin's, 1979.

Laliberté, Norman, and Alex Mogelon. *Drawing with Ink: History and Modern Techniques.* New York: Van Nostrand Reinhold, 1970.

Laliberté, Norman, and Alex Mogelon. *Drawing with Pencils: History and Modern Techniques.* New York: Van Nostrand Reinhold, 1969.

Lohan, Frank J. *The Drawing Handbook: Comprehensive, Easy-to-Master Lessons on Composition and Techniques Using Pencil and Pen & Ink.* Chicago: Contemporary Books, 1993.

Martin, Judy. *Encyclopedia of Colored Pencil Techniques.* London: Quarto, 1992; Philadelphia: Running Press, 1997.

Nice, Claudia. *Sketching Your Favorite Subjects in Pen and Ink.* Cincinnati: North Light Books, 1993.

Simmons, Gary. *The Technical Pen: Techniques of Artists.* New York: Watson-Guptill, 1992.

EMBROIDERY: HAND TECHNIQUE

Barnden, Betty. *The Embroidery Stitch Bible.* Iola, WI: Krause, 2003.

Beaney, Jan, and Jean Littlejohn. *A Complete Guide to Creative Embroidery: Designs, Textures, Stitches.* London: Batsford, 1991.

Beaney, Jan, and Jean Littlejohn. *Stitch Magic: Ideas and Interpretations.* London: Batsford, 1998; Chicago: Quilter's Resource Inc., 1999.

Box, Richard. *Color and Design for Embroidery: A Practical Handbook for the Daring Embroiderer and Adventurous Textile Artist.* Washington, DC: Brassey's, 2000.

Brown, Pauline. *The Encyclopedia of Embroidery Techniques.* London: Quarto, 2016.

Campbell-Harding, Valerie, and Pamela Watts. *Bead Embroidery.* London: Batsford, 1993.

Eaton, Jan. *Mary Thomas's Dictionary of Embroidery Stitches.* North Pomfret, VT: Trafalgar Square, 1998.

Embroiderers Guild of the United Kingdom. *Getting Started.* Embroidery stitch tutorials and videos.

Ganderton, Lucinda. *Stitch Sampler: The Ultimate Visual Dictionary to Over 200 Classic Stitches.* New York and London: Dorling Kindersley, 1999.

Greenlees, Kay. *Creating Sketchbooks for Embroiderers and Textile Artists.* London: Batsford, 2005.

Grey, Maggie, and Jane Wild. *Paper, Metal & Stitch: Creating Surfaces with Color and Texture.* Loveland, CO: Interweave, 2005.

Hedley, Gwen. *Drawn to Stitch: Line, Drawing, and Mark-Making in Textile Art.* London: Batsford, 2010.

Hedley, Gwen. *Surfaces for Stitch: Plastics, Films & Fabric.* London: Batsford, 2002.

Hoskins, Nancy Arthur. *Universal Stitches for Weaving, Embroidery, and Other Fiber Arts.* Atglen, PA: Schiffer, 1985.

Howard, Constance. *The Constance Howard Book of Stitches.* London: Batsford, 1979.

Howard, Constance. *Embroidery and Color.* New York: Van Nostrand Reinhold, 1976.

Lemon, Jane. *Metal Thread Embroidery: Tools, Materials, and Techniques,* 2nd ed. London: Batsford, 2002.

Parrott, Helen. *Mark-Making in Textile Art.* London: Batsford, 2013.

Samples, Carole. *Treasury of Crazy Quilt Stitches.* Paducah, KY: American Quilter's Society, 1999.

Stanton, Yvette. *The Left-Handed Embroiderer's Companion: A Step-by-Step Stitch Dictionary.* Horsby Westfield, NSW, Australia: Vetty Creations, 2010.

Tellier–Loumagne, Françoise. *The Art of Embroidery: Inspirational Stitches, Textures, and Surfaces.* London and New York: Thames and Hudson, 2003.

Wellesley-Smith, Claire. *Slow Stitch: Mindful and Contemplative Textile Art.* London: Batsford, 2015.

EMBROIDERY: MACHINE TECHNIQUE

Beaney, Jan. *Vanishing Act.* Berkshire, UK: Double Trouble Enterprises, 1997.

Campbell-Harding, Valerie, and Maggie Grey. *Layers of Stitch: Contemporary Machine Embroidery.* Chicago: Quilter's Resource, 2002.

Campbell-Harding, Valerie, and Pamela Watts. *Machine Embroidery: Stitch Techniques.* London: Batsford, 1989.

Grey, Maggie. *Raising the Surface with Machine Embroidery.* Chicago: Quilter's Resource, 2003.

Harker, Gail. *Machine Embroidery.* London: Herehurst, 1990.

Shinn, Carol. *Freestyle Machine Embroidery: Techniques and Inspiration for Fiber Art.* Loveland, CO: Interweave, 2009.

Wolff, Colette. *The Art of Manipulating Fabric.* Radnor, PA: Chilton, 1996.

HISTORY: ART AND DRAWING

Gardner, Helen. *Gardner's Art through the Ages: A Global History,* 14th ed. Edited by Fred S. Kleiner. Boston: Wadsworth, Cengage Learning, 2013.

Ingold, Tim. *Lines: A Brief History.* London and New York: Routledge, 2007.

Janson, H. W. *Janson's History of Art: The Western Tradition,* 8th ed. Edited by Horst Woldemar. Upper Saddle River, NJ: Pearson Education, 2011.

Lindemann, Gottfried. *Prints and Drawings: A Pictorial History.* Translated by Gerald Onn. New York: Praeger, 1970.

HISTORY: EMBROIDERY

Barber, E. J. W. *Prehistoric Textiles: The Development of Cloth in the Neolithic and Bronze Ages with Specific Reference to the Aegean.* Princeton, NJ: Princeton University Press, 1991.

Beaudry, Mary C. *Findings: The Material Culture of Needlework and Sewing.* New Haven, CT: Yale University Press, 2006.

Bridgeford, Andrew. *1066: The Hidden History in the Bayeux Tapestry.* New York: Walker, 2006.

Browne, Clare, and Jennifer Wearden. *Samplers from the Victoria and Albert Museum.* London: V & A Publishing, 1999.

Kettle, Alice, and Jane McKeating. *Machine Stitch Perspectives.* London: A & C Black, 2010.

Paine, Sheila. *Embroidered Textiles: Traditional Patterns from Five Continents.* New York: Rizzoli, 1990.

Parker, Rozsika. *The Subversive Stitch: Embroidery and the Making of the Feminine.* New York: Routledge, 1984.

Parmal, Pamela. *Samplers from A to Z.* Boston: Museum of Fine Arts, 2000.

Sawyer, Alan R. *Early Nasca Needlework.* London: Lawrence King, 1997.

Smith, Barbara Lee. *Celebrating the Stitch.* Newton, CT: Taunton, 1991.

Springall, Diana. *Inspired to Stitch: 21 Textile Artists.* London: A & C Black, 2005.

Weissman, Judith Reiter, and Wendy Lavitt. *Labors of Love: America's Textiles and Needlework, 1650–1930.* New York: Alfred A. Knopf, 1987.

TEXT AND TYPOGRAPHY

Bringhurst, Robert. *The Elements of Typographic Style,* 4th ed. Seattle, WA, and Vancouver, BC: Hartley & Marks, 2012.

Clayton, Ewan. *The Golden Thread: The Story of Writing.* Berkeley, CA: Counterpoint, 2013.

Nakanishi, Akira. *Writing Systems of the World: Alphabets, Syllabaries, Pictograms.* Tokyo and Rutland, VT: Tuttle, 1980.

Robinson, Andrew. *Lost Languages: The Enigma of the World's Undeciphered Scripts.* New York: McGraw-Hill, 2002.

Robinson, Andrew. *The Story of Writing: Alphabets, Hieroglyphs, and Pictograms.* London: Thames and Hudson, 2007.

Sacks, David. *Letter Perfect: The Marvelous History of Our Alphabet from A to Z.* New York: Broadway Books / Random House, 2003.

Materials, Tools, and Equipment

In my stitching practice, I first determine the types of materials and tools best suited to a project, and then use the highest quality I can afford. If necessary, I choose quality over quantity, because good beginnings are more likely to lead to pleasurable creative experiences and successful aesthetic outcomes. And I generally use the same materials for "studies" as I expect to use in the project itself, because learning how materials can be "worked" and feeling what they "want" to do (or not to do) is part of the creative process.

While the following overview provides some reliable brand names at the time this book was written, vendors come and go with the passage of time, product offerings change, or a particular product may not be readily accessible where you live, work, or shop.

Regardless of when you first encounter this book, you can use the following information to locate similar or alternative products.

BEADS

Desirable characteristics:

- Uniform bead size for each type
- Evenly cut and drilled
- Consistent color
- No chips, cracks, or blemishes
- Avoid beads with painted interiors or exteriors, as these are apt to fade, chip, or wash away

My stash includes:

- Glass seed and bugle beads
- Bone rounds, bugles, and roundels
- Wood
- Sterling silver
- Plastic (very selectively, and avoiding those which look "cheap")

Sources: Bead shows, bead shops, and online bead vendors.

DYES, PIGMENTS, AND TEXTILE PAINTS

Desirable characteristics:

- Pre-mixed products, ready to apply directly from a bottle or jar, are the easiest to use in your home or studio and the mostly likely to minimize the toxicity and "clean air" issues of trying to mix your own.
- Stock a small range of colors that can be mixed (e.g., magenta, scarlet, turquoise, blue, golden yellow, chino, brown, black).
- Detailed instructions and good chemical support information from the company, in writing at a minimum, with additional support online and/or by phone if possible. Follow manufacturer recommendations to avoid illegal and unhealthy contamination of your local water supply.

My stash includes:

- Textile pigments and paints (nearly always safer to use than dyes)
- MX fiber reactive dyes. I have long used products from ProChemical & Dye and Dharma Trading.

Sources: Online dye and pigment vendors. Marketers at textile-related conferences and trade shows.

FABRICS

Desirable characteristics:

- Strong fibers and even weaves; solid construction
- Dimensional stability (minimal stretch)
- Looser weaves for larger-scale threads, tighter weaves for smaller-scale threads, in-between for combinations of both. (Generally, the choice of weave scale for the background fabric will need to accommodate the largest type of thread you expect to pass through it.)
- Pre-wash the fabrics to remove dirt or finishes, to pre-shrink and soften, and to minimize puckering.
- For dense stitching or to mask show-through of back-side threads, stabilize the fabric with interfacing, cotton flannel, or thin cotton batting.

My stash includes:

- Natural fiber fabrics from plant or animal sources. Cotton: print cloth, sateen, sheeting, gauze, or muslin. Silk: noil, organza, or organza netting. Linen: softened linen, handkerchief linen, or heirloom linens.

- Nylon netting is the main exception to my preference for natural fibers, and is the only synthetic fabric I use with any frequency.

- I generally avoid fabrics with coatings or finishes added during the manufacturing process, because I find that uncoated fabrics feel better in the hand and more easily accept dyes, pigments, and the threaded needle.

- Pre-treated fabrics, pre-cut and paper-backed, sized to fit my printer, are the main and necessary exceptions to my preference for uncoated products.

Sources: Online fabric companies specializing in untreated fabrics. Marketers at textile-related conferences and trade shows.

HOOPS AND STRETCHER FRAMES

Desirable characteristics:

- Look for continuous contact between the inner and outer hoops.

- Durable wooden hoops resist cracking or splitting under tension and hold the fabric stretched tightly. Look for smooth edges or use sandpaper to smooth them yourself.

- High quality plastic hoops with interlocking grooves also work well.

- Wrap the inner hoop, whether plastic or wood, with a strip of muslin, or apply hoop tape to enhance the fabric grip.

- Hoops with grooved screw heads tighten easily with a standard screwdriver; thumbscrews are harder to grip and tighten sufficiently.

- "Square" hoops (actually rounded rectangles) expand the stitching area.

- Stretcher, slate, or scroll frames hold the fabric more tightly than hoops, provide access to all sections of the design simultaneously, require the support of a stand or tabletop blocks, and are generally less portable than hoops.

My stash includes:

- Edmunds (high quality) or Hardwicke Manor (very high quality and expensive) quilting and embroidery hoops

- Simple modular wooden scroll frames

- Hand-built wooden slate frame

Sources: General and specialty online vendors. Fabric, stitching, and quilting stores.

NEEDLES

Desirable characteristics:

- Needle sizes are numbered: the larger the number, the smaller the needle diameter. Keep a selection of types and sizes on hand.

- Needles should be strong and straight, but flexible enough to bend repeatedly without breaking or remaining bent.

- Match the needle diameter to the thread diameter and the fabric density.

- Needle eyes should be large enough to thread easily and allow the thread to move freely during stitching.

- Use sharp needles and discard when they become dull (they start to catch on the fabric or resist piercing it).

My stash includes:

- A variety of embroidery, sharp, crewel, and millinery needles from Bohin (a very fine brand made in France).

- Older John James, manufactured in the UK prior to 2012, before the company outsourced production abroad.

Sources: General and specialty online vendors. Quilting and stitchery shops.

SCISSORS

Desirable characteristics:

- Sturdy stainless-steel construction.

- Comfortably shaped handles that fit your dominant hand. (If you are left-handed, invest in left-handed scissors.)

- Continuous contact between the inner and outer blades to allow clean cutting out to the points without hitches that leave ragged or chewed edges.

- Choose scissor sizes to fit the task: shears for large fabric cuts, medium-sized "craft" scissors for small fabric cuts, and embroidery scissors or snips for cutting threads.

- Buy the best quality scissors you can afford, have them re-sharpened regularly, store them in a dry location, and use them only on fabric and threads. (Use of good fabric scissors on paper or other non-fabric materials quickly dulls the blades.)

My stash includes:

- Gingher: shears, embroidery scissors, and snips for the studio (high quality and dependable)
- Mundial: shears, craft scissors, and snips (adequate for workshops and travel where the chance of loss or damage to tools is greater)

Sources: Fabric, quilt, or stitchery shops. Online sewing vendors.

SEWING MACHINES

Desirable characteristics:

- Heavy-duty construction with metal parts, in particular the internal cams. (This may involve buying an older machine, made before the industry increased the number of plastic components.)
- For ease of free-motion stitching, feed dogs which easily disengage with a simple lever, knob, or button.
- Attachments include a quilting, darning, or open-front free-motion foot.
- Freely-moving dial or rheostat to control stitch width smoothly during stitching.
- Sturdy carrying case.
- Do not skimp on regular sewing machine maintenance. Locate and use your local sewing machine repair shop.

My stash includes:

- Bernina 930 (manufactured in 1985). Heavy, all-metal, versatile, and ideal for free-motion work. Mine was purchased new, but the 930 is still available second-hand, online, and at select Bernina stores. Well worth the price.
- Juki TL-93E home industrial machine. For straight-stitch only, with added governor for speed control. Very fast for extensive straight stitch free-motion work.
- Singer Featherweight (manufactured in 1966). Small, lightweight, and portable. Straight-stitch only. Throat plate cover for feed dogs facilitates free-motion work.

STANDS

Desirable characteristics:

- Strong clamp that holds a hoop or frame to provide a "third hand" during stitching. The clamp must grip the hoop or frame tightly and hold it firmly in place without working loose or slipping as you stitch.
- Well-balanced metal stands are more sturdy, durable, and dependable than most wooden stands.
- Look for smoothly-finished, strong, and easily-turned gears, screws, clamps, joins, levers, and knobs.
- Modular stands can be disassembled for storage or travel.
- Choose a stand that allows easy access to the back of the work during stitching without loosening a screw or knob.

My stash includes:

- For a permanent location in my studio I use a K's Creations floor stand. It is heavy (stainless steel), durable, sturdy, well-balanced—an industrial-looking "work horse."

- For travel, when packing space is tight, I have a lighter-weight heavy-gauge aluminum Lowery stand (from the UK) which disassembles easily to stow in carry-on luggage. As a bonus, its base slips easily beneath a lounge chair or sofa, enabling use in a more casual sitting position, even in a reclining lounger with your feet raised. (It may be necessary to place a weighty object on the base as "ballast" to prevent the stand from tipping when using larger hoops or attached frames.)

- For flexibility, portability, and light weight, I use the modular Needlework System 4, whose well-designed, sturdy, and cleanly-finished clamp can alternately be attached to four different types of aluminum stands (floor, travel floor, table clamp, or laptop/tabletop) with stainless steel fittings. The clamp is made of thick, high-density "space-age plastic" (as the manufacturer describes it) which grips hoops or frames solidly and without creasing the wood.

Sources: Stitchery shops and online vendors.

THREADS

Desirable characteristics:

- Strong enough to avoid breakage as threads rub through the eye of the needle.

- Sufficiently friction-resistant to resist shredding when pulled repeatedly through fabric.

- Sufficiently colorfast to avoid bleeding dye onto the fabric or adjacent threads when wet.

- Consistent and even thread weight (diameter), quality control (no weak spots, bumps or knots), and dye lot accuracy (in case you need to buy more of that color).

- Instead of buying specific threads for each project, keep a broad inventory of threads on hand to allow spontaneous choices and interesting or unusual color mixes. Inventory suggestions: Variety of natural and synthetic fiber types and weights in both tight and loose spins. Wide ranges of colors from many areas of the color wheel, light to dark and bright to muted. Variegated threads in subtle, sophisticated, jarring, or high contrast color mixes. An assortment of textures, e.g., shiny, matte, rough, smooth, wiry, stiff, soft, or furry.

My stash includes:

- Flosses and machine embroidery threads (cotton, silk, rayon, nylon, polyester); pearl cottons; gimps and cords; narrow tapes and ribbons.

- Wool threads and yarns, such as those spun for tapestry, needlepoint, knitting, or crewel work.

- Bast fiber threads: various spins of linen, ramie, jute, and hemp.

- Leaf fibers: raffia (stripped length of palm).

- Metallic threads: synthetic flosses and real gold (gold purl, passing).

- Mixed fiber content yarns and novelty threads: wide assortment originally intended for weaving, crocheting, tatting, or knitting, in small amounts.

- Hand-dyed threads from small specialty hand dye companies or individual dye artists (the latter are often encountered by fortunate chance).

- When I need very specific colors (color matching) or absolute color control, I buy un-dyed threads on large cones and dye the colors myself with chemical or natural dyes.

Sources: Fabric, quilting, weaving, and stitchery shops. Marketers at textile-related conferences and trade shows. Online vendors.

For an up-to-date list of current vendors, please consult the website for this book at:
http://www.schifferbooks.com/theintentionalthread

Index

Abstraction, 57, 64, 150

Activities ("Try this!"), 25, 35, 49, 63–64, 75–76, 92, 99–100, 105, 125, 137–138, 150–151, 171, 182–183

Airbrush effects, 82–84

Analogous colors, 109, 118, 211, 214

Appliqué, letterforms, 53–54

Beads, 103, 115, 130, 132, 137, 162–163, 168, 170, 172, 220

Chalk, 78, 135, 159

Chipping, 162–163, 214

Color, 108–124, 144–148, 167–168

Color context, 109, 111

Color matching, 115

Color mixing in the needle, 119, 145

Color perception in the studio, 115

Color proportion, 115, 120–124

Color tips, 115

Color wheel, 110, 214

Complementary colors, 117, 214

Composition tips, 10, 30–34, 131, 214

Contour drawings, 104, 214

Contours, 13, 101–104

Crayons, 75

Cross hatching, 153–158, 215

Delicate lines, 77, 85–90

Diagonal lines, 28–29, 30–34, 38, 120, 127, 142, 165

Digital printing on cloth, 147

Dissolvable web, 97–98, 214

Elemental mark-making, 36–48

Emotion, 211–213

Equipment, 220–223

Exercises ("Try this!"), 25, 35, 49, 63–64, 75–76, 92, 99–100, 105, 125, 137–138, 150–151, 171, 182–183

Expressive marks, 205–213

Fabric marking, 38

Feathering, 77–84

Fills, 107, 126–136, 139–149, 152–170

Fine line stitching tips, 85

Floats, long, 127, 215

Free-motion machine stitching, tips, 41

French knots, tips, 143

Gradation, 152–170, 214

Hair (human), stitching with, 90–91

Haloing, 168–170, 215

Heavier weight lines, 15,18

Horizontal lines, 27–28, 30–34

Hue, 111, 215

Illusion of three-dimensional space, 31–33, 152–170

Intensity, color, 113–114, 215

Knitting yarns, 18, 84

Large-scale marks, 65–74

Lettering, 50–62

Line character, 13, 14, 54–56, 204–213

Line direction, 26–34

Line weight, 14–24, 35, 70–74, 78, 85, 89, 101–103, 112, 124, 155, 165–166

Lines, fine, stitching tips, 85–90

Lines, long, 66–69

Machine stitching, 17–19, 22–24, 39–44, 53–54, 149

Machine text, programmed, 56

Marking fabric, 38

Materials choices, 37, 93–98, 172–173, 220–223

Metal mesh, 98

Mimicking traditional drawing materials, 87–89

Nylon netting, 96

Oblique lines (see diagonal lines)

Opaque fills, 139–149

Optical color mixing, 115–116, 120–124, 215

Organza, 94–95

Organza, silk, machine stitching on, 95

Organza mesh, 95

Outlines (see contours)

Overcasting, 18, 28, 68, 79, 179

Perspective, atmospheric, 31

Perspective, linear, 31

Projects ("Try this!"), 25, 35, 49, 63–64, 75–76, 92, 99–100, 105, 125, 137–138, 150–151, 171, 182–183

Rhythm, line, 34

Rhythmic stitching, 127–129, 137

Samplers, 62, 196–202

Satin stitch, machine, 17–19, 23–24, 40, 50

Scale, large, 65–74

Scale, small, 77–90, 133–136

Seeding, tips, 133–136

Shaded fills, 152–170

Small-scale marks, 36–48, 131, 133-136, 142, 144, 159-170

Stabilizing large pieces of fabric, 71

Stippling, 145, 159–170

Stitches, layering, 122

Tacking stitch (machine), 149

Tension, stitch 22, 41, 48, 68, 92, 95, 127, 143, 185, 215

Tension, visual, 28

Text, alternative styles, 50–62

Texture, 172–181

Thin lines, 15, 77, 85–90

Thread painting, 148

Three-dimensional illusions on cloth, 31–33, 152–170

Tools, 220–223

Transparent fabrics, 93–98, 126

Transparent fills, 126–136

Try this! (activities, exercises, projects), 25, 35, 49, 63–64, 75–76, 92, 99–100, 105,125, 137–138, 150–151, 171, 182–183

Valdani cotton threads, 22

Value, color, 81, 112–114, 216

Vertical lines, 26–27, 30–34

Wool threads, 18, 22, 73, 84, 112, 118, 133, 166, 172, 174, 176, 183

Susan Brandeis is Distinguished Professor Emerita at North Carolina State University's College of Design and is a member of the university's Academy of Outstanding Teachers. She holds graduate degrees in both art education and textile art and is a studio artist who has been making, exhibiting, teaching, and writing about textile art and design for over 35 years. She founded the Southeast Fibers Educators Association. Her work has been pictured in leading publications in the field and exhibited throughout the United States; in Canada, Great Britain, Japan, Finland, South Korea, Colombia, the Netherlands, and the Philippines; and at the Textile Museum in Washington, DC, and the International Biennial of Tapestry in Lausanne, Switzerland. She is represented in numerous private and public collections, including the Smithsonian Institution's Renwick Gallery. http://susanbrandeis.wordpress.ncsu.edu